TRANSPEOPLE:
REPUDIATION, TRAUMA, HEALING

Transgendered people face myriad forms of prejudice in their everyday lives, not only from social conservatives, but even from many left-
ists, psychiatrists, feminists, and lesbians and gays. In *Transpeople*,
Christopher Shelley provides an in-depth study of the repudiation and
indignity many transpeople suffer, and looks at what society can do to
improve understanding of transpeople and trans-related issues.

In this work, Shelley uses an interdisciplinary approach that
includes extensive interviews with both male-to-female and female-to-
male transpeople. Addressing both mainstream and radical psychological, feminist, and political theory, he examines the serious challenges that transpeople present to traditional sex and gender norms, as
well as the often intense reactions of non-trans people when these
norms are called into question.

Combining rich theoretical perspectives and qualitative research,
Transpeople provides valuable insights into both the experiences of
transpeople and the root causes of gender-based discrimination.

CHRISTOPHER SHELLEY is Clinical Director of the Adler Centre of the
Adlerian Psychology Association of British Columbia and lectures in
gender relations at the University of British Columbia.

CHRISTOPHER SHELLEY

Transpeople

Repudiation, Trauma, Healing

UNIVERSITY OF TORONTO PRESS
Toronto Buffalo London

ISBN 978-0-8020-9784-2 (cloth)
ISBN 978-0-8020-9539-8 (paper)

Printed on acid-free paper

Library and Archives Canada Cataloguing in Publication

Shelley, Christopher
    Transpeople : repudiation, trauma, healing / Christopher A. Shelley.

    Includes bibliographic references and index.
    ISBN 978-0-8020-9784-2 (bound).   ISBN 978-0-8020-9539-8 (pbk.)

    1. Transsexuals. 2. Transsexualism. 3. Sex discrimination. 4. Social isolation. 5. Transsexuals – Psychology. 6. Transsexualism – Psychological aspects. 7. Gender identity. I. Title.

HQ77.9.S44 2008   306.76'8   C2008-901281-X

This book has been published with the help of a grant from the Canadian Federation for the Humanities and Social Sciences, through the Aid to Scholarly Publications Programme, using funds provided by the Social Sciences and Humanities Research Council of Canada.

University of Toronto Press acknowledges the financial assistance to its publishing program of the Canada Council for the Arts and the Ontario Arts Council.

University of Toronto Press acknowledges the financial support for its publishing activities of the Government of Canada through the Book Publishing Industry Development Program (BPIDP).

To Kimberly Nixon,
a trailblazer in the struggle for transpeople's social emancipation
and a feminist of fortitude, wisdom, and compassion.

Contents

Preface

This book is written for those who desire a better understanding of the ubiquitous issues that many transsexual and transgender people face. The intent is to outline the field of trans studies by noting some of the controversies that exist and to situate these descriptions within some of the existing discussions and debates in the overlapping fields of women's and gender studies. While many books exist that discuss transpeople's lives and the services that they can receive from medicine, psychology, and other specializations in the helping professions, there are few texts that discuss the institutional and interpersonal *reactions* that many transpeople face in their everyday/night lives. As knowing subjects of the barriers and asymmetric social power that characterize their experiences of inequity, this book consults transpeople to aid in a project of *conscientization* about those signified or otherwise inscribed as trans.

Transpeople commonly use the term *transphobia* in a dual sense to describe and explain the negative barriers and interpersonal experiences that they are regularly forced to encounter. This book explores the topic with an appreciation that the term 'transphobia' carries enormous experiential and emotional weight for many transpeople and their allies. Yet it is a tightly knotted word that, when loosened, opens up its connections to broader social and intrapsychic processes that point to a range of repudiations. These repudiations, painfully, entail some form of rejection of transpeople as subjects, objects, or both. These repudiations are widespread and are perpetrated from all corners of the political spectrum, including those who portray themselves as enlightened or progressive on social issues.

I have endeavoured to re-present the voices of a group of transpeople who have generously shared their narratives of transphobia with me. Some readers will be entirely unfamiliar with the issues and debates that trans studies traverses, and the book aims to review them. Yet, I have also set out to plumb aspects of theoretical and clinical psychology in analysing the perpetrators of 'transphobia,' noting that these discourses and practices, for better *and* for worse, have long been tied to *trans* lives and, separately, the study and treatment of *phobia*. This dimension of the book may interest trans scholars and will certainly be useful to psychologists, psychotherapists, clinical social workers, and counsellors. Those in gay, lesbian, queer, and women's studies may also find the theorizing on perpetrators' motives, from the insights garnered from depth psychology (psychoanalytic, Jungian, Adlerian), translatable into other categories of subjugation, such as those based on the well-trodden categories of homophobia and misogyny. Furthermore, feminists will note that I have not overlooked the deep and at times acrimonious debates that transpeople pose(d) on the controversial question: who is a woman? The book also aims to provide activists, allies, legal reformers, academics, clinicians, administrators, employers, students, and all parties concerned with building inclusive and diverse communities, with a better understanding of the complex difficulties that often beset transpeople's lives.

My final motivation is consistent with an important message conveyed in the TRANSMIT allies toolkit (http://web.mit.edu/trans). Here, allies of transpeople are asked not to add the 'T' to LGB(T) without first 'doing the work.' This book promotes the understanding of transpeople's struggles for well-being in the face of widespread injustices and aspires to bring together a sense of the everyday voices and scholarly work that exist in the field. Hence, as an ally of transpeople, I wish to persuade others of the importance of soundly adding the 'T' to the LGB in more than merely script and rhetoric. This entails joining with transpeople in order to work for equity, inclusiveness, and a just community for all. Education on trans issues is widely acknowledged by transpeople and their allies to be a crucial aspect to 'the work.' This book represents a modest contribution to this work, one that raises issues that require it while, hopefully, provoking greater discussion and debate regarding trans issues in the overall pursuit of a fair and just society.

Christopher A. Shelley
Vancouver, BC

Acknowledgments

Numerous individuals – some in small ways, others in greater ways than they may know – were crucial to the evolution of this book. I wish to offer deep thanks and appreciation to all of the following: Professor Valerie Raoul (Emeritus, UBC-Vancouver, Women's and Gender Studies; French), Dr Becki Ross (UBC-Vancouver, Women's and Gender Studies; Sociology), and Professor Dawn Currie (UBC-Vancouver, Sociology), for their invaluable mentorship as feminist scholars; Tina Arsenault and Caroline Magnier of Victoria, BC, who provided valuable assistance with the interview transcripts and related equipment; my colleagues at the Centre for Research in Women's and Gender Studies (UBC) for their tremendous support (with special thanks to Professor Sneja Gunew, Dr Tineke Hellwig, Dr Wendy Frisby, Bianca Rus, Jane Lee, Dr Dorothy Seaton, and Dr Kim Snowden); Caroline White, Women's Studies at Langara College, Vancouver, for her scholarship, trans allied activism, and assistance with critical feedback on earlier drafts of this study; Lukas Walther of Vancouver Coastal Health's Transgender Health Program, for his tremendous assistance, friendship, and trans activism; Dr Patricia Elliot of Wilfrid Laurier University, Waterloo, Ontario, for her dedication to trans studies and patience with reading earlier drafts of this work; Dr Rachael St Claire, of Boulder, Colorado, for permission to cite from her sagacious, unpublished paper on Jungian psychology and transpeople; Dr Derek Hook of the Department of Social Psychology at the London School of Economics and Political Science, for permission to cite from his unpublished manuscript on postcolonial psychoanalysis; Professor Irmingard Staeuble of the Department of Psychology at the Free University of Berlin, for permission to cite from her unpublished manuscript on psychology and colonization; barbara findlay, QC, a remarkable lawyer and trans activist in Vancouver, who is staunchly committed to transpeople's rights; my dear friend Susan Cosco for her tremendous personal support; the key informants who participated in this study, for their enormous help in aiding me to meet with a sufficient number of interviewees; and, most especially, all of the transpeople who participated in the study, for educating me, generously sharing their narratives, and for immeasurably enriching my life.

Abbreviations

APA	American Psychiatric Association
BC	British Columbia
DSM-IV-TR	*Diagnostic and Statistical Manual of Mental Disorders,* 4th edition, text revision (American Psychiatric Association)
GID	gender identity disorder (*DSM*-IV-TR, category #576)
IS	intersex
FtM	transsexual (TS) female-to-male

Usual trajectory of surgeries: any one, or combination of, hysterectomy, oopherectomy (removal of ovaries), mastectomy, metoidioplasty (release of the suspensory ligament of the clitoris so that it resembles, according to Lawrence [2000], 'a micro penis'), vaginectomy (removal of the vagina), scrotoplasty (creation of prosthetic testicles), phalloplasty (abdominal flap, radical forearm flap, or fibular flap).

LGBTTQI	lesbian–gay–bisexual–trans–Two-Spirit–queer–intersex
MtF	transsexual (TS) male-to-female

Usual trajectory of surgeries: vaginoplasty with or without labiaplasty and with or without orchiectomy (with orchiectomy: [1] removal of testes; [2] without orchiectomy: relocation of testes up and into the abdominal wall).

Optional surgeries: breast implants, facial reconstruction (FFS), voice-box surgery, Adam's apple reduction/shave, hair transplant.

SRS	sexual reassignment surgery
TG	transgender
trans	Utilized tentatively in this book as an umbrella term to denote 'transsexual' *or* 'transgendered.'
TS	transsexual
TV	transvestite

TRANSPEOPLE:
REPUDIATION, TRAUMA, HEALING

1 Introduction: Transpeople and the Problem of Re/Action

Subjugation and 'Cure': Transpeople as 'Phobogenic Objects'

Transpeople are among the most subjugated and marginalized of social groups. In the West, they experience a daunting array of institutional barriers and (inter)personal repudiations, either in addressing a mis-sexed body (transsexuals: TS), or in seeking the freedom to live partially or fully outside of the sex/gender binary (transgender: TG). This book engages with trans narratives and relevant theories, in an attempt to understand the barriers transpeople face in the external social world and the internalized world of the subject/self. Attempting to understand how the two intersect in the complexities of trans lives entails traversing multiple discourses and bringing them together. The result is a hybrid project that is trans-disciplinary. Trans-disciplinarity follows and extends (through hybridity) a long tradition of interdisciplinary research on the lives of transpeople (Denny, 1998). Discourses as divergent as hermeneutics, feminism, postmodernism, poststructuralism, psychiatry, and depth psychology, as well as the personal accounts of people interviewed for this project, will be drawn on to aid in 'understanding' what I will call *trans repudiation*. The overall approach is hermeneutic (Gadamer, 1960), since the aim is understanding, through the interpretation of theoretical master-narratives, how these pertain to the personal narratives of individuals.

In this book, transpeople are assumed to be the primary experts on their own lives. For too long, academics and clinicians have adopted an Archimedean standpoint, perpetuating politically loaded notions of neutrality and inscribing their own authority over the lived experience of transpeople. Such inscriptions often radically diverge from the points of view that transpeople voice, so much so that 'expert' inscriptions often represent in themselves a radical repudiation of trans subjectivity, a subjectivity that I believe ought to be seen as meaningful and valuable on its own terms. Scientific claims to expertise over trans lives, purporting to be the products of clinical experience and research, have in fact added fuel to overtly political rejections of transpeople's assertions to being either fully (TS) or partly (TG) mis-sexed/gendered. One of the most surprising aspects of rejection or condemnation of trans-ness is that it comes from all points of the political spectrum: from religious conservatives, liberal humanists, radical feminists, and lesbians and gays. Repudiation of trans subjectivity also lies at the heart of sectors of the 'helping' professions that seek to 'assist' transpeople, usually with the aim of making them disappear into 'normativity.' The specific helping professionals most relevant to transpeople are psychiatrists and psychologists. They are responsible for the initial authorization and referral for sex reassignment surgery (SRS) and hormonal treatments. In this study, I intend to critically appraise the general theoretical premises that psychology and psychiatry assume in describing and clinically managing 'gender disorders,' with an understanding, based on my own experience as a psychotherapist, that these disciplines are, in practice, especially conflictual for transpeople. The clinical discourses of psychiatry/psychology are in many ways the worst (but not the only) offenders in producing authoritative inscriptions over and about the lives of transpeople. Hence, these intertwined disciplines are a good place to substantiate the necessity of elaborating and following suggestions for better procedures generated by transpeople themselves.

Psychology and psychiatry both include clinicians who are trans advocates, but they simultaneously harbour others whose aim is to produce conformity to 'acceptable norms.' Those upholding the aims of normative adjustment for those with 'gender disorders' range across the following positions: (1) outright denial of the authenticity of *all* claims to being mis-sexed and an associated rejection of sexual reassignment surgery (SRS) – patients must be adjusted to conform to their 'sex of origin'; (2) denial of the authenticity of the claim to being mis-sexed but a willingness to accede to the idea that SRS is the only solution for those with persistent 'delusions'; (3) a parsimonious acceptance that a small number of subjects are genuinely mis-sexed, with authorization of SRS contingent on the patient's agreement to cross into stereotypical sex/gender conformity; or, (4) acceptance of the legitimacy of TS claims to being mis-sexed, accompanied by rejection of TG requests for partial surgeries or hormone treatment alone, eliminating acceptance of border-crossing and in-between-ness as legitimate. These positions coalesce around the notion that persistent trans-based distress points to a serious form of psychopathology that requires clinical management, which may or may not include hormone therapy and SRS.

There are philosophical traditions inherent within these disciplines that, when critically examined, can explain the tendency of some psychiatrists and psychologists to consider trans-ness as a form of madness, one that requires a normative prescriptiveness (although they often disagree on how this can be achieved). For example, historians of psychology have traced the ways in which the discourse of psychology as a discipline is rooted in 'Eurocentric and Orientalist patterns of thought' that broadly reflect the colonizer's view of the world. This view operates through a 'civilising mission' based on 'European modernity as subject and the colonised world as object' (Staeuble, 2005, p. 2). Defined as a category of psychopathology, transpeople are often subjugated, as I will demonstrate in this book, by the gaze of some ('sane/civilized') clinicians whose intent ('mission') is to cure ('insane/uncivilized') 'sex and gender deviants.' Hence, psychiatry and psychology name/categorize and then control the means of addressing trans-embodied distress under the diagnostic rubric of 'gender dysphoria' (APA, 2000). Through these clinical discourses, transpeople have become an object of fascination, similar to the postcolonial conception of the 'phobogenic object' (Fanon, 1967, p. 151).

Hook (2005), in critiquing the concept of 'race' as it pertained to apartheid policy in South Africa, analyses the psychodynamics of the 'white' gaze upon 'black' skin/bodies; the latter become a 'phobogenic object,' which produces a 'volatile polarity of affect ... criss-crossed with relations not only of dread, disgust and fear, but also with relations of attraction, fascination, exoticism and desire' (p. 2). A parallel example pertaining to transpeople can be seen in the work of the evolutionary psychologist Michael Bailey (2003), a contemporary and controversial figure in sexology. At times, Bailey is sympathetic to transpeople, attracted to them as an 'object' of study and opposed to social discrimination against them. Elsewhere, however, he endorses a view that transsexual subjects embody a disorder and maladaptiveness which must ultimately be resolved (controlled) through genetic prevention. In essence, he views transpeople as unfortunate, wayward mistakes of nature, which science might one day be able to fully correct (civilize). In the interim, granting sex changes where warranted must suffice; but the overall aim is to prevent the necessity for such surgical interventions, for science to preclude these spoiled products of nature. Evolutionary psychologists like Bailey yearn to decipher the genetic codes said to produce the mis-sexed body, to more fully control transsexual and transgendered embodiment and prevent it from occurring in the first place. Such evolutionary/eugenic views ultimately aim to preserve the sanctity of the sexed binary, which is deemed undoubtedly desirable. Whether or not transpeople agree, most are forced into dealing with psychologists and psychiatrists, some of whom hold evolutionary points of view, if or when they seek medical assistance.

The scientific status of psychological/psychiatric studies suggests, by a 'halo effect,' that their conclusions on transpeople are authoritative and impartial. This clinical gaze Others trans-embodied people as exotic oddities who cannot be healed through the talking cure. Failing to cure transpeople of their psychic distress, psychiatry/psychology maintains the role of gatekeeper to other medical interventions such as endocrinology, involving hormone therapy, and various plastic surgeries. This gate-keeping function usually, but not always, dissuades those who might come to regret a sex change, and indeed a persistent, though very small,[1] minority of people do vehemently regret transitioning (Pfäfflin, 1992; Batty, 2004). These exceptions are frequently cited as evidence that sex 'change' is not a solution, and/or that the originally assigned gender must be the 'true' one. The existence of people who regret transitioning points to the need for gate-keeping, as problematic as this function often is. Nonetheless, the health sciences are consistently met with legitimate medical demands made by people who claim, in autobiographical accounts, to have been mis-sexed since their early childhood. That medical technologies are capable of helping most of these people to live lives that are liveable is not the issue. The issue is that such technologies are embedded within a broader culture of almost universal rejection of transpeople. As psychiatry and psychology demonstrate, this repudiation is found even within the very disciplines that purport to assist those with mis-sexed bodies. The health sciences express an uneasy ambivalence towards tampering with the embodied sexed binary, which remains sacrosanct in Western culture. This ambivalence is replete with paradoxical contradictions that continue to render issues related to transsexuality/transgenderism controversial.

All Western sexed and gendered selves are interpellated subjects of a culture (language and social structure) that cannot readily accommodate infringement of the sexual binary. Surgery is usually willingly applied to genitals only in a limited number of 'extreme' cases, such as intersex (IS) subjects, born with both, or some of both, female and male organs/anatomy (Preves, 2002). In IS subjects, surgical transgression of the binary does not actually take place; rather, the binary is clarified and imposed, etched onto a body that cannot be allowed to continue to represent sexed ambiguity. The quest for conformity, however, is not infallible, and surgery can produce gross, even inhumane, errors. Chase (2000) draws attention to the physical and psychological management of some intersex (IS) babies/children. This management prescribes and enforces the sexed binary, as sexologists such as the late John Money (1986) have long instructed, inscribing sex and gender in ways that frequently amount to mutilation. In the case of IS babies, these medical decisions do not respect or reflect any future agency or control on the part of the patient.[2] Later, as adolescents and adults, many IS people are outraged at the extreme intrusion of unwanted and unnecessary surgeries[3] (e.g., removal of a 'small' penis or a 'large' clitoris).[4] This is so when the surgical decisions do not concur with the gender identity adopted, or when some IS people would prefer to have retained bodies that reflect their natal 'ambiguity,' to adopt third or other sexed and gendered identities, similar to the aims of other TG people.

In contrast, transsexuals, some of whom recognize only later in life that they have been assigned to the wrong category, have to go through a taxing and burdensome appeal to medical authorities to achieve the opportunity to live in a re-sexed body through sex-change technologies. The right for TS subjects to be granted sex change was a hard-won battle. Historically, some medical specialists eventually acquiesced to the wishes of TS people, performing operations justified by a humanitarianism that dictates the surgical treatment of a purportedly deep and chronic 'psychopathological syndrome.' Surgery is granted as a last resort, in response to the persistence of the request in otherwise 'sane' persons and in light of the failure of psychiatric treatments to extinguish the request. Psychology and psychiatry are charged with giving/denying consent for accessing these procedures. The end effect is that psychiatry and psychology as discourses and clinical practices entail a fundamental contradiction and conundrum for transpeople (including some IS people): they mis/serve these subjects.

The discussion so far already reveals a basic paradox or tension that is at the heart of studies related to trans-sexuality and trans-gender. Those who wish to 'change sex' (TS) frequently subscribe to the dominant view that two sexes (and only two) are both inevitable and desirable. They wish to belong socially (in the eyes of others) to the sex to which they feel (mentally/emotionally) they belong, and want their body to conform to the expectations for that sex. Subsequent problems are often related to issues of 'passing.' Such individuals are not anxious to change dominant gender expectations, but to conform to them. Many transgender (TG) people (some of whom also undergo SRS), on the other hand, would prefer to be able to retain ambivalence, either in body or in comportment. They suffer because society does not accept a third sex or indeterminacy. However, as we shall see, TS and TG people, in reality, face similar issues of discrimination and repudiation.

The Importance of Ethical Agency

In researching this area of sex/gender conformity and its transgressions, it is essential that the 'subjects' themselves exert their own agency. Trans academics like Jacob Hale (2004) have posited necessary principles for researching transpeople without compromising their integrity, voice, and intrinsic worth. It is significant that it took an academic transman like Hale to articulate such a proposal, in response to the way that ordinary transpeople have been largely ignored by the authorities on their lives. In adopting a hermeneutic approach for this study, I recognize that dialogue with transpeople is a compulsory component to researching trans lives in the social sciences. In undertaking a trans-disciplinary project involving qualitative research (interviews), political perspectives, and a review of depth psychology in relation to trans-ness, I will be attempting to bring together approaches that might appear irreconcilable. Nevertheless, together they show why transpeople's position is fraught with inner and outer tensions.

Hale asks non-transpeople like myself to 'approach your topic with a sense of humility' (p. 1). Transphobia, regardless of speculations on its causes or even semantic arguments over the appropriateness of the term itself, conveys an arrogance intrinsic to its expression, one that compromises principles of equity; if you, for example, are trans and I am afraid of you or disturbed by your transgressiveness, what right have I to bar you from proper health care, an education, a job, a public lavatory, a restaurant, to make a spectacle of your body, and so on? Worse, what right have I to unleash my unconscious rage at your body, to threaten you, to harass you, or to physically assault you? I have no such right. And yet, as this study reveals, these arrogant assumptions and disgraceful acts are very common, the source of unwelcome experiences in transpeople's everyday/night worlds. Perpetrators may not know or understand their reasons for subjugating the lives of others. They may very well be expressing an unconscious sense of feeling threatened by an otherness that is deeply disturbing to those whose own sense of security is bound up in sex/gender distinctness.

Placing myself as researcher in the Socratic stance, beginning with 'I know that I do not know,' has allowed the possibility for transpeople to take a pedagogic role in this book, to educate me and my readers as 'knowing subjects' in their own right, rather than being seen as deviant objects, exotic Others, or colonized victims waiting to be rescued by their very colonizers. In pursuing this study, I have attempted to be critically self-reflexive, to become aware of my own gaze, discomfort, and so on. This gaze can be reflected back to researchers from transpeople themselves, who usually know when they are being repudiated. Dialogue based on the 'hermeneutic circle' (Gadamer, 1960) returns speech to the subjects for reconsideration, for the production of self-knowledge. Hence, Hale asks researchers if they can travel in transpeople's worlds. If the answer is no, then the researcher probably will not understand what transpeople are talking about. I have travelled in transpeople's worlds and hope to continue to do so. These are not easy journeys to take and challenge non–trans-embodied people profoundly. To be a trans ally requires such fellow-travelling, and if transpeople agree to guide you, it is a gift to be cherished.

Researching Trans Repudiation: Narrative 'Method' and Study Participants

In approaching the topic of transpeople's lives and the repudiations they experience, I have taken transcribed interview material and considered these dialogues in relation to a range of theories, in order to better understand the myriad problems that transpeople face. This is, I believe, a hermeneutic exercise. Gadamer (1960), in reviving the term 'hermeneutics,' did so to critique the Romantic hermeneutics that had preceded him. Those hermeneutics claimed that a meta-Truth was inherent in texts such as the Christian Bible and that if one were to read such texts correctly, Truth would objectively emerge. The title of Gadamer's treatise, *Truth and Method*, does not evoke a means to achieve Truth, but rather a critique of *method* as a means of uncovering Truth. Gadamer's hermeneutics is not a complete rejection of methodical work. It is a rejection of complete understanding as an achievable goal, of totalized grand vision, and of any particular method as the one and only means to uncover absolute Truths. For Gadamer (1960), *'the hermeneutical problem ... is clearly distinct from "Pure" knowledge detached from any particular kind of being'* (p. 314; italics in the original). There is no 'pure' knowledge; rather, as Gallagher (1992) comments, 'knowledge is always imperfect knowledge' (p. 341), or as Haraway (2004) puts it, 'rational knowledge is always interpretative, critical, and partial' (p. 93). The interpretative, critical, and partial assumptions that Haraway speaks of parallel Gadamer's insistence that dialogue gradually comes to produce only partial understandings, which, in turn, require an ongoing interpretation. Furthermore, these assumptions also parallel the central tenets of the depth psychologies,[5] discourses which suggest that an ubiquitous unconscious dynamic operates in human subjectivity and relatedness, that our knowledge of self and others is only partial.

My approach utilizes a hermeneutic and dialogic engagement with transpeople as 'knowing subjects.' This approach emerges thus: (1) between myself and the interviewees (qualitative research that gives authority to personal experience, foregrounds the power of narrative in the form of reflections and stories, and offers concrete examples as voiced by the subjects themselves); and (2) between this material, gathered from transpeople, and theories about sex and gender: both sociopolitical and psychological (especially depth psychology). The analysis of the depth psychologies, and related issues pertaining to contestations between the self and the subject, emerges following reflection on the interviews as a whole, by extending the sociological conception of *discrimination* into the intra/interpersonal phenomenon of *repudiation*. This theoretical explication and analysis *frames* what I have 'understood,' what Gadamer (1960) terms *foregrounding*. In this study, it is hermeneutic/narrative exchanges that produce theoretical foregrounding. My ultimate aim is to return this analysis to transpeople and their allies as part of an ongoing conversation, which, I shall argue, is also relevant to feminists and other scholars in the field of sex/gender studies.

My approach to narrative is consistent with its use as a distinct category in qualitative psychology, one that has gained strength in recent years (White and Epston, 1990; Josselson, Lieblich, and McAdams, 2002; Parker, 2004). Narrative research is construed as a means to insert the importance of storied lives, of retaining voice, of providing a counterbalance to an over-emphasis on quantitative methods, as evidenced particularly in mainstream psychology (Rennie et al., 2002). Narrative is about deeply listening to human experience, emphasizing the framing of research questions with which to generate dialogue. Combining this approach with hermeneutics foregrounds the striving for understanding as a result of listening to narrative accounts.

What I have tentatively 'understood' from consulting transpeople is that their everyday/night lives are troubled by pervasive repudiations. These reflections have produced three clusters that inform my tentative 'conclusions.' These research questions are generated and presented as analytic frames, as an outcome of hermeneutic dialogue, and focus on three tensions:

1 The *Internal/External* distinction as evidenced by a split between psychology and sociology: to what extent does this dyad function as a complex interrelationship evident in trans discrimination, repudiation, and consequent subjugation?
2 *Paradox*: What are the paradoxical dynamics that surround the phenomenon of trans repudiation and transphobia?
3 *Contradiction*: To what extent are there splits within the unified referent 'trans'? How do current social/political conditions produce contradictions that transpeople are forced to navigate?

In considering these three clusters, it becomes clear that transpeople embody in a most striking way post/modern issues and debates regarding social relations, the self, and subjectivity. These issues point to nostalgia for a lost wholeness/home, as expressed by TS people, and a resistance/refusal of the sex/gender binary as expressed by TG people. Externally, TS people are often frustrated in their attempts to recover/live in this lost home, while TG people find that a third space is an unavailable social position. These issues do not merely point to what is troubling in transpeople's lives, but also to the ways in which trans-ness itself becomes troubling to theory. Trans-ness as conceived in either modern or postmodern terms both valorizes and questions

'wholeness' or 'integrity' as a goal (belonging to the *right* sex), implying a degree of essentialism and certainty. It also valorizes and questions border-crossing, in-between-ness, fragmentation, or indeterminacy as an attractive, transgressive alternative. Both positions have
utopian aspects in theory, but prove to be uncomfortable, even infer-
nal, in the real lives of transpeople.

The Research Project

This book began as a qualitative research project, based on twenty in-
depth interviews with transpeople living in the Greater Vancouver district of British Columbia. Without any prior contrivance to achieve an
equal ratio of FtM or MtF participants, narratives were produced that
reflect upon and reveal aspects of the lived experiences of ten MtFs
and ten FtMs. The categorization of MtF or FtM was based at
minimum on full-time pronoun use (excepting those instances where
a person's safety is compromised) contrary to the sex/gender assignment at birth. My trepidatious use of MtF/FtM categories reflects the
fact that many of the interviewees do not themselves use the MtF/FtM
designation yet do acknowledge its tentative validity for representation in this study. Difficulty in ascertaining the appropriateness of
MtF/FtM labels points to the lack of consensus about the binary in
trans communities, since, as mentioned above, some transpeople see
the binary in essentialist terms and are loathe to leave it, while others
view it as a major impediment to achieving their desired identity and
an object for overthrow.

At the time of the interviews, nineteen of the twenty interviewees
were taking hormones; five were pre-operative; thirteen were post-
operative; and two were 'no-ops' (no surgery intended at the time of
interview). In terms of the last category, one was taking hormones, the
other was unable to at the time due to health reasons. Both 'no-op'
interviewees hold relatively stable identities as TG and offer interesting perspectives on trans repudiation from a TG standpoint. It must be
said, however, that a TG standpoint more broadly may also include
those who have had sex reassignment surgery (SRS), and should not
be construed as synonymous with 'no-op' intentions. In contrast, TS
identity is synonymous with those who have, or expect to have, SRS.

The interviews focused on these people's experiences *as* trans. My
initial working assumptions, which I revisited after the completion of
the interviews, included the use of the term 'transphobia' in the inter-

views, as it is well known among transpeople. Upon reflecting on the transcripts after all interviews were completed, I noticed that what was being termed 'transphobia' was often actually a range of types of repudiation, which might include phobia. Listening between the lines, I heard: 'phobia, yes, but more than just phobia.' Hence, my initial assumptions were eventually revised, including the appropriateness of the use of the term 'transphobia' in the interviews themselves. My initial assumptions included the following:

- Transphobia affects *all* transpeople.
- Transphobia is a 'fact' regardless of one's race, class, or sexual orientation. Race, class, and sexual orientation as intersectional issues were not addressed directly but certainly welcomed when they emerged, usually spontaneously, in the interviews. Those who did draw attention to racialized/ethnic/cultural identities wanted them noted: one is Jewish; four First Nations, and one Metis. Two First Nations identify in the tradition of *Two-Spirit*; however, they also make use of the TS/TG identifications and inscriptions when they deem it necessary (for example, at a medical office).
- Transpeople are not suffering from a mental illness but rather live lives that, in and of themselves, have intrinsic worth and are not compromised by psychopathology on the basis of trans-ness alone.

All interviewees were given the option to use a pseudonym, indeed encouraged to do so. However, some adamantly refused, insisting that their actual names be used. Justifications were offered, such as 'I am already known through media attention,' 'I don't care,' 'I am not interested in masquerades,' and 'I wish to retain ownership over my own life story.' I am charged, however, with protecting the privacy of those who chose not to reveal their true identities. As a compromise, I will not indicate whose name is, or is not, an assumed one. Moreover, for privacy reasons, I regret being unable to introduce each of the twenty participants in more detail. Had I done so, the participants might have inadvertently identified each other. Many of the interviewees are acquainted with each other, in some cases through activism. Also, transpeople as a group *appear* to be small in numbers despite their strong local networking. Hence, the disclosure of general profiles (e.g., TS: x to x + sexual orientation + ethnicity + years since surgery) could give strong clues to the other participants that could potentially compromise confidentiality. The participants are listed in table 1.

Table 1
List of participants

FtM		MtF	
TS	Dean	TS	Aiyanna
	Frank		Jamie-Lee
	Hank		Jenny
	Jeb		Kimberly
	John		Patricia
	Keenan		Robin
	Trevor		Roz
	Yossi		Sabrina*
			Tami
			Wynn
TG	Alex		
	Nick*		

* Denotes coexistence of Two-Spirit identity

Upon analysing the finished transcripts, I noted institutional sites and specific issues where transphobia and trans repudiation were relayed, proceeding to a thematic analysis familiar to qualitative researchers. I then coded each transcript to mark the institutional sites and other issues identified. Ten analytic categories emerged, pointing to the ways in which the interviewees' lives were/are challenged and affected:

1 *Health Care:* This category relates to aspects of physical care (diagnosing/treating) and institutional (hospitals, clinics) interactions. The emphasis is on relations with professionals in medicine and psychiatry/psychology.
2 *Lavatories / Change Rooms:* In public, trans subjects are forced to choose gendered geographic spaces, with a notable lack of a third space. This category often pertains to issues of passing, evoking fear on the part of others who cannot deal with ambiguity and on the part of those unable to pass.
3 *Family and Personal Relations:* The issue of being (or not being) the *same* person as before, and dealing with the sense of loss and the need for adjustment on the part of others. Psychodynamic issues raised include defensive reluctance or refusal by others to accept

the subject's 'new' sex/gender position, commonly evoking a range of affective issues: mourning, desire, trust, rejection, and repudiation.

4 *Employment:* Difficulties in securing and retaining paid employment; and experiences of on-site harassment from co-workers and/or supervisors.

5 *Education:* Difficulties in pursuing one's education on the primary, secondary, and post-secondary levels of education. These difficulties range from insensitivity to trans issues through to harassment from teachers, instructors, administrators, and peers.

6 *Threat/Violence:* The degree of negative reactions towards trans subjects ranges from verbal threat to physical assault.

7 *Problems with Law Enforcement:* To what extent are transpeople comfortable with accessing law enforcement services? Are transpeople subject to prejudicial treatment from law enforcement?

8 *Relations with (Other) Lesbians and Gays:* Are transpeople accepted in lesbian and gay communities? Are non-trans gay, lesbian, and bisexual subjects less likely to perpetuate trans repudiation than heterosexuals?

9 *Reactions from Radical Cultural Feminists:* Tensions exist between radical cultural feminists and many transpeople. This divisive and controversial subject was raised by several of my interviewees.

10 *Self-Oppression:* Trans repudiation can also be found in transpeople themselves, especially in the form of self-oppression.

The interviews became only one element or dimension of this transdisciplinary study. They provide a good deal of information on the interplay between *external* circumstances and *internal* reflections/experiences, and on the reaction of others to those perceived as shifting gender boundaries. The internalized conflicts disclosed in the stories of these transpeople also prompted me to rethink feminist, queer theory and depth psychology theories about identity formation and the sex/gender relationship. Specifically, the analysis I provide both confirms and adds to the sociological material collected by Devor (1997) and Namaste (2000, 2005), and also the trans theorizing provided by Elliot and Roen (1998), Prosser (1998), and Hird (2000, 2003). More broadly, I noticed that transpeople un/wittingly serve as a lightning rod, challenging the assumptions and prejudice of those who believe themselves enlightened on sex/gender oppression (such as some gays/lesbians and feminists). In sum, transpeople challenge us inasmuch as they embody the postmodern condition – illustrating both nostalgia for a lost/desired *whole*/integrity, and the desire for indeterminacy, not to have to choose, to become something that either does not yet exist or is not recognized as legitimate in the broader culture. What emerges is a fundamental split or tension within the category of 'trans' itself, which is always present but not always acknowledged in the growing field of trans studies.

Issues in the Field of Trans(gender/sexual) Studies

It is difficult to speak of a 'field' in a unified sense when referring to trans studies. 'Trans,' as White (2002) points out, is a problematic term, an inadequate umbrella for transgenderists (TG), transsexuals (TS), transvestites (TV), cross-dressers, some Two-Spirit, some queer, and some intersex (IS) people (all of whom may interchange trans with other identities). *Transgender*, moreover, is sometimes used to refer to all of these various categories of identity and embodiment, as in the quest for 'transgender rights' and associated protections against discrimination sought through 'gender identity' provisions. However, trans scholars such as Namaste (2005) reject the term, citing unthought imperialist motives such as anglophone-generated scholarship over francophone contexts. She contends that the French language does not have an equivalent term for 'transgender,' and in contexts such as francophone Quebec, many transsexuals find the word meaningless. Outside of Quebec, the Canadian trans activist Mihra-Soleil Ross, in an interview with Namaste (ibid.), argues that 'the concept of "transgender" still makes little sense. It constantly has to be "explained" to the average TS/TV person – especially to prostitutes and show girls – by the "leaders" ' (p. 102). It is more important, argues Namaste, to focus on the location of transsexuals in the social world and to clarify subjugation based on class rather than based on Anglo, middle-class, academic arguments that supposedly digress into identity politics.[6]

I have tenuously maintained the trans umbrella (e.g., in referring to 'trans-people'), not to elide these categorical splits but to try to comprehend a common theme expressed by TS and TG people: their experiences of repudiation, including transphobia. The acrimony over the legitimacy of the term 'transgender' requires that I abandon it as an umbrella category in favour of 'trans.' However, I disagree with those theorists and activists who disavow transgender altogether. What this study argues is that transpeople, regardless of their status as TS, TG, and so on, grapple with the problem of repudiation. Social location *and* identity are equally important in this analysis. To better understand the significance of these splits within trans studies, it is imperative that I discuss the contested status of queer theory in relation to transpeople's lives.

Queer Theory

The fairly recent rise of queer theory in relation to trans lives is important to consider, not only for its celebration of transpeople as transgressive, but also because many (but certainly not all) transpeople also identify as queer. Briefly, queer theory takes issue with a number of 'common-sense' postulates regarding sex/gender/sexuality, especially the seemingly unproblematic, historically constructed naturalism that flows from the traditional binary of an elevated 'normal/natural heterosexuality' versus a debased and 'deviant/unnatural homosexuality.' Queer theory analyses the hegemony that this asymmetrical relationship between the poles of this binary imposes. Judith Butler (1993) refers to the regulating norm of the *heterosexual imperative*. The concept echoes Adrienne Rich's (1980) earlier introduction of the notion of *compulsory heterosexuality*, which continues to constitute the normative expectation of sexual identity and behaviour in most societies, in the West and elsewhere. Homosexual relations between men, for example, are in fact still punishable by death in seven nations, with the beheading of convicted homosexuals as one form of execution inflicted upon the condemned (Hari, 2004).

In the West, through discursive and historical analyses, queer theory tells of the creation of homosexuality as an identity and practice that were pathologized only in the latter part of the nineteenth century, as part of a regulative ideal of sex/gender difference (Butler, 1993). The medicalization of homosexuality accompanied sexological and psychiatric discourses that classified as deviant those with persistent same-sex desire. Yet legal and moral statutes, which tended to focus on male same-sex behaviour and its prohibition, were already implemented under the earlier, pre-medicalized view that considered such behaviours as sinful or immoral, rather than the result of a medical condition. These laws echoed mid-seventeenth-century attitudes that saw the temptation to 'debauchery' as widespread and something to which anyone might succumb (Jagose, 1996, p. 11).

Following the gay and lesbian liberation movements, launched in the late 1960s in America with ripple effects elsewhere, slow but continued change has occurred, such as the decriminalization of sodomy laws and the de-listing of homosexual behaviours as mental illnesses in many countries. In some jurisdictions, common-law and marriage rights have been extended to same-sex couples, giving homosexuality broader social recognition, though this issue is currently being vigorously contested, especially by social conservatives and many religious groups. Attention has also been drawn to the dangers of derogatory language, as 'hate speech,' while gays and lesbians have reclaimed pejorative terms such as *queer* to designate an analytic category for theorizing. For some gays and lesbians, queer emerges as a new identity that replaces the previous categories of gay, lesbian, and bisexual. 'Queer,' however, resists an exact definition. Jagose (1996), for example, points to the plasticity and indeterminacy of this term, which connotes its roots in constructivism, poststructuralism, and postmodernism. It resists essentializing the allegedly natural relationship between chromosomal sex, sexual behaviour, identity, and desire. The term disrupts the stability of identity (including gay and lesbian identities) and posits fluidity rather than innateness or crystallization. Queer speaks to the importance of:

1 the theoretical power of *difference* (queer profits from the techniques developed by deconstruction to uncover difference and show how grand narratives previously glossed over contingent variances);
2 problematizing assumed points of consensus and questioning umbrella terms (covering may also have the effect of masking);
3 maintaining an attitude of incredulity towards metanarrative (as conveyed by Lyotard), one that challenges absolutes; and
4 *plurality*, which might very well be the force that breaks apart stubborn dualisms such as good/evil, sane/insane, straight/gay, and male/female.

Queer theory suggests pursuing an understanding of gendered subjectivity that includes the complexities and instabilities of desire that dualisms such as straight/gay overshadow. Queer tends to favour, somewhat problematically, TG as a category over TS since TS subjects tend to prioritize the desired stability of material embodiment over politically expedient categories within identity politics. In attempting not to overlook the materiality of lived lives as they are located in the concrete social world, I have also not overlooked the power of discourse to produce the realm of the material itself (Butler, 2004). When considering trans repudiation, the material importance of embodiment is especially relevant to all issues of gender, and here specifically in drawing distinctions between transsexuals and trangenderists. In relation to queer theory, these divisions circulate contentiously in discussions of identity and material embodiment (Prosser, 1998; Elliot, 2004a). This seems so since queer theory at times veers rather closely to an idealization of fragmentation and disintegration, of mystification and categorical failure. So long as it does not fall over into the illegible abyss of chaos, its insights will remain strong and provocative; for example, Butler's (1990, 1993) notion of gender as a fiction based on an inscribed performativity, a repetition of a stylization of constructed codes that *materializes* over time. Here, gender approximates 'the natural,' so that it appears innate, it emulates the essential. This analysis builds on Foucault's (1978) uncovering of the discursive construction of sexuality as part of the power/knowledge axis. Butler (1990) asks, 'How does language itself produce the fictive construction of "sex" that supports ... various regimes of power?' (p. ix.). Other queer theorists such as Halberstam (1994), Noble (2004a, 2004b), Pratt (1995), and Stryker (1998) emphasise the ways in which queer theory undoes the binary by creating a third space for gender transgression. Stryker defines queer as follows: '(1) the sense of a utopian, all-encompassing point of resistance to heteronormativity and (2) a "posthomosexual" reconfiguration of communities of people marginalised by sexuality, embodiment, and gender' (p. 151). This definition reflects the rise of transgender activism in the 1990s, which at times militantly rejected conformity to the sex/gender binary (Califia, 2003).

However, not all transpeople are satisfied with total rejection of the sex/gender binary valorized by queer theory. Prosser (1998) argues that Butler overemphasized performativity and language in her 1990 book *Gender Trouble*. He suggests that she has failed to account sufficiently for embodiment in both *Gender Trouble* and *Bodies That Matter* (1993). In challenging the postmodern 'third space' assumptions that emanate from Butler's and other queer theorists' positions, Prosser wonders what happened to the 'first' and 'second' spaces. He contends that these spaces still matter in ways that go beyond the poststructural thesis on the productive nature of power:

> Constructing trans into the very 'fin' of the millennium, postmodernism
> has challenged the key binaries of modernist identity grand narratives by
> idealizing the middle ground – the '/' or transition itself ... this promo-
> tion of trans comes at a price ... it leaves unattended differences that con-
> tinue to matter on either side of the slash. (P. 201)

In her book *Undoing Gender* (2004), Butler seems to tacitly affirm the
spirit of Prosser's statement. In this book, she sensitively comments on
the injustices that TS people face in addition to affirming transpeople's
right to 'realize their autonomy' (p. 77) or 'what we might call transau-
tonomy' (p. 76). Nevertheless, queer rejection of the possibility of
being entirely or definitely a man or a woman does not automatically
equate with the embodied experiences of transsexuals. Their experience tends to differ from that of a congruently embodied, non-trans
female or male subject who is queer identified. While transgender
activists privilege the crossing and fluidity of queer, many transsexuals disagree. Firstly, TS people express a variety of sexual orientations,
and while some might change these, others retain a stable sexual orientation over the course of their lives (e.g., always feeling like a
straight man). TS people may be queer identified, but certainly not all
of them are. Many FtMs, for example, are heterosexual in their orientation following transition, a transition that lends social and physical
embodiment to their sense of having been heterosexual males in
female bodies prior to transition (Devor, 1997). Such heterosexual
persons might, but also might not, resonate with the identity 'queer.'

To return to the problem that White (2002) noted, 'trans,' as an
umbrella term, supposes a sense of unity amongst TG, TS, IS, gender
liminal, and Two-Spirit people, as well as some bisexuals, cross-
dressers (transvestites, drag Kings/Queens), gender benders, and
queer identified people, a sense of unity that often does not exist.
There might be issues that produce strategic solidarity (e.g., eradication of transphobia), yet even here one cannot assume that all trans
people will come forward to support such a campaign. There are
transsexual people who, upon transition. disappear into the world to
live straight lives and may not want to be reminded of the past or to
be activists in any way (Prosser, 1998). They may be more motivated to
maintain the gender binary than to blur it.

Some TS people insist that their ontology is medically rooted, seeing
themselves as having a sexed brain that is in contradiction with their
mis-sexed body. For those who accept these causal attributions, an

essentialist physiology is at the root of the mis-sexed body, not culture, language, environmental factors, psychodynamic factors, or other aspects raised by queer theory. The 'trans' discourse, for such persons, is not an accurate one. They do not wish to move from one sex to another – they have always been of *one* sex, with medical issues that require correction. Hence, queer theory is of little or no relevance to such subjects. As Prosser (1998) writes:

> ... the current [TG] campaign to remove gender identity disorder entirely from the DSM does not consider that, for some transsexuals, gender identity disorder may be experienced precisely as a disorder, a physically embodied dis-ease or dysphoria that dis-locates the self from bodily home and to which sex reassignment *does* make all the difference. (P. 203)

Prosser argues that some transsexuals adamantly disagree with those TG activists who wish to remove the clinical status of gender dysphoria from the *DSM* psychiatric nomenclature of mental disorders. Burnham (1999) concurs that there is a lack of unity between TS and TG people. Namaste (2000) also challenges the umbrella definition, arguing that it 'may erase the specificity of all different transgendered and especially transsexual individuals' (p. 267). Moreover, she decries the way that queer theory neglects the everyday lives of TG and TS people in terms of their location in the institutionalized social world. She charges that queer theory, including the imposition of queerness on all trans subjects, constitutes 'a remarkable insensitivity' that overlooks the 'lives, bodies and experiences' of transpeople (p. 23).

For TG people, resistance to the binary is imperative. Noble (2004b) argues that he refuses to be a man and emphasizes 'the need to think paradox: I'm a guy who is half lesbian' (p. 26). This paradoxical hybridity is typical of TG identity, entailing multiplicity and related configurations. While such identity conclusions are important to TG people, they are not necessarily the same conclusions that TS people arrive at. Meyerowitz (2002) emphasizes the historical development of the TG movement. She notes that it arose after well-known figures such as Harry Benjamin and Christine Jorgensen died, and cites the relevance of the Internet as an element in postmodern culture, something that also came about after the demise of Jorgensen. The Internet, moreover, facilitates transnational crossing through non-embodied means, nodes with no centre (such as chat rooms), and opportunities for organizing global communication and protests. Internet interactions allow for cyberspace crossings and the hosting of cyber identities in performative, language-based modalities (Rothblatt, 1996). These might be valuable attributes for TG activists, or those who wish to play with gender distinctions, yet such technological sophistications elide the embodied incongruity that TS people live with in their concrete everyday/night worlds. Leading TG activists, such as Feinberg (1993), nevertheless call for the revolutionary overthrow of the binary, a militant rejection of a fixed sex/gender identity, of passing, of duality, in favour of reconfiguring oneself as s/he. Prosser (1998) rejects this universal call, emphasizing that in point of fact, TG crossings, fluidity, and indeterminacy are about gender and not sex. TS is not so much about the fluidity of gender crossing as it is about 'substantive transition: a correlated set of corporeal, psychic, and social changes' (p. 4): hence, Prosser's project to 'wrest the transsexual from the queer inscription of transgender' (p. 56). Further problems with the trans umbrella emerge when one looks more closely at Indigenous expressions of gender, and whether they do or do not belong within the constructed category of trans.

Two-Spirit People

In North American Indigenous cultures and traditions, prior to colonization, there was no such thing as a sex/gender binary. The binary appeared in First Nations people's worldview following colonization, when Western religious traditions intruded, often violently, as in the history of the residential schools in Canada and the United States. In this instance, Indigenous children were forcibly removed, cut off from their families in order that they might be 'civilized.' This process involved inculcating and indoctrinating these children in Christian traditions, of which the gender binary forms a major aspect. Historically, in New France, French colonists noted the phenomenon of gender and sex variance among Indigenous people, using the pejorative inscription *berdache*. Brown (1997) traces this term to Arabic, from which it migrated into Italian, Spanish, and French. Its root meaning is sodomite. In English, 'berdache' was used as a standard term for the gender liminality perceived among First Nations, especially by anthropologists, who thought the term innocuous. However, during the Third Native American / First Nations Gay and Lesbian Conference held in Winnipeg (1990), 'berdache' was denounced for its colonial imposition and its insulting connotations (Jacobs, Thomas, and Lang,

1997). Alternatively, conference attendees agreed to adopt the more appropriate *Two-Spirit* designation. 'Two-Spirit' captures the spiritual aspects of Indigenous gender liminality that the pejorative 'berdache' misses, spirituality being of central resonance in the phenomenon (Hall, 1997). The newer term is not without its own problems. Although widely adopted and recognized, for example, in gay and lesbian studies, Two-Spirit poses some translation problems in certain Indigenous languages. Jacobs et al. (1997) cite its literal translation into Navajo or Apache as signifying a person with two spirits, one living and one dead. In Shoshone, the translation means 'ghost' (p. 3), implying a person of whom one should feel frightened.

In denouncing the term 'berdache,' First Nations scholars noted the ways in which English and French anthropologists focused on bending the phenomenon to fit their more limited focus on sexual deviance, seeing the berdache as simply a 'male homosexual' (Herdt, 1997). The traditional anthropological reading also tended to mitigate or ignore the special cultural, spiritual, and gender roles of Two-Spirit persons. Prior to colonization, First Nations children who displayed certain characteristics were identified, usually by a grandmother, as Two-Spirited, as having the spirits of both male and female simultaneously. In adolescence, they were bestowed with a unique initiation ceremony that affirmed their special significance to the tribe. Two-Spirit people were (and are, in terms of reclamation) seen as gifted, endowed with unusual spiritual powers that warranted special status within their communities. Attributions of clairvoyance, prophecy, healing abilities, and so on, were common (Brown, 1997). Two-Spirit people were called upon to offer counsel to other tribe members experiencing marital problems or to assist with matchmaking prospective marriage couples. They were valued for their special insight into male/female relationships since they embodied the spirit of both sexes and could therefore impart extraordinary wisdom. Prior to colonization, Two-Spirit people were not subject to repudiation. On the contrary, they were honoured with special status.

Western anthropologists tended to dismiss the Two-Spirit claim, usually identifying and focusing on male-bodied 'berdaches' and the fact that they often took a male-bodied husband. While the anthropologists classify Two-Spirit people negatively as homosexual, the tribe itself did not view their marital and sexual relations with men as homosexual. Across tribes, in fact, the only consistent restriction placed upon Two-Spirits is that they could not marry or engage in sexual relations with other Two-Spirits. The traditional Western view of Two-Spirit persons, which focused on the assumed sinful debauchery of male homosexuality, as supposed evidence of 'uncivilized behaviour,' tended to overlook the multiplicity of the phenomenon. It seems that female-bodied persons could also be identified as Two-Spirit. Some First Nations scholars, however, dispute this assertion. Blackwood (1997), for example, argues that the 'manly-hearted women and warrior women of the Plains nations were alternative roles for women, not two-spirit genders' (p. 290).

The tendency to clear-cut classification is not necessarily – in the case of gender – an Indigenous tradition. Kehoe (1997) argues that many non-Western cultures 'value dynamic shifting, transformations, and existence in more than two dimensions' (p. 266). Colonization has, however, meddled with Two-Spirit traditions. The imposition of Western religious morals and values on First Nations put the special status of Two-Spirit people into disrepute among most North American Indigenous peoples. Having mostly lost their traditional roles, Lang (1997) notes that many First Nations people, who would have been initiated and socialized into Two-Spirit roles, instead found themselves rejected by their families and communities. Those who remained on their reservations often had to closet themselves, and those who could not do so usually left for urban centres, assimilating into gay and lesbian subcultures. Western gay and lesbian activists who forged the LGBT identity configuration have recently broadened it to be more inclusive of Two-Spirit people: LGBTTQQI.[7] In any case, the attempted eradication of Two-Spirit people by Western colonial traditions was not absolute in effect. Lang (1997) tells us that some of the grandmothers still remember the traditions of gender liminality and try to ensure that a Two-Spirit child is afforded the chance to claim the role within the community. Moreover, in Indigenous cultures that were not subject to colonization, as in parts of Polynesia, gender liminality retains its cultural significance (Roen, 2001).

Two-Spirit people in postcolonial society may or may not seek SRS. They may also hold an ambivalent position in regard to queer theory and the trans umbrella. In queer theory, the emphasis on sexuality and gender liberation tends to obscure the primacy of culture that many Two-Spirit people espouse. Lang (1997) argues that for most Two-Spirit people, their identities as First Nations people are usually the primary element of self-understanding. Recent reclamation of the status of Two-Spirit, damaged as a result of Western imperial adventures and coercive colonization, privileges ethnicity and cultural heritage. This cultural heritage is sufficient to allow for gender liminality in ways that do not require Western queer theory or a trans umbrella. That some First Nations Two-Spirit and gay and lesbian people are in agreement with queer theory and seek solidarity under a trans umbrella is not to be overlooked under postcolonial conditions. That racialized oppression can erase gender liminality and force its limited reclamation under newer Western discourses, such as queer theory, points to the tangled ways in which intersectionality manifests itself. Whether through queer theory or the undoing of racist oppression of traditional Native ways, the challenge for trans studies and TG activists is how to make space for addressing racial subjugation, abandoning their hitherto singular critical focus on the Western sex/gender binary.

Interiority and Exteriority

The current situation of Two-Spirit people illustrates the impact of social and cultural change in a particular context, in conjunction with a personal identity that does not conform to the sex/gender binary. This brings us back to the discussion of the tensions between exteriority and interiority. Exteriority pertains to the social world, its navigation by transpeople and the barriers they encounter. Interiority refers to the phenomenology of the subject and sedimented psychodynamics. The latter include identity configurations and intersections, trauma, fictional goals, and so on. There has been a tendency among academics to focus on one or the other: psychoanalysis has often focused on interiority to the exclusion of exteriority, while sociology on exteriority to the exclusion of interiority (Elliot, 2004a). For transpeople the body, in its flesh and blood corporeality, becomes the crux of these two dimensions. This is especially so for transsexuals, most of whom at one point or another must broach the issue of 'passing.' The body, as matter, matters, as Fuss (1989) wryly notes and Butler (1993) theorizes in responding to earlier misperceptions of her theory of *performativity*. How the body is socially read and how one feels about one's own body meet at the primary intersection between interiority and exteriority, where gender is concerned. This division between interiority and exteriority points to a broad paradox that TS and TG people tend to face, as exemplified in table 2.

Table 2
Interiority/exteriority

Interiority	Exteriority
TS – wants to conform to binary	TS – not always allowed to conform
TG – does not want to conform to binary	TG – is often forced to conform

Interiority pertains to the subjectivity of the gendered and transgendered self, the dimension psychoanalytic and other depth psychology discourses are concerned with. Exteriority refers to the location of gendered and transgendered subjects in the social world, their sociological and legal status, and so on. The issue of passing as male or female or the refusal to do so lies at the crux of this paradox. TS subjects generally want to pass (conform) in the social world in ways that are congruent with their gendered subjectivity, and yet are often refused and repudiated (read as non-conformist or aberrant). TG subjects often do not want to pass (preferring to be non-conformist) and yet are frequently forced to conform to the sex/gender binary (as when having to choose a lavatory or to tick a male/female box on a government form).

The paradoxes between interiority/exteriority have produced some acrimonious debates within trans communities. While TG activists have called for an end to transsexual passing (the striving to be socially read as male or female), many TS people have rejected the call. Prosser (1998) suggests that TS desires to pass are predicated on matching 'corporeal interiority (internal bodily sensations)' (p. 43) with external perceptions. Prosser argues that TS passing relieves the trauma of having been mis-sexed, it becomes 'a step towards home' (p. 184). SRS and exogenous hormone treatments are not really far removed from general social passing, as they help to align the felt and visual body. Social passing (dress, gesture, gait, accoutrement, and so on) aligns with external expectations. That passing might, as TG activists charge, be detrimental in the long run to a project of rejecting sex roles is not the issue. The issue is that TS people seem to be targeted for hyper-performing a gender by stereotypical presentations; pejorative accounts such as Germaine Greer's (1999) dismiss MtFs as 'pantomime dames.' Such criticisms place an unfair burden on TS people, who need to undo the trauma of psychological homelessness by going home to a body that feels right, to be/long, to be in the right sex. Conformity to sex and gender norms may be necessary for TS people to heal from the trauma of having been mis-sexed, but their performance of the role may still appear as acting rather than being (in the *performative* sense of bringing something to pass).

Namaste (2000) defines passing thus: 'Passing is about presenting yourself as a "real" woman or a "real" man – that is, as an individual whose "original" sex is never suspected. Passing means hiding the fact that you are transsexual and/or transgendered' (p. 144). In a society rife with transphobia and trans repudiation, and in subjects already traumatized by having been mis-sexed, the desire to struggle for home and to not be detected (passing) seems reasonable, even if attempts at passing rely on prevailing stereotypes of how males and females should ideally look and act.

Some feminist theorists, such as Lorber (1994), call for a society in which men and women, as currently understood, would no longer exist. Many of us would like to see this happen. If such a change were to occur, perhaps *then* TS people might feel more comfortable with SRS/hormones alone, with no further need to 'pass.' Why are TS people singled out and condemned for their passing, when natal males and females with a wide range of physical and behavioural characteristics pass in the world all the time, usually without any such criticism? The extent to which transpeople carry social stigma is an important consideration for the field of trans studies. *Stigma*, as Erving Goffman (1963) famously pointed out, is a term that goes back to ancient Greece, where criminals, slaves, or traitors were marked in the flesh, branded in such a way as to carry a tarnished and immediately identifiable status that was always visible, so that they might be avoided. The trans subject, like those maimed Greek outcasts, often carries a visible social stigma. Transpeople remain branded, marked as identifiable, yet they are also curiously 'erased'[8] from the social world (e.g., denied legal documents), as Namaste's (2000) ethnographic study of transpeople in Quebec argues. In this instance, they do not fit into any categories and remain *personae non gratae*.

Transpeople have historically been denied their selfhood. Faced with stigma, social barriers, and a widespread lack of understanding, many have turned to writing as a way of articulating their embodiment and associated struggles.[9] Prosser (1998) analysed fifty autobiographies written by transpeople from 1954 to 1996. He asks, 'Why do so many transsexuals write autobiographies?' (p. 103). The contested site of the body is a major factor. Prosser notes that in these autobiographies 'being trapped in the wrong body' becomes a transsexual's motivation for writing the self; the 'wrong body' theme becomes their 'most famous rhetorical trope' (p. 104). Those TS subjects who do not write their life story must nevertheless become master narrators of their own mis-sexed stories. The inevitable requirement to narrate the trauma of being mis-sexed from childhood onwards, in order to gain authorization from psychologists/psychiatrists, enforces a need for self-narration. Narrating the body becomes a necessary skill, and self-narration is a key element in persuading the authorities to permit SRS. The interiority of memory, and the need to ex/press trauma in a cohesive storied form, intersects with negotiating the exterior social world and its institutions. The self as an integrating story is re/called in pursuit of healing or repairing the mis-sexed body, in appealing to the authorities for aid, for medical help in hope of achieving congruity. Success depends on the ability to convey 'who they are,' in order to remain or become what they want to be. This was evident in the stories shared in the interviews conducted for this book.

Trans-scribing: Theory and Interviews

Following this Introduction, chapter 2 proceeds to an analysis of the terms *repudiation* and *trans/phobia*. Transphobia assumes and insinuates that phobia is the sole motivation for social discrimination against transpeople. While acknowledging the colloquial importance of 'transphobia' in trans communities, and pragmatically making use of the term in the interviews, I point to the less universalistic and less causal implications of *repudiation* as a process that intersects the interior (intrapersonal) with the exterior (interpersonal/institutional). Repudiation often includes a phobic reaction, yet might also include ideological forms of rejection/negation of both identity and trans subjectivity of a non-phobic cast. Hence, repudiation complements the more common usage of transphobia and is not intended to replace the term. Chapter 3 provides reflection on the thematic topics that emerged from my interviews with transpeople. Nine of the ten primary categories of social repudiation are covered in this chapter (with the tenth category discussed in the Conclusion). Salient excerpts from the interviews are concentrated in chapters 2 and 3; however, they also appear throughout the book when appropriate or when relevant, so as to ensure that transpeople themselves are substantially heard as they narrate the social and internalized barriers they experience. Examples of political repudiation and prevailing contradictions follow in chapter 4, which provides a socio-political and clinical context to the myriad issues raised in the interviews. Chapter 5 replies to these varied political/clinical rejections of transpeople's embodied claims by means of 'talking back,' to refute the arguments of those who mis-comprehend trans subjectivities.

The latter part of the book pursues a more sustained analysis of the depth psychologies in order to 'return the gaze' of the perpetrators of trans repudiation. These discourses are shown to be central to an understanding of the dynamics of unconscious repudiation. The notions of trauma, distress, conflict, defence, compensations, ideal strivings, unconscious fictions, and subjectivity in its (un)conscious aspects, are all part of trans experience. The challenges transpeople pose to the psychic sedimentation of the sex/gender binary in non-trans subjects requires a reconsideration of depth psychology for an adequate theorizing of the complexity of trans repudiation. A return of the clinical gaze onto the discourses/narratives of the depth psychologies provides a means of reclaiming them to account for trans repudiation, without maintaining the conservative analyses of psychopathology that have commonly appeared in these discourses. Chapter 6 looks at Adlerian theory – since this is the psychological orientation I am best familiar with – and its usefulness to these debates. The study concludes in chapter 7 by considering aspects of the subject/self debate. For transsexuals especially, the concept of *self*, implying integrity and cohesion, may be an effective healing fiction for those with mis-sexed bodies. In contrast, the perpetually fractured *subject* (as favoured by poststructuralism), which emphasizes fluidity, disintegration, and multiplicity, is often more relevant to those TGs who are seeking to escape from the sexual binary. The fact that repudiation denies both subjectivity and selfhood to transpeople points to the need for profound change on both the social and psychological levels, so that transpeople might be considered subjects/selves in their own right. Healing the self for many transpeople entails a physical transition *and* an emotional/psychological evolution, to make peace with oneself, to end self-oppression. Self-oppression is an all too common feature found in the histories of many trans subjects.

In keeping with the feminist thrust of this work, I call for solidarity with trans struggle, for their emancipation from sex and gender oppression. This oppression might seem uniquely targeted towards them, but it may, in fact, be part of something broader, something that affects all of us in differing and perhaps unthought ways.

2 Repudiation and Transphobia: Concepts, Theory, and Experience

In their status as Others, transpeople are frequently positioned within an alterity that is not of their own making; whether they like it or not, they are often forced to endure the primal reactions of others. These reactions are often complex and not well understood, least of all by perpetrators. I have therefore introduced the term *repudiation* in striving to understand an array of reactive dynamics directed towards transpeople, which are often hostile and threatening. As an analytic category, repudiation includes phobic reactions, as well as other dynamics of negation, in relation to trans alterity. Yet repudiation also goes beyond those interpersonal experiences that transpeople routinely describe as *transphobic* in nature. In going beyond transphobia, I do not purport that there is no such thing. On the contrary, it signifies a troubling set of dynamics that often disrupts transpeople's everyday/night lives. However, I intend to critically appraise the term and demonstrate its limitations. Expounding upon 'repudiation' as a concept and a process will, I believe, strengthen the legitimacy of the experiences that transpeople disclose when they speak – in a global sense – of the far too frequently encountered phenomena of 'transphobia.'

The Limits of Trans/phobia

The term *transphobia*, while understood within trans and queer communities, generally remains unfamiliar everywhere else. A search in the randomly selected 2005 edition of the *Oxford Canadian English Dictionary* does not reveal the word. The term *transsexual* is listed, and *transgender*[1] has been recently added to this reference tool. *Trans* and *phobia* are separately outlined in different categories, both of which provide clues as to the potential meaning of the full term. 'Trans' is defined as follows:

> **Trans-** / traenz, -ns / prefix **1** across, beyond (*transcontinental; transgress*). **2** on or to the other side of (*transatlantic*) (opp. cis-) **3** through (*transcutaneous*). **4** into another state or place (*transform; transcribe*). **5** surpassing, transcending (*transfinite*) ... [from or after Latin *trans* across]. (P. 1540)[2]

'Trans' carries with it a sense of motion, movement, process, and so on. These connotations explain the term's appeal in critical fields such as feminism and postcolonial theory, fields concerned with change. These discourses have begun to consider the action-oriented and dis-locating power of *trans* through trans-disciplinary inquiries into transnational and transcultural issues in relation to oppression and various subject positions. 'Trans,' in its conceptual and etymological complexity, is a term ripe for social, theoretical, and praxis implementations.

In the interviews with the twenty transpeople consulted for this book, none of the participants problematized the term 'transphobia'; all agreed that it connotes an identifiable, menacing force that is often perceived as ubiquitous, or a dynamic that may have traumatized them in the past. Regardless of the multiplicity of identity configurations that emerged in the study, participants identifying as Trans, transsexual, Two-Spirit, or transgender, all acknowledged the problem of transphobia. While many transpeople disagree with one another about matters of identity and politics, none seem to disagree with the notion of transphobia. Indeed, that transphobia exists constitutes one of the major points of consensus that has emerged from my research. Moreover, that transpeople themselves have not necessarily critically appraised the term may have more to do with the urgency of the political issues that transphobia signifies, rather than academic debates surrounding its semantic interpretation.

Transphobia ultimately suggests a causal explanation for the subjugation of trans lives, the thesis that transpeople incite – by their very existence and presence – *fear*. Undoubtedly, within perpetrators' reactions, the affect of fear is dynamically a part of many instances of trans discrimination. Yet is it universally so? Does not the invocation of the universal transphobia, therefore, automatically conjure the trans subject as fearsome? Having listened carefully to transpeople on this matter, I argue no, there is little evidence to suggest that all forms of trans-based discrimination are rooted in fear. Rather, and in fact, it is transpeople who more often have reason to be afraid.

We are reminded that phobics know what they are afraid of – their fear of the phobic object is *conscious*, though the root of the fear may be obscured. Yet it is apparent that those who consciously negate or otherwise reject the legitimacy to trans claims to having been missexed/gendered may do so for reasons other than fear, such as loyalty to social and religious ideals, or moral convictions predicated by an 'ought.' There are political ideologies, for example, that do not accept the legitimacy of trans lives. Subscription and faithfulness to a conscious or default political ideology does not necessarily point to the primacy of fear as the affective motivation for rejection and hostility. Hence, repudiation, a process of disavowal and negation that often includes fear yet also contains other schematic dynamics, is a less limited explanatory position.

Repudiation evokes conscious and unconscious dynamics that are inter/intrapersonal. It constellates a range of affective and cognitive elements such as sympathy, pity, and a saviour attitude for the 'misguided' (a colonial mindset), through to enmity, hatred, and repulsion. The latter are aggressive qualities that may or may not be laced-in with fear/threat. While phobia is a known complex caused by conscious fear of an object, repudiation connotes a multifaceted dynamic, often unconscious, a reactive process of ambivalence to an object that can evoke simple defensive negation through to extreme responses.

Because transphobia is analogous to homophobia, it certainly bears mentioning some of the problems that the latter term manifests. Kitzinger (1996) points out the insufficiencies of the concept of homophobia:

> Unlike terms such as *sexism* or *heterosexism*, which were developed within the Women's and Gay Liberation Movements and modelled on *political* concepts, the word *homophobia* derives from (and is used within) the academic discipline of psychology: *phobia* comes from the Greek for 'fear' ... The notion that some people might have a phobia about gay men and lesbians first began to appear in psychological writing in the late 1960s and early 1970s, and homophobia was defined as 'an irrational persistent fear or dread of homosexuals.' (P. 8)

Kitzinger argues that there are two critical dimensions to the concept of *phobia*. Firstly, as with other forms of psychopathology, psychology exercises its individualizing power under prevailing social conditions in ascribing a personal diagnosis such as phobia. This notion suggests that the phobic flaw is one merely residing within an individual. Rather than prioritizing historical and cultural aspects to an aetiology, the mental distress is addressed solely as an individual problem in need of diagnosis and adjustment through individual treatment. Homosexuality, itself formerly considered a sexual neurosis, is an apposite exemplar of the problem. Historically, psychology conceptualized homosexuality as a sexual deviation or dysfunction, a fault within an individual, requiring individual treatment and adjustment towards an unproblematic, normative heterosexuality. This view, Kitzinger argues, shifted the emphasis and responsibility for social discrimination from the oppressor to the oppressed. It is the homosexual and not society, in this myopic gaze, who must change. Her second point is that there are legitimate reasons for the heterosexual establishment to fear, for example, lesbians (since, she argues, lesbians hold revolutionary power). Yet 'homophobia' tells us, following affirmative models of therapy, that this is simply an irrational fear. One need not be afraid of lesbians according to the discourse of homophobia, suggesting that it is just an 'irrational phobia,' one that can be tended to like any other ailment. While there is no diagnosis of 'homophobia' in the *Diagnostic and Statistical Manual of Mental Disorders* (APA, 2000), there remain legal precedents that argue for 'homosexual panic' as a reason to mitigate the consequences/sentencing for perpetrators' acts of hostility and violence directed towards gays and lesbians (Steinberg, 2005).

A phobia is an irrational fear that is out of proportion to the danger at hand, though some of these fears have a sound foundation in the historically lived experience of both humans and animals. Fears of snakes, spiders, and heights, for example, are legitimate, but only 'psychopathologically' significant if they control a person's life beyond what is reasonable. Undoubtedly, there are people whose fear of lesbians, gay men, or others constituted as queer may cause them to experience great anxiousness, palpitations, sweat, shortness of breath, alarm, and so on. Whereas one would be hard pressed to find a rational evolutionary or individualized reason to justify a fear of queer people, examples abound of institutionalized enmity of them in the social world. This is the root of the problem: 'homophobia' is not rational; rather, it mirrors historical problems, related to the ruling of bodies, internalized by subjects through the *social world*. While the phenomenon often manifests as a psychological effect, there is no homophobia that can be attributed simply to the psychologized individual. For this reason, like Kitzinger, I therefore prefer the term *heterosexism* over 'homophobia.' I also acknowledge, however, that 'homophobia' is useful as an everyday term, and its entry into common parlance renders it a simple if inadequate referent. It is easy to surmise that this too is a rationale for why transpeople continue to use the analogous concept of transphobia: it approximates 'homophobia' in ways that can readily borrow the latter's increased familiarity as a political issue commonly discussed in public discourse. As with related attempts to describe the socio/political fear of various groups (e.g., xenophobia, Islamaphobia), linking phobia to a subjugated group lends rhetorical, analytic, and descriptive clout to urgent social problems. This is especially so in the current political climate of fear ('the war on terror').

Conceptually, transphobia is also used to describe the concrete effects of trans subjugation that produce the 'daunting array of obstacles' (Califia, 2003, p. 1) that transpeople face in the course of their everyday/night lives. And while homophobia and transphobia overlap, they are also quite distinct in some ways. For example, many transpeople are straight in their sexual orientation, and this makes it erroneous to posit homophobia or heterosexism as the social force that explains their oppression. And yet the fearful antagonist who utters transphobic insults may very well be unaware of being transphobic. The matter is also complicated by the probability that perpetrators may either misread transpeople as queer or reject the heterosexual transperson's claimed orientation and impose homosexuality on them. As Califia (ibid.) argues, 'straight culture reads much of the public expression of gay identity as gender transgression. To them, we're [trans] all part of the same garbage heap of sex-and-gender trash' (p. 256). The issue is that of gender transgression, of refusing to be what one 'is' or was ordered to be and inscribed as, of resisting the Law of the Father[3] which defends the sanctity of the sex/gender binary system. Since transphobia also signifies the obstacles and barriers that transpeople face, the concept is often used to justify an end to the deficit of rights that they clearly lack. Yet, as we shall see, the call for trans rights often demonstrates the schisms between TS and TG interests.

Riki Wilchins (2002a) uses the term *genderism* rather than 'transphobia' to describe the systemic oppression that queer and transpeople are subject to. On the model of racism, she describes genderism as provoking the 'civil rights movement of our time' (p. 17). Wilchins

(2002b) places herself as an activist in the transgender camp, arguing that the binary gender system is the object for overthrow: 'binaries ... They are not really about two things but only one, power' (p. 43). This drawing of attention to the effects of binary-based oppression on TG people is laudable. However, her analysis tends to overlook the conscious use and approval of the binary by some transpeople. It also overlooks the fact that many transpeople are not, will not, or cannot be TG activists. Furthermore, Wilchins's declaration – 'the civil rights movement of our times' – suggests that the racialized struggles of yesteryears have been resolved, or only belong to another time. It is important, I contend, that the struggle for trans liberation not be separated from other struggles, or placed above them, including the ongoing struggle to end racism. Other trans scholars such as Namaste (2005), who emphasizes the needs of TS people, oppose campaigns for 'transgender rights,' suggesting that a rights strategy often conceals imperialism.[4]

Aside from conveying the need for attention to rights and the debate that surrounds a rights-based strategy, transphobia as a dynamic concept also highlights the interpersonal fears that many transpeople themselves express. Burnham (1999), in her study of the social barriers confronting transpeople, writes about the prominence of transphobia, which points to 'lack of support and understanding, fear of losing spouse, family, friends ... fear of an unpredictable future, and fear of losing a job' (p. 29). She believes that addressing and eradicating transphobia will require a 'monumental effort' (p. 29).

While Burnham makes an important point, the use of the concept 'transphobia' requires cautionary limits. Her example points to the genuine internalized fears that many transpeople express, yet these understandable fears are not necessarily of the intensity of a phobia. A totalizing 'transphobia' can also have the perhaps unintended effect of erasing 'race'/culture as analytic categories. Roen (2001), in her discussion of a Maaori trans woman, illustrates the complexity of intersecting identities and how the repudiation of Indigenous 'trans embodied' people has further ramifications; for example, in view of

> ... the Maaori conception of identity as something which is never based in the individual alone but relates to the extended family (*whaanau*) and to genealogy (*whakapapa*) ... to deride [a Maaori] for being transsexual would be to denigrate her entire ancestral line: a far more risky and grave action than merely discriminating against an 'individual.' (P. 259)

Transphobia, as a Western concept, can mask the history of colonialism and imperialism if one assumes that it connotes merely a fear of transgressing the dominant Western sex/gender binary. Moreover, 'transphobia' conceals the Western denigration of Indigenous Others, including cultures and histories that often celebrate what the West views as gender transgression, as in Two-Spirit tribal roles and statuses. In this case, the repudiation is actually refusing a whole culture and not just an individual's sex/gender.

When it does occur, there is necessarily a relational quality to transphobia. As Dorothy Smith (1999) writes, 'It is the relations that rule, and people rule and are ruled through them' (p. 82). Smith is specifically referring to institutionalized ruling relations between men and women. What is needed is an extended understanding of how the same/other binary also rules transpeople. This is a complex undertaking, as many transpeople themselves are enmeshed in the gender binary and do not wish to overthrow it, perceiving themselves simply as mis-assigned. Hence this book raises issues around belonging and being rejected simultaneously, of being on both sides at once. If someone is TS, for example, living as a man or a woman legally and post-surgically, yet meets with consistent barriers that reject that person's embodied and phenomenological claims, can transphobia wholly account for such obstacles? In some cases perhaps, but more broadly I suggest that another process is also going on.

Trans Repudiation

To repudiate is to reject, refuse, condemn, repel, disown, renounce, and back away from that which engenders repulsion. Repudiation entails dynamics of denial, and for psychoanalysis is primordially related to the early experiences of separating from the mother, for example, by rejecting her breast. In the moment when the infant rejects the mother's breast, s/he also repudiates it, making it ab/ject (refuse-d, thrown out). The etymology of repudiation is linked to the Latin *repudiare* and *repudiatus*, pointing to the foot (*ped* or *pes*), recoiling, backing away from something or kicking it away. Harper (2001) also links the origins of the word to *pudere*, or that which causes shame. The word migrated into Old French by means of *repeller* from *re* or back, and *peller* meaning to strike at or to drive back the 'repellant.' It was linked to eighteenth-century medicines created to treat tumours, which had a rank flavour, a vile taste that was repelling.

Together, transphobia and trans repudiation point to the complexity of re/actions that many transpeople are forced to endure from others. The *re* in reaction is the motivating factor that prompts an action, whether the stepping-back in re/pudiation, the pushing away of the object (the re/ject), the affective defence exemplified in the psychoanalytic concept of the *reaction formation*, or the re/press-ion of one's own lack of gender certainty that is stirred up when encountering the trans object. Ironically, psychoanalytic and depth psychology discourses may aid greater understanding of the repudiation of trans subjectivity since these discourses consider *prima facie* the ways in which the past (re)impinges on the 'present,' how presence is undermined.

Butler (1993) suggests that repudiation is a crucial act involved in the formation of subjectivity:

> ... the subject is constituted through the force of exclusion and abjection, one which produces a constitutive outside to the subject, an abjected outside, which is, after all, 'inside' the subject as its own founding repudiation. (P. 3)

Kristeva (1982) speaks of abjection as located 'at the crossroads of phobia, obsession, and perversion ... overtaxed by a "bad object," [the subject] turns away from it, cleanses itself of it, and vomits it' (p. 45). She contends that repudiation is a form of negation, '*negation* and its modalities, *transgression, denial, and repudiation*' (p. 6; italics in original). It can be witnessed in the repulsion that is expressed in food loathing or the urge to vomit on seeing something repulsive. Repudiation carries with it deep ambivalence and hence is complexly linked to desire, to being pulled to an object that one loves and hates; 'repudiation affects desire itself' (ibid., p. 7). It is also linked to the precariousness of self and identity, a response to a sense of threat. The prohibition against eating foods such as shellfish or pork in some cultures has little to do with the food items themselves; rather, it becomes symbolic of identity and threats to identity, of engulfment or annihilation.

The reasons for a specific repudiation, importantly, may have conscious or unconscious roots. Stephen Frosh (1994), in his psychoanalytic study of masculinity, notes the tendency to repudiation: 'identifying and feeling at ease with men's "own" sexuality seems to be something both necessary and hard to manage, at times producing violent repudiation of anything too threateningly "other"' (p. 93). Adam Jukes (1993) believes that the formation of male selves, traced to traumatic separation issues with the mother, is the source of 'male misogyny' (p. xxvii). He contends that misogyny is a 'potential' in all people, male or female, though more 'debilitating' in males, who may remain unconscious of their enmity towards women. Jukes suggests that relational circumstances 'call out' misogyny, where it may spill into rage or crystallize into a more conscious sense of hatred. The object of such enmity is viewed as a threat to the self, and in more extreme cases (such as the complex of phobia as in transphobia), fear and paranoia become so intense that they must be projected outwards onto an object. Loss of the self, so laboriously built, is threatening to the subject; hence, s/he marks the boundaries of an 'unstable identity by reifying and repudiating the other' (Frosh, 1994, p. 122). Whether this Other is a woman, queer person, or transperson may not matter since, for the most phobic, they *all* may threaten the (male) self.

McAfee (2004) suggests that abjection, an early form of repudiation, is part of a tenuous self-formation in the process of separating from the mother, of drawing lines between 'you' and 'me,' 'the state of abjecting or rejecting what is other to oneself – and thereby creating borders of an always tenuous "I" ' (p. 45). The phenomenon is saliently dramatized in the film *The Crying Game* (Jordan and Wooley, 1992). Fergus (a.k.a. Jimmy), a former IRA member living incognito in England, is dating Dil, an anatomical male who is assumed by Fergus to be a natal female. Dil, in turn, wrongly believes that he knows of her trans embodiment. When they are about to make love, Fergus discovers Dil's penis. He reacts with a look of horror, assaults her, then turns and violently vomits. He vomits out her penis, attempting to abject it.

Fergus's reaction is somewhat akin to Kristeva's (1982) observation that certain cultures engage in purification rites and other religious practices that establish boundaries between groups (e.g., men and women) to prevent 'pollution' or 'defilement.' And yet the abject also exerts a fascination, similar to Fanon's (1967) phobogenic object. McAfee suggests that the abject is 'both sickening yet irresistible' (p. 47). In our culture, trans repudiation is rife, yet the success of films like *The Crying Game*, and of magazine articles, television spectacles, pornography, etc., that portray transpeople, is evidence of a fascination with transgressive gender/sex bodies. According to Merleau-Ponty's philosophy of *alterity*, the flesh of the Other is contained within the subject's own self (Smith, 1990). Yet Emmanuel Levinas (1990) sees this 'carnal subjectivity' (p. 57) as inter-subjectivity, a 'flesh of one's flesh ... an intercorporeity' (p. 63). The anachronistic dynamic surfaces in Fergus's attempt to vomit the penis; the Other in Levinas's thought is irreducible – it cannot be abjected since the penis, flesh of one's flesh, is already a part of, for example, Fergus's narcissistic self. Psychodynamics are implicitly operative in the phenomenon, the past impinging on the 'present' through the *re* as Levinas argues: 'Here is vision turning back, re-turning into non-vision ... into vision's denial at the heart of vision, into that of which vision, already espousing a plastic form, is but forgetfulness and re-presentation' (p. 60). Throughout the remainder of *The Crying Game*, Fergus remains drawn to Dil, yet also ambivalent towards her trans status. His initial fear of her penis dissipates into a generalized repudiation – at times he insists that she dress and behave like a man, while at other times he tolerates her femininity. This example illustrates how fear (phobia) often operates – in varying degrees – within the domain of repudiation.

Since the term 'transphobia' is used in trans communities, I likewise made use of it in my interviews. Yet, following reflexive theorizing on the interviews as a whole, I tend to use the term 'repudiation.' In doing so, I see transphobia as an aspect of repudiation, but repudiation is more than just fear; it conveys an ongoing narcissistic need to preserve the 'purity' of the self, to draw borders between the self and Others. Moreover, I am aware of sociopathic syndromes, such as those discussed in Duncan Cartwright's (2002) study of violent, imprisoned offenders, in which dehumanization of objects occurred during sadistic acts (such as murder) and there is little or no evidence of emotionality (inclusive of fear). In some cases, tracing the childhood history of such offenders reveals physical and sexual abuse, where identification with the aggressor defensively protects against fears of annihilation. In this case, fear may have sedimented since that time, yet not all sadistic offenders have such histories (ibid.). Most sadistic, violent offenders are men, and all of the participants in Cartwright's study were men in prison. In the West, men commit at least 90 per cent of violent crimes (Campbell and Muncer, 1995), which may indicate that their male/masculine identity is experienced as in need of protection or assertion.

'Repudiation' is a term related to a number of concepts in depth psychology. For example, it shares aspects of Freud's concept of *Verwerfung* (from the verb *verwerfen*, to throw away), often translated as 'distortion.' Freud used the concept to evoke differing meanings, as Laplanche and Pontalis (1972) summarize:

(1) In a rather loose sense of a refusal, which can, for example, occur as repression; (2) ... a casting-out in the form of a conscious judgement of condemnation; (3) [in the Lacanian re-reading] ... the ego rejects (*verwirft*) the incompatible representation ... and behaves as if the representation had never occurred to the ego at all. (P. 187)

Repudiation of trans subjectivity can be seen on a spectrum ranging from a conscious yet unexpressed distaste through to extreme forms of reaction that precipitate violence and destructiveness based on rage (sudden and explosive) or hatred (stable, integrated aspects of enmity towards an object). In *Instincts and Their Vicissitudes*, Freud (1915) writes:

Hate, as a relation to objects, is older than love. It derives from the narcissistic ego's primordial repudiation of the external world with its outpouring of stimuli. As an expression of the reaction of unpleasure evoked by objects, it always remains in an intimate relation with the self-preservation instincts. (P. 135)

There is the potential to theorize the unconscious and defensive mechanisms of repudiation, especially concerning transpeople. Yet, to date, very little appears to have been done. While issues related to transpeople's experiences of being-in-the-world are rarely addressed in these discourses, several central concepts are useful in the attempt to understand their experiences and the reactions they are often forced to endure. I shall proceed to discuss some of these psychoanalytic concepts in relation to transpeople's status as Others.

Psychoanalysis, Repudiation, and Alterity

However flawed and context specific one might consider Freud's original account of psychosexual development, it has undoubtedly had widespread influence. As for its relevance to transpeople, some elements of Freud's theory may potentially help us to understand the difficulties transpeople face as a result of being trans. This utilization of Freudian theory is ironic since, as we shall see in chapter 5, psychoanalysis has been used to repudiate TS people. It has long denied their status as genuinely mis-sexed, clinically explaining away embodied incongruity under the disabling discourse of psychopathology.

Re-harnessed, psychoanalysis can nevertheless explain aspects of people's reactions to transpeople and, in particular, their intensity. Concepts such as repression, projection, envy, defence, and abjection are essential to maintaining sexual difference, a difference Freud sees as necessary but constantly under threat. Human psychology, in general, employs various defence mechanisms, or what Alfred Adler (1956) termed *safeguarding* strategies. These strategies are of shared interest among the depth psychologies (Freudian, Adlerian, Jungian) and often centre on material that is concerned with sex and gender. Western culture has developed, over time, tremendous ambivalence in these realms, and ambivalence is the stuff of defence and the unconscious.

Frosh (1994) claims that 'psychoanalysis at its very core is about sexual difference; it is constituted in it and through it, acting it out as it tries to pronounce upon it' (p. 12). The key element embedded in Freudian theorizing on sexual difference is to be found in its foundational concept of *repression*. Classical psychoanalysis contends that human subjects actively seek pleasure and avoid pain, particularly in the first few years of life. In neurosis, the pain most often avoided is that associated with anxiety. Anxiety serves as a warning signal, alerting the ego (consciousness) to the danger of overwhelming anxiety or panic (flooding). Anxiety may surface, should an unconscious wish break through the barriers guarded by the censor, and subsequently overwhelm the ego. Once the ego has been warned of impending danger, of flooding, the individual may then (unconsciously) seek a particular mode of defence.

Anxiety is often related to uncertainty about one's gender identity – an uncertainty built into the problematic binary established only with difficulty by both sexes. Samuels (1993) suggests that the deeper, unconscious roots of a conscious gender certainty produce patterns that are 'rigid, conventional, and persecuting' (p. 130). This position is echoed by O'Connor and Ryan (1993): 'the unconscious challenges the circle of certainties by which the human recognises itself as ego' (p. 140). Psychoanalysis contends that the human infant is born undifferentiated or *polymorphously perverse*: initially there is no gendered aim to innate sexuality. Through stages of maturation and experiences such as breast-feeding and toilet-training, the infant comes to direct her/his sexual impulses onto certain objects. With regard to the acquisition of a particular gender, it would appear that Freud's phallic or Oedipal phase (ages 3–6) is paramount. Repression becomes a feature as the child moves through stages of psychosexual development, culminating in the latency stage (beginning around ages 7–8), a period of more comprehensive repression.

In the Oedipal phase, castration anxiety in boys is said to develop through the discovery of the difference between male and female genitals. This phase is the most significant for any child's development of gender identity and sexual orientation (Freud, 1925). 'Proper resolution' of the phase ensures the establishment of 'correct' (hence heterosexual) sexual objects, the foundation of erotic attraction in adult life. The Oedipal phase emphasizes the development of the superego, a mental agency that operates through self-recrimination (guilt), said to be of more significance to boys due to castration anxiety. The judicial function of the superego was controversially asserted as evidence of male moral superiority and female lack of moral rectitude, something that feminists have strongly contested (Gilligan, 1982).

For girls, penis envy is said to characterize the phallic phase, motivating a shift in erotic attachment from mother (women) to father (men) – from homosexual to heterosexual. In boys, identification shifts from mother (desired object) to father (feared object) due to the threat of castration associated with the incest taboo. Submission to the father ensures the safekeeping of the boy's penis, and offers the incentive of masculine privilege. This aspect of the theory was contested, however, by women psychoanalysts such as Karen Horney (1937). She polemically suggests that unconscious 'womb envy' in males is of greater influence in gender politics than any penis envy in females. Today, it appears that psychoanalysts are somewhat less one-sided than Freud was on the issue of envy and the other sex's reproductive bits. As Colette Chiland (2005) notes, 'Many three- or four-year-old boys have wept when they learned that they would never be able to carry a baby in their tummy, or that their breasts would never contain milk' (p. 66). Chiland is nevertheless a controversial figure since, as we shall see in chapter 5, she maintains the Freudian tradition of repudiating and pathologizing transpeople.

I suggest that *envy* is a useful concept for considering a range of trans repudiations, from slight discomfort through to more extreme repudiations such as those witnessed in violent attacks. Psychoanalysts such as Melanie Klein (1975) claim that a range of destructive forces are contained within the sedimentation of the psyche, including potent affects such as envy. Kate Barrows (2002) argues that 'it is *difference* that arouses envy' (p. 20; italics in original). In psychoanalytic theorizing, envy is considered a deeply uncomfortable affect, which can be experienced consciously yet is also a powerful unconscious force. Conscious envy, especially that caused by social deprivation (poverty, material inequality), is an understandable reaction to social injustice. However, unconscious envy, such as that expressed in an intolerance of difference, is a more complex dynamic to understand. Envy appears in early childhood and can manifest itself at any age. In children, Barrows outlines various 'objects' that stir up envy: 'the penis ... for its potency, the breast for its feeding capacity, the mother's body for being able to contain babies and both parents for being, in their different ways, sources of life' (ibid., p. 19).

Psychoanalysts suggest that envy is a painful emotion, so much so that it must be disowned through defensive manoeuvres such as *projective identification*. Drawing on Klein, Cartwright (2002) suggests that projective identification is about the infantile 'splitting off of "part-objects" that have become "bad" through their association with destructiveness' (p. 14). In attempting to comprehend why some sadistic, violent offenders have no previous history of violence or instability, Cartwright suggests that the seeming irrationality of such acts can be understood by recourse to psychoanalytic theory. He ascertains that 'hatred and dread are central to primitive [*sic*] experience and it is only if these can be contained in some way, that love and the "good object" can be found' (p. 17). I suggest that a range of trans repudiations might be linked to the problem of envy for a number of possible reasons. Transpeople may be envied for shifting into bodies that the hostile perpetrator may unconsciously desire to have. Or envy may incite rage to crystallize into hatred, as Adam Jukes (1993) suggests regarding *misogyny* (which he believes to be a universal problem in males and females), an often unconscious hatred of women that, when roused, threatens 'the psychological well-being of the subject' (p. 5).

Transpeople (and non-trans 'homosexuals') are deemed by some psychoanalysts to have failed to resolve the Oedipus complex. Male-bodied trans children (pre-MtF) are said to remain pathologically attached to their mothers, failing to shift their identification to the father. Female-born transpeople (pre-FtM) are said to have failed to resolve their penis envy, falsely believing that if they shift identification to father, they will (in tandem) grow a penis. Their mistake is to have identified with the father, rather than with what he represents (the correct erotic desire of difference). 'She' fails to shift, as the *Electra complex* demands, 'her' clitoral arousal to the vagina, remaining active rather than becoming passive. In both instances, failures in sexual identification are the primary culprit that produces 'gender identity disorders' (GIDs) (APA, 2000).

The violation of the binary, as perceived by those who have negative reactions on encountering the trans body, may elicit a number of primordial reactions, manifestation of deep fear, since trifling with reproductive organs, genitals, and breasts evokes not only castration anxiety but also an unconscious terror of dismemberment and death. The repudiation of SRS (sexual reassignment surgery) may be based on the irrational fear that it represents the annihilation of the human species, as does abortion for some anti-choice campaigners. Negative reactions to the idea of mastectomy for FtMs may be stirred up by infantile ambivalence towards the breast, or fear of women refusing to be mothers, of a permanent withholding of the breast, the death of the mother. That trans men have abjected a mis-sexed breast is not recognized as a type of maternal abjection tied to the desire to keep the body clean and hygienic, 'proper,' as Kristeva (1982) explains. FtMs may be seen as rejecting the mother's body, which has been partly internalized, but improperly so. Those who repudiate FtMs do not comprehend this abjection. Without surgery, the abject hounds the FtM subject, since binding practices do not remove the mis-sexed breast. He must fully abject the breast in order to finalize his separate self. SRS in this sense is not a mutilating practice; rather, it is a necessary and final abjection to assist the construction of the integrity of the sexed and gendered self.

In regard to MtFs, their breasts may be encountered as not akin to the mother's breast, as an impostor devoid of milk, a 'bad breast'; and the thought of vaginoplasty may arouse castration anxiety in some men. Moreover, images of a woman with a penis may evoke the pre-Oedipal, all-powerful phallic mother. Conversely, the removal of the FtM breast may be seen as an unconscious savaging of the mother's 'good breast,' while phalloplasty and scrotal closure of the vagina forecloses/annihilates the desire/dread of the mother's genitals.

Falling back into ambivalent and irrational reactions to an early object when confronted with the trans body points to the lack of effectiveness of the internalized Law of the Father (the superego). In many cases, such repudiation of a transperson assumes they are 'really queer,' which may or may not be the case. Queer or not, transpeople might evoke intense feelings of *envy*. Tim Dean (2001) speaks of the

Lacanian concept of *jouissance*, 'the conviction that others are enjoying themselves at our expense, and it is this conviction that sparks the desire to injure others' (p. 129). Transpeople might be hated for shifting into envied bodies, of doing the 'unthinkable,' imagined to have access to forbidden forms of pleasure 'that responsible, law-abiding citizens are denied' (ibid., p. 129). This disavowal is really about their status as trans, and repudiating the trans body is connected with refusing same-sex desire. Trans repudiation conveys the fragility of the perpetrator's own identity as belonging to one well-defined sex/gender and as heterosexual.

For TS subjects, in particular, to be socially read as *being* the proper embodied sex speaks to a desired metaphysics of presence. The ideal is to never be socially read as trans, to 'pass.' Yet, in the shadow of passing, of sufficiently approximating this ideal, is the contradistinctive possibility of failing. Sara Ahmed (2004) speaks of the 'failure of presence' in which those constituted as Other generate a misreading of the relationship between 'subjects, objects, [and] signs' (p. 46). This misreading produces an effect that is affective. When one doesn't pass, they are forced into a position of alterity and subject to reactions. If the Other is laughed at, interpreted as having failed to pass, this may constitute a reaction formation that 'conceals' embarrassment or fear, of dredging up border anxiety. Ahmed suggests that 'fear works by establishing others as fearsome *insofar as they threaten to take the self in*' (p. 64; italics in original). This cannibalistic threat, of seemingly being forced to ingest the Other, produces a defensive dynamic of self-border constriction. The unconscious is roused to trigger autonomic responses: the stomach clenches, the gag reflex readies itself, and the subject prepares to vomit out the offender, to abject. Encountering an Other may then entail the stepping back or repudiation of that Other. Yet, since the Other is fascinating, an ambivalent two-step may follow – I step back and then step forward again. This see-saw effect – rocking back and forth – is the desire to find steady ground, to regain balance, to determine where I end and you begin.

There are times when the reaction to the Other is extreme. In some cases, transpeople have been severely beaten, raped, and even murdered by male perpetrators. The occurrence of such intense violence, whereby they are not only slain but mutilated beyond recognition, suggests a force of enmity that implies extreme repression and subsequent projection on the part of the attackers, who may be motivated by their own severe, unresolved Oedipal conflict. This unleashing amounts to an act of hatred. Jukes (1993) defines hatred thus:

> ... essentially a state of enmity for an object, with its attendant wishes to dominate and control it. In most cases these impulses are reinforced by a – not always unconscious – desire to exterminate – that is, kill – the object if one fails to dominate it. (Ibid., p. 6)

With this dynamic in play, it is not surprising that many transpeople view passing, to move through the world undetectable as trans, as a complex issue. If one can pass, one may avoid the threat of extreme reactions. Yet through no fault of their own, many transpeople do not pass some or most of the time.

Narratives of Trans Repudiation and Transphobia: The Conundrum of Passing

Male perpetrators of violent attacks on those perceived by them as 'sexually deviant' often claim 'self-defence' as the reason. This 'defence' is related to the psychoanalytic concept of *defence mechanisms*. Transpeople's stories confirm that serious incidents of violence remain both a threat and a reality in many of their everyday/night lives. The case of a murdered teenaged trans woman in the United States, Gwen Araujo, exemplifies violent repudiation constituted through subjective dynamics of defence. On 3 October 2002 four young men discovered that their friend Gwen was a genetic male with a penis. Three of these men had previously engaged in sexual relations with her, not knowing that she had male genitals. They subsequently

> ... kneed her in the face, slapped, kicked, and choked her, beat her with a can and a metal skillet, wrestled her to the ground, tied her wrists and ankles, strangled her with a rope, and hit her over the head with a shovel. (Steinberg, 2005, pp. 1–2)

At trial, one man pleaded guilty, another denied any direct role in the murder, while two others sought to mitigate their crime using a 'trans panic' defence, an extension of the homosexual/gay panic defence. The latter two argued in court that Gwen had betrayed them by deliberately being deceptive about her 'true' sex. Steinberg summarizes their defence in court:

... two defendants' immediate reactions to the news 'provoked emotional reactions.' One defendant appeared 'disillusioned' and had a 'look in his eyes ... like his illusion as to normality and the way things are supposed to be had been shattered.' He acted as if he had heard 'the craziest news you could ever hear.' A second defendant cried, and 'throughout all the events was very emotional.' While killing Araujo, he exclaimed, 'I can't be fucking gay, I can't be fucking gay.' *Defense* counsel claimed that the men acted out of 'shame and humiliation, shock and revulsion.' (P. 16; italics added)

In analysing the case, Steinberg argues that the reaction of these men to Gwen's trans status entailed a feeling of threat to their (hetero)sexuality, exemplifying 'a desire to hide from imperfections and a wish to be perfect, whole, and impenetrable' (p. 19). She counters the trans panic defence as a mitigating factor, suggesting that 'to the extent that one's own dislike of another person is related to a vulnerability in his own personality or identity, it is illogical and unfair to mitigate punishment for his violent acts towards that other person' (p. 20). This unwarranted defence[5] of the unthought fragility of the perpetrator's masculine identity and heterosexuality is, the author argues, not substantially different from past legal defences, used until the late 1970s, whereby a man sought to defend or mitigate 'homicidal rage' committed upon the discovery of marital infidelity, to defend his 'manly honour' (ibid., p. 21). The case of Gwen Araujo also interestingly portrays the complex intertwinement between interiority and exteriority with the internal defence mechanisms of the accused paralleling the external institutionalized role of the defence counsel.

Invariably, when discussing transphobia with transpeople, the matter of navigating the sex/gender binary surfaces. Does one desire adhering to the binary in all situations or just some? Alternatively, is the aim to defy it, again in all situations or contextually limited to some? In my interview with Trevor, for example, I asked how passing relates to transphobia, for which he replied:

I think there are two dimensions here. One is that passing is the avoidance of transphobia and the other is, where is your comfort level? Early on I had a lot to say about queering the binary, I don't have anything to say about that now. I realized as I moved along that I was in a box and that I wanted to be in another box. I am aware of the limitations of that but it's also where I'm comfortable. I'm a man and I'm quite happy to say this with all its limitations and all its problems. I'm quite fine with being in that box.

Trevor is happy with the essentialism of 'being a man' and feels most comfortable in that location. For him, the issue of passing is no longer an issue at all. As Trevor explained, he had a greater sense of trying to 'pass' when he was living as a woman:

> Trevor: Now it no longer feels like passing. Before transitioning I was living in a pretend place. Passing is about putting out the façade. I passed to the world for decades, now I'm not passing, I'm being ... now I never think, am I being perceived as a man? I mean that was a moment-to-moment conversation when I was trying to live as a woman. With every interaction I had as a woman there was this internal dialogue, 'Is this how a woman would respond? Would a woman say it this way? This person is seeing me as a woman so how would a woman respond?'
> Chris: So passing was an issue for you when you were trying to live as a woman?
> Trevor: Always, all the time. I mean I didn't even know that dialogue was there until it stopped. It was so deeply ingrained. And then I thought, 'Oh my god I've been doing this all my life.'

Another interviewee, Jenny, decried the 'Real Life Test' requirement that many gender clinics enforce for their SRS applicants. That is, those requesting SRS must live in their 'aspired' gender role for one or two years prior to surgery. This requirement is construed as a test that one can *pass*. Jenny offered her analysis:

> I hate the word 'passing' because not passing denotes failure, that's why it's just a lousy word. By saying 'passing' you're implying, if I'm not passing I'm failing. I think being able to look at yourself in the mirror after you start going full-time and like the person that you see, it doesn't matter what anyone else thinks ... It's like a test, you're going to pass or fail. Even the word 'real life test' is a bad one too, because it implies that it's not an actual experience. Like today I'll be a woman – tomorrow I won't, I did pretty good, 'A.' The life I came from was no life and there is no going back. It's always just going forward and I think for a lot of the girls that's what it is, the life was so miserable that this is the only choice. And to call it a 'test' belittles it.

Passing is a complex and politically loaded issue in trans communities. Those who pass well generally move through society with little stigma unless they are out as trans. At the same time, the ability to pass does not make a person entirely immune to trans repudiation. There are circumstances in which one's status as trans can be called out for even the most pristinely passable of gendered subjects (by family, medical history, or jurisdictions where official documents such as birth certificates cannot be changed). Nevertheless, Califia (2003) notes that an inability to pass risks making someone a constant target for harassment. On this basis, he argues that transitioning earlier in one's life (assuming this allows one to pass better than a later transition) is to a transperson's benefit. He also notes that some transgender activists view passing as a privilege and disparage the practice as conformist. This point is echoed by Elliot and Roen (1998), who argue that 'both crossing and passing unwittingly reify positions of sexual and/or gender identity' (p. 234).

For Hank, successful passing is a conundrum with benefits and its own set of problems:

> I think the day-to-day, when you're on the bus or just trying to get a cup of coffee, that level of transphobia dies down the better you pass. But then the worry around disclosure increases, because the better you are at passing then the more stake there is in that claim. Whereas when I'm not very successfully passing, people aren't that surprised to find out I wasn't born male, people wont be shocked.

Passing can be burdensome for some transpeople, denoting a persecutory feeling and a demand on oneself that one pass at all times. Gender ideals can carry this persecutory function for all people trans and non-trans (*cisgender*) alike. Those with poor self-esteem, for example, may harshly judge themselves according to these ideal standards.

Roz found that when she abandoned the internal demand to pass (which for all gendered subjects has external reference points), her sense of well-being increased:

> The minute I stopped worrying about trying to pass and trying to be that immaculate woman, my whole life brightened up. I just stopped trying to hide and got to this place saying, 'Well I'm Roz and I'm outrageous and my life's outrageous. I have this journey and mission to tell my story and be who I am and it doesn't matter anymore, you know?'

The issue of passing carries a different complexion for TG people. Alex (TG) spoke to me about tensions in trans communities around passing:

> I've run into some stuff in the broader trans communities that privileges TS over TG, TS being the 'real' transpeople; that TG is just a phase or experimenting, or isn't a real identity, or is about getting attention, or is 'just' a political statement meant to challenge the system. When I think of the stuff around 'just' a political statement, well what else accomplishes change?

Alex spoke of his experience of feeling pressure to relinquish his TG identity, of being pushed into the TS end of the trans continuum:

> I feel sometimes like there's pressure to identify as TS if you're trans, or for folks to focus only on TS issues. And I'm happy to be an ally to TS folks, and to talk about or get involved in activism on issues and concerns that don't directly affect me, but when I hear TG experiences being devalued, it's hard not to take such negative stereotyping personally. With any marginalized community, infighting is both a risk and a reality.

Tami believes that it is generally harder for trans women to pass in society than it is for trans men:

> Tami: You know, it's so much easier for transsexual men to pass in public, take some testosterone, wear baggy pants, a pair of work boots, a baseball cap, buzz all your hair off ... The next thing you know you're growing facial hair and your shoulders are filling out. For us we've got to shrink our shoulders, soften the facial features, get rid of the facial hair, you know, do something with our hair, our nails and waxing and breast augmentation and on and on, right? Wow!
> Chris: And do you think trans men experience less transphobia?
> Tami: Very much and most will probably tell you that too.

Indeed, most of the trans men I interviewed readily acknowledge that trans women generally have a much harder time passing:

> Yossi: I know there are FtMs who experience sexualized violence from other men, there are FtMs who don't have the same experience as mine. I don't mean to dismiss them but in talking about broad patterns I think

that trans women do have a much rougher time of it than trans men, especially in trying to access gender-specific spaces.

Kimberly views transphobia as ubiquitous. She provided a rationale for the reasons that transpeople themselves are also prone to express it:

Transphobia is like one of those invisible things, it's like racism or homophobia or sexism or ableism. It's these unconscious things that we do and say in our everyday lives and they affect other people and they oppress other people, they limit other groups' liberties and freedoms and that's what happens with transgendered people.

Frank spoke of his current position, having fully transitioned, and totally passing as a man in his self-perception and social experience. This existential and social shift provides him with a new standpoint from which to deal with transphobia:

I go under the radar, the transphobic radar in society, because I pass as a man, I look like a man now so no one gives me a second glance anymore. I'm not offensive to society's judgmental eye, I fit into one of its bloody slots. I think a lot of the transphobia is just superficial, visual, brutal as it is. If someone's deemed offensive to someone's eye, then they're going to get targeted. Fat people get targeted all the time for the same skewed reason; anyone considered ugly gets targeted, anyone not fitting. Transpeople get targeted when we're visible, period. You know, though, trans friends of mine who pass as women, they don't get targeted ... they know they're safe as long as nobody finds out. And as soon as my beard growth came in the assholes couldn't find me and that's a fact. I was all of a sudden privy to conversations I never even wanted to hear from these guys. The same guys that would be obnoxious to me up and down the street don't even see me anymore, they're like, 'Hey buddy, how's it going?' Because I look alright to them, even guys that are obnoxious, guys who know I've had a sex change. I look alright, act alright, and it's just not going to get deeper in there. They're not deep thinkers, these guys; if it looks alright, they don't put up a fight. But before, all those decades before, when I didn't fit into either of the binary slots, I was a target ... some of the trans women, they were able to hide before transitioning if they wanted to ... they could hide it, but now they're a target. I think they are absolutely way more in danger, not to say that if I was in a group of men and it was discovered, say I was in a locker room and it was discovered, I believe then I could be in danger. My carpentry class, I believe I could have been in danger if those guys, knuckle draggers that they were, if they'd found out. I certainly was really invested in them not finding out, they were straight knuckleheads. They were really straight, really rough guys. I sure didn't want them to know I peed sitting down, let alone that I didn't have a penis then at all.

Frank illustrated the trans aspect of transphobia, that depending on one's place in the temporal trajectory of transitioning, differing levels of repudiation may be experienced. In this sense, transphobia and repudiation may be more of an issue at certain points in a transperson's life than others. The self-knowledge of being trans, and the threat of discovery, may compel transpeople to constantly conceal their status in order to preserve their safety. Frank recounted the following story about a class he took with other males who were 'transphobic' and did not know of Frank's trans status:

In the carpentry class, there was a trans woman who came to teach the class one day. Many of the guys were making crude comments loud enough for her to hear. I wanted to wave both my hands and say, 'Here I am, hello, I'm over here, it's okay there's another one in the room with you.' But I didn't say a peep, I channelled it to her with interesting questions and sincere appreciation for the effort she put into the answers that she gave us. I interacted that way so she could get a really strong and warm supportive vibe off of me, she had no idea I was a trans man. And with my questions I kept a couple of the guys in check, as if 'Hey, that's not cool.' Not outing myself and putting myself on the line but as one of their chosen brothers, if you like, I just sort of shamed them with a look or not laughing at their stupid jokes. So they stopped because they looked up to me, I was an older guy they respected ... I was able to use some advantage of power over them without outing myself.

Frank skilfully uses the social privilege of being seen as a (natal) male to help diffuse trans repudiation when it appears. In this case, he acted as a hidden ally, attuning himself to the atmosphere of repudiation in the classroom, expertly taking the winds of repudiation out of crude, disrespectful, and potentially escalating harassment. He also demonstrates the power of being a 'silent' ally.

For other transpeople such as Alex, who does not want to pass one hundred per cent of the time as a man, different kinds of trans repudiation are often manifested. While the following example might be viewed as affirmative, it carries with it an underlying ambivalence that is uncomfortable to transpeople, as Alex revealed:

> The other day, after doing focus groups with a group of street-involved youths, I was talking to one of the guys and out of the blue he said, 'You're a chick!' and at first I thought he said 'you're Chuck,' so I said no, my name is Alex. And then I realized he was referring to my gender, so I said no, actually, I'm trans, and he thought that that was really cool, he'd never met a transperson before, and he looked fascinated and kept on staring at me. So, while it wasn't an overtly transphobic experience, having that kind of intense energy focused on figuring my body out rather than engaging in the conversation is disconcerting and makes me uncomfortable.

Alex brings a particular perspective to the debate, since he sees the range of reactions that he experiences as reflecting back to him the challenges his varying and shifting gender presentations pose:

> Because my identity is TG rather than man or woman, in some ways when people are confused whether I am a guy or a woman, or when I am getting one person saying one thing and another person saying another, it reflects back to me my gender identity more accurately than if I was being perceived as just one or the other. So even, I think, when I am getting some stuff that might be in that transphobia kind of category, it might reflect my gender identity back to me rather than if someone was identifying me purely as male or as female ... it is more affirming than if I was getting only 'sir' or only 'ma'am,' though I hate – I really dislike – ma'am, even before I identified as a trans man (laughter). And there are some days when I want one response more than another, which also makes it complicated.

TG people's fluidity and non-conformity with respect to the binary challenges perception and language. Their being-in-the-world can also challenge the perceptions of other transpeople and allies. Alex shared more of his experience and thoughts:

> It's also challenging for my partner in ways that I don't think the partners of TS people generally experience. Before I decided to go with male pro-

nouns out of practicality, all my trans guy friends were calling me 'he,' but other people in my life were calling me 'she.' My partner varied what pronoun she used for me, and I was really comfortable with that. However, she felt like she got attitude from and was judged by transpeople and trans allies for calling me 'she,' like they thought she was being an unsupportive, 'bad' partner. Also, for TG folks, I think partners' responses to our bodies can be different from what the partners of TS folks experience, once the TS folks are finished their transition process – particularly for trans women, since most trans guys can't afford or for various other reasons don't get genital surgery. Especially for TG folk who choose to take hormones or have some surgeries, but don't fully transition – we have bodies that really don't fit with binaries – whether it's trans guys who have chest surgery but don't take hormones and otherwise have a female body with no breasts, or trans guys who take hormones but don't have surgery and may end up bear-ish with breasts.

These experiences are not confined to TG people since trans-ness is not a prerequisite for mis-reading a subject's gender. One can be a congruent man or woman and yet still be mistaken as the opposite by others. Many TS people can identify with TG experiences since periods of embodied ambiguity often precede the completion of transition. For those TS people dealing with the surgeries, or waiting for them, the issue may take on heightened significance, as trans repudiation may surface at times in acute ways at different stages of the transition process. Jeb was taking testosterone but had not yet undergone chest surgery. He was frustrated with the delays and the long wait to get a mastectomy:

> Chest surgery can be pretty important for people's safety, and because I'm low-income I have to wait a long time to get it. I can't hide my chest in the meantime ... I mean ... to wear eight sweaters in the summer and that seems ridiculous. I don't know what the actual waiting lists are, but if I had to get breast reduction because I had back problems or something, I'm sure it wouldn't be as long of a wait ... I'm absolutely putting myself out there. And I think it's worse than (before), like right now if people read me as female they think 'dyke.' If I have a beard and a low voice with a chest, people will look at me and think 'freak,' you know?

Wynn spoke of similar difficulties as she moved through the earlier stages of transition, for example, in preparing for her electrolysis sessions:

... you have to grow your facial hair out too, to do it. So it's hard, people get pretty stressed out when you're even slightly feminized, and having facial hair, I get stared at a lot. People give you disgusted looks in public constantly.

The importance of passing as it pertains to legitimate safety issues can also mask the deeper anxiety that Western cultures exemplify with those who resist sex/gender categorization. Sabrina (Two-Spirit) reminded me of this fact when I asked her about passing. Two-Spirit people embody two spirits. For Two-Spirits, it does not necessarily make sense to pass only as One:

I am who I am and my physical features are my physical features and I have no desire to change them. Some people see me as female, others have their doubts, others see me as male ... I'm a Two-Spirit person, that's who I am.

Trans repudiation spans all points of the political spectrum, from the right wing through to the left. Wynn described her experiences with some 'progressive' activists:

Some of my friends have been very supportive and lots have ... been that kind of politically correct type, especially political activists. Like it's not cool to be transphobic, but they are and they just treat me really weird, especially a lot of the guys, they feel really uncomfortable around me now. They don't talk to me much anymore and treat me like I've got 30 less IQ points, don't act like I think about stuff anymore. Or a lot of them will come up to me and like touch me and stuff now, it's like they think that I want to have my gender identity validated by them, you know?

John had an especially pointed view on the trans repudiation of government institutions:

John: One thing that makes me very angry and frustrated is the transphobia of institutions, the issue of gender identification on your driver's licence, your birth certificate, or in your SIN[6] or medical records. I resent this very much. Depending on the extent of your physical transition, you may never be able to correct those records. I feel very fortunate because I've been able to get most of this changed. But there are a few important records that remain F, essentially because I have chosen not to have a hysterectomy. Those Fs are an invasion of my privacy and a discrimination against me as a man and as a transsexual person.

Chris: Do you have any idea why they want to take the gonads, the ovaries, to take them out, why is that so important to the authorities?

John: I don't know, but I would guess that it has to do with who they decide will 'count' as a man or a woman.

In John's case, trans repudiation exemplifies itself in textual coercion to have surgery (a hysterectomy) that he does not want, in order to be counted as male. In ruling and legitimating sexed bodies, the government at times repudiates some transpeople in highly essentialized ways. Robin, however, cautioned that transphobia is often less obvious and even invisible. She had these final words to say on the topic:

> Transphobia exists everywhere ... it is more pervasive in society than most people will realize. And ... many of us have probably seen examples of it and have not even recognized it or have been able to walk by wondering ...

Trans Repudiation and Intersectionality

Analysis of the interview transcripts as a whole reveals that trans repudiation is often not experienced as a clear and one-sided expression of prejudice, discrimination, and stigma. Indeed, many of the interviewees, while able to clearly identify transphobia itself, indicated that it is frequently tied up with other intersectional issues based on racialization, class, sexual orientation, and ability. Trevor elaborated:

> If you are trans and you don't have a job, you are living in poverty, a low income level, and depending where you have come from, the trans stuff is tied into all this other stuff. And if they are wearing kind of alternative clothing, are young or maybe they aren't fully white, all that stuff gets mixed in there, race, class, and so on. The transpeople I know who experience that, they get it all at once in a ball of wax.

The ball-of-wax metaphor that Trevor uses sums up the often complex dynamics of Othering, of targeting those marginalized on more than one level. Yossi, for example, spoke of living with a disability in addition to being trans, Jewish, and queer:

My experiences as a transperson have been, I would say, relatively calmer than say my experiences as a Jew. You know, my experiences as a Jew have been shit in this society – being trans has had its ups and downs and it's certainly had lots of verbal harassment and some threats of violence, but it's not been the same kind of daily shame or stigma or feeling like a freak, you know? I experience that mostly around my ethnicity, so by the time it came to trans stuff I kind of knew the process.

Yossi draws attention to the ways in which intersectionality needs to be taken into account when considering the lived experiences of transpeople. As we discussed the matter, he continued to draw attention to further intersectional dynamics:

Chris: So in terms of dealing with people who have some kind of uncomfortable reaction to you, I guess you need to sort of sift through. You mentioned your ethnicity, so, 'Is this a reaction to my Jewish-ness, is this a reaction to my being queer, or is this a reaction to my being a transperson?'

Yossi: Or being fat or having a disability. I often walk with a cane and people will often come up to me and say, 'What's wrong with you?' and I'm like, 'on which level,' you know? (laughter), 'what are you referring to?' They often mean the cane, so it's very difficult to know what's actually going on and thus how to address it. I think the more visible your stuff is, that's probably what people are responding to. So when I have the cane, I usually get ableism before I get transphobia. When I don't have the cane, I often get homophobia and transphobia together because that's the next most visible thing about me.

Nick expressed the problems he has experienced as a TG person living with disabilities. He grapples with wanting to change his body but faces obstacles that prevent him from doing so: 'I want to try and physicalize more how I feel inside and I think hormones will help me do that, I can't do surgeries for a lot of reasons. Politically, physically, my health, my disability.' Nick would like to explore alternative and holistic therapies to assist him with actualizing the changes he would like, especially in light of the effects that pharmaceuticals would have on his body in view of his already precarious health.

In approaching the interviews from a hermeneutic perspective, I have underscored the position that trans repudiation, at least in part, is rooted in a lack of understanding. Understanding and its lack is a dynamic that often surfaces in trans lives. John spoke of the realization that he came to in regard to a somewhat difficult relationship with his fundamentalist Christian father:

> You know it's strange, because one day my sister said to him, 'I'm sure you must have trouble with it because of your faith.' And he said, 'No, it has nothing to do with my faith, I just don't understand it' ... I had always assumed that it was a biblical issue, but he told my sister that it had nothing to do with that. He thinks I've done something unspeakably stupid. I have a sense that I've lost his respect and esteem as a good, intelligent person, which is painful. You want your parents to be proud of you, but you can't arrange your life around what they want.

The Problem of Trauma

The lack (loss) of understanding from others is just one of several areas of trauma to consider in relation to trans lives. First, there is the trauma of the mis-sexed body, which is especially evident in TS people, a trauma that needs medical interventions in order to repair/heal the person. Second, the trauma of repudiation and the constellation of issues that emerge from it, including hostility and violence. Prosser (1998) draws on Freud's 1917 essay 'Mourning and Melancholia' to differentiate between the meanings of these two terms in relation to transpeople. In mourning there is the resolvable grief surrounding loss, as with the death of a love object. In melancholia, the unconscious masks what is lost, not necessarily the actual death of an object but rather an unnameable loss, such as loss of love buried deep in the past. Melancholia, so long as it remains unconscious, is irresolvable. The unconscious dynamic suggests that the individual is unaware of what has been lost.

When the mis-sexed body is prevented through repudiation from loving and being loved in the style and ways that it desires, a sense of melancholia may prevail. In MtFs there might be a melancholia for the historical loss of the gendered love that a daughter would have received rather than a 'son.' In FtMs there might be melancholia for loss of the mother who did not love him as she would have loved a son. There might be melancholic loss of non-existent adolescent boyfriends or girlfriends, the missing and ghost-like figures of memory, of lost relations that could not develop, that might have otherwise been possible. And there might be melancholic loss regarding those years of having been forced to move through the world under a punishing binary that refuses to acknowledge the pain of incongruency, which in some cases is so threatening as to be banished, buried. So long as a person's trans-ness is repressed, hence unconscious, there is danger of melancholia; the malady is nameless.

Kristeva (1989) cites the nineteenth-century French poet Gérard de Nerval's sonnet 'The Disinherited,' grasping at his phrase 'the black sun of melancholia,' in titling her book *Black Sun: Depression and Melancholia*. For Kristeva, melancholia is related to something unutterable, something nameless, presymbolic. Perhaps those transpeople who have not accepted their trans-ness and struggle to keep it repressed (often for decades), this nameless thing is the mis-sexed body and the distorted, early familial and social relations that flowed from mis-comprehending it. In studying the pre-transition lives of those transpeople who only much later acknowledge their trans-ness, it is clear that the repression of trans feelings takes a chronic course. Repression and denial do not make the problem disappear. Melancholic loss is especially relevant in understanding those transpeople with long pre-transition histories. Those who try to deny their trans-ness move through life with a pervasive sense of wrong-ness, of inauthenticity, of chronic melancholia, with which a host of compensatory behaviours, such as alcohol and drug abuse, may very well be associated. The untenable strategy of repression usually leads to a narrative of emergence, of accepting one's status as having been mis-sexed, clearly because one can no longer tolerate life under a black sun.

For Nerval, his black sun was inescapable, as he committed suicide after a final mental breakdown. For transpeople, their black sun may be extinguished with the emergence and integration of the repressed, and in some cases the healing of both the mis-sexed body and the associated melancholia. Cartwright (2002) underscores the necessity of healing trauma: 'Psychic states induced by trauma often cannot be contained and worked through adequately and thus cannot be mourned. As a consequence, these experiences remain concrete volatile objects suspended in the psyche' (p. 43).

Freud held that an overwhelming event in one's personal history could be internally censored and repressed, yet interminably return in the present under the guise of somatic symptoms, as in hysteria.[7] So long as the forgotten event remains unresolved, it continues to haunt the present. The traumas of the past do not necessarily disappear, but can reverberate and menace the future. Berger (1997) outlines the problem:

But 'trauma' is not simply another word for disaster. The idea of catastrophe as trauma provides a method of interpretation, for it posits that these effects of an event may be dispersed and manifested in many forms not obviously associated with the event. Moreover, this dispersal occurs across time, so that an event experienced as shattering may actually produce its full impact only years later. (P. 572)

The trauma of the mis-sexed body can be exacerbated by repudiations that psychically re-wound the already troubled corporeal body. The sedimented histories of transpeople, when unearthed, may reveal an extensive assortment of traumatic experiences associated with the mis-sexed body. With so much emphasis placed in popular culture on the physical surgeries undergone by transpeople, there needs to be more space made for transpeople to give voice to their trauma, to heal not only the mis-sexed body but also the traumas resulting from the wounds of the past.

This discussion of trans repudiation hopefully will add to recognition of the complexity of issues related to transphobia and trans repudiation, which can come from all parts of the socio-political spectrum. These aspects will be looked at more closely, before returning to the questions raised by depth psychology.

3 Social Repudiation

In representing salient points and storied fragments from my interviews with twenty transpeople, I begin with Dorothy Smith's (1987, 1999) feminist contention that subjects are located in their everyday/night worlds as embodied beings under ruling relations. Her sociological contention is confirmed and illustrated by the narrative evidence I cite, which reveals that navigating one's life in the social world can be, and often is, traumatic for transpeople. The rules enforced carry institutional and textual bases that come to mark embodiment, expressed in flesh-and-blood gestures through the dynamics of interpersonal relations.

Hook's (2006) analysis of racism argues that no matter how advanced its various forms, 'racism never loses its localization in the body' (p. 208). Similarly, trans repudiation begins viscerally with embodiment and with the concomitant rousing of the abject. Butler (1990) agrees with Kristeva (1982) that the abject object is rendered so by virtue of having been expelled, of being cast out, akin to excrement. Such objects become 'an affront to wholeness be it of the body, of identity, of socio-symbolic structure' (Hook, 2006, p. 218). Hence the colloquial protest, feeling as though one has been 'treated like shit,' emphasizes the potential treatment that all abject objects – in their embodied status as Others – are subject to. Being *treated as* refers to interpersonal dynamics, the social realm, to which the attention of this chapter turns to.

The gaze of repudiation directed at transpeople, which often leads to overt, punishing acts, is consonant with Foucault's (1984b) concept of *panopticism* (all-seeing), drawn from Jeremy Bentham's *panopticon* or model prison. Such a prison contains a tower with observatory windows on all sides that permit the authorities to observe inmates' cells at all times in such a way that the surveillance is undetectable. There are few places in the world where transpeople, especially those who do not 'pass,' can escape the panoptic gaze associated with surveillance and condemnation. In their narratives, the interviewees often evoked painful events that point to violence. They corroborated, by the experiences they shared with me, Namaste's (2000) definition of violence as it pertains to transpeople's lived experience, whereby violence ranges,

> ... from verbal insults (e.g., calling someone a 'fag'), to an invasion of personal space (e.g., throwing a bottle at a lesbian as she walks by), to intimidation and the threat of physical assault. 'Violence' also includes the act of attacking someone's body – whether through sexual assault (rape), beating, or with weapons like baseball bats, knives, or guns. (P. 139)

There are a myriad possible motivations behind transphobia and other forms of trans repudiation. These range from sudden, irrational rage (reflecting serious unconscious conflicts) to more stable and conscious forms of enmity, such as those related to the defence of political ideologies that view transpeople as a threat to a cherished sex/gender binary. That transpeople often un/willingly stir up and rouse defensive reactions, because of the (un)'certainty' of perpetrators' own tenuous positions as sexed/gendered subjects, points to the phenomenon of projection, which causes stigmatized transpeople to be (unfortunate) targets. These defensive reactions may surface due to the triggering of unresolved Oedipal conflicts (castration anxiety), unconscious misogyny, abjection, a sense of threat to a subject's unconscious gendered fictions, or because the 'freak' unwittingly throws light onto a perpetrator's own shadow – surprising and disturbing what is disowned in the self. In many cases, what is roused is an unacknowledged sense of threat to the perpetrator's own tenuous gender order (the 'common sense' sex/gender binary), which is circularly thrown back onto those who are seen to disrupt or potentially annihilate it.

The gender 'order' is, I suggest, sedimented in the perpetrator's unconscious yet *does not originate there*. The problem is ultimately generated in the socio/political fabric of the culture, since the symbolic order within (interiority) reflects something that is internalized from outside (exteriority). That acts of threat and intimidation are not limited to individual perpetrators, but often extend to groups (e.g., swarmings), suggests that the unconscious defences stirred up in one individual can quickly spread to others, igniting a collective response that seeks to defend the 'normal' binary against a supposed threat. For Kristeva (1982), the threat of the abject is the threat of death. Ironically, such perpetrators do not recognize that it is the transperson who is vulnerable and actually threatened with real violence, violence that can lead to death.

The following discussion and examples of incidents exemplify the seriousness of the problem of repudiation and transphobia, the dangers that transpeople face. These storied fragments are organized under eight thematic categories:

1 Health Care
2 Lavatories and Change Rooms
3 Family and Personal Relations
4 Employment
5 Education
6 Threat/Violence
7 Problems with Law Enforcement
8 Relations with (Other) Lesbians and Gays
9 Reactions from Radical Cultural Feminists

The list is not comprehensive since there are other important issues that transpeople could raise. The aim is to demonstrate the potency of social repudiation in the everyday/night lives for those who live as trans.

1. Health Care

Darke and Cope (2002) write that, 'perhaps nowhere is the brutality of institutionalised transphobia so apparent as in the treatment of trans-people by the health care system' (p. 37). The narratives that transpeople shared with me further corroborate their observation. Transpeople, especially TS and those TGs who transition, need the health care system to intervene and correct the mis-sexed body. Lawrence (2000) reports, in a review of extensive, multiple longitudinal studies of post-operative transsexuals, that SRS and hormonal treatments are an effective way to alleviate the chronic embodied distress that transsexuals experience. Indeed, it is often disastrous should their somatic incongruency not be addressed by the health care system. In short, transpeople require the services of competent health care professionals to facilitate transitioning (if so desired), or to attend to unrelated health concerns or crises, just as do any other human beings. While I have listened to narrative accounts of good health service rendered, where transpeople have been treated without apparent repudiation or discrimination, there remain far too many instances of traumatic encounters with health care service providers. The health care system mis/serves this population.

As 'phobogenic objects,' transpeople often encounter unwelcome dynamics of fascination, the polar swing of desire/disgust, and repudiation in their everyday/night lives. Yossi (FtM) lives with multiple disabilities and often requires medical assistance. He finds that health care professionals often get 'hung up' on his trans-ness, regardless of his reason for consulting them. He recounts once being rushed to the emergency department at a hospital. After he revealed his trans status, he was asked several questions: 'They got all caught up in asking about my genitals, "have you had genital surgery *yet*, or *do you plan to?*" And, you know, when you've been hit by a car, those are not really the kinds of questions you want to go through.'

Yossi's recollection reminded me of a similar incident that ended in tragedy. Califia (2003) tells the story of Tyra Hunter, who was gravely injured in a hit-and-run car accident. When emergency personnel arrived, they were compelled to cut off her pants in order to enable treatment of injuries. Discovering that Tyra had a penis, the first attending paramedic jumped back and yelled, 'That ain't no bitch!' (p. 233). They refused to continue treating Tyra's serious injuries, and she later died. More than two thousand people attended her funeral, outraged with the discriminatory treatment, the dereliction of duty displayed in a life-or-death situation.

Yossi has also been denied essential and emergency medical services:

> My most recent experience was definitely after transition, I'd already had chest surgery. I had acute meningitis and went in for treatment and the doctor just refused to see me and said, 'I don't work on people like you, you'll have to go see your GP.' And I didn't know at that time that I had meningitis, I just had really severe neurological symptoms. So I went to see my GP and he kind of said, 'Oh my God, we need to get you some care right away.'

When health care service is not denied to transpeople, it can never-theless be accompanied by undue intrusiveness, including a sexual-ized gaze of fascination. When asked if he had ever been made to feel uncomfortable as a result of his trans status, John (FtM) replied:

Yes, mostly in the medical world. When I go to a doctor, I don't necessar-ily want to answer irrelevant questions about my transsexuality. One doctor wanted to know if I took the 'male position in sex.' I didn't know what he was talking about; what did he mean by 'the male position'? It was an awkward, irrelevant question and I didn't know how to respond to it ... I was just there to get my shot because my regular doctor was away, and he was asking me these odd questions.

As authority figures, medical doctors can be intimidating to trans-people, who, considering the complexities of sex reassignment surgery, need to feel comfortable in discussing future treatments. Like many TS people, Frank (FtM) has acquired considerable expertise on various SRS procedures, having spent years looking into his options. This amateur yet detailed grasp of available data often exceeds the physician's own professional knowledge, a common situation for TS people seeking surgery (Namaste, 2000). Frank wishes to take an active and collaborative role in discussing the transitioning of his body with physicians, and was dismayed at the response he received:

Suddenly he's an expert after just telling me he doesn't know very much about [FtM surgery], and he just wants to go in there and cut this and cut that ... and when I hesitated he said, 'We don't have time for this,' and then flat out: 'Forget it, I won't help you. You don't trust me so this won't work.' I've known him for what, ten minutes? ... yet still he refused to listen to any research or input I had for him. Now I don't know if that's just doctor arro-gance or if it was because I was trans. I wouldn't have allowed him to touch me after that, no way he's coming anywhere near me with a sharp instru-ment. Jeez, if his privates were on the chopping block, I bet he'd have some questions! He wasn't thrilled to meet me, time-consuming and complicated and uncommon. That's why he was so bugged about me taking more than my allotted fifteen minutes, literally telling me three times that I had to think of the other patients [waiting outside].

Some interviewees expressed their frustration at the seeming impos-sibility of accessing necessary health services. Sabrina (MtF) told me about her difficulty in finding a gynaecologist, preferably female. Most of those she approached refused to take her on as a patient. Eventually she found a male gynaecologist who provided her with good service. Sabrina remarked, 'When he examined me, he was totally fine, he just seemed surprised when he didn't find any uterus. "You know," he said, "I'd never have known."' Yet female gynaecologists are not, as I discovered with John, immune to trans repudiation. Indeed, John experienced negation of his gender following consultation: 'The visit was fine, but during the follow-up I saw the letter she wrote to my GP about me. I was referred to as "she, she, she, young woman, female," I felt very angry about that.'

Jenny (MtF) spoke of her difficulty in finding a surgeon willing to perform an orchiectomy (removal of the testes). In frustration, she lamented that 'women can get hysterectomies easier than I can get an orchiectomy. And hysterectomy's a dangerous operation ... they can't find anyone to help me.' Jenny also had a difficult time locating a psychologist to sign SRS authorization letters, which are required before surgeons will perform any SRS procedure. Without the stamp of approval that a psychiatrist or psychologist can provide, transpeople might be categorically dismissed as 'not trans' or something Other. When Tami (MtF) was asked what barriers she faced before transitioning, she replied that the most difficult was 'having the health care providers believe me.'

Jeb (FtM) has also experienced problems finding a psychologist or psychiatrist. Not knowing where to start with the transition process, he began by consulting his GP, who he described as having 'zero knowledge' on trans health issues. After persisting for several months, he was referred to a psychiatrist in another, distant city. Being unemployed, the travel expenses were hard to bear. Eventually, Jeb managed to arrange the travel but found his rapport and experience with this psychiatrist unsatisfactory: 'He and I had stylistic differences (laughter) and I had no other options. That's the guy I had to see even if I couldn't stand him ... I was supposed to go back again and I flat out refused.' Jeb's disclosure is consistent with Namaste's (2000) study, which shows the considerable dissatisfaction that transsexuals often express towards psychological and psychiatric service providers. She also found, citing a separate study, that physicians (such as GPs) are often woefully under-prepared and under-trained to deal with the complex health needs of transsexuals.

Some of those interviewed had a better impression; for instance,

Kimberly (MtF), who recalled her positive memory of dealing with a hospital-based gender clinic: 'For me it was a very good experience and I can't say enough about the people I encountered there, the doctors [including the psychiatrists].'

It can take time before pre-transition TS people can obtain the required referrals and appointments needed with various specialists. It is understandable why medical and psychological authorities charged with giving/denying consent for surgery need to take the required time to ensure that SRS is the right way forward for the patient. Hence permissiveness, or *immediate* affirmative acceptance for referral to SRS from gatekeepers (contrary to Harry Benjamin International Standards),[1] is not necessarily the answer to all transpeople's embodied distress. While delays and diagnostic probing may very well be an irritant to those seeking SRS, the diagnostic process tries to attend to those who may presently want SRS but might come to regret transition later in life. In Britain, Batty (2004) interviewed some of those among the very few of SRS recipients who later came to regret their transition. These individuals blame psychiatry and inadequate medical diagnostic procedures for recommending SRS too quickly or even inappropriately, often with devastating consequences. These narratives of regret include examples of a return to living as best as one can in their natal sex, or feeling stuck between sexes in a way that leads to distress. While longitudinal studies consistently demonstrate that SRS leads to alleviation for most with a GID diagnosis (Pfäfflin, 1992), conflicting data report that between 1 and 18 per cent of recipients later regret transitioning (Batty, 2004). It is not clear if there are those within this group who may have ignored the advice of physicians not to pursue SRS. For example, some patients will go abroad for surgeries to jurisdictions where authorization requirements are less stringent.

The medical and psychological authority that gives transpeople the green, amber, or red light to proceed with SRS constitutes an expression of social power that can have both positive and negative effects. In this sense, an interesting incident was relayed during the course of my interviews. What happens when health care professionals *push* transgendered people to go into full transitional directions? Is it appropriate to press for a 'green light' for SRS or hormones, when this is not necessarily the person's present desire, and an 'amber light' approach might be the more appropriate one? Alex's (FtM) story deals with this controversial issue. At the gender clinic, he wanted to *explore* gender issues: 'I went in saying: "I'm not sure what's up, I've got gender issues going on, I want some help and support in figuring things out, I don't know whether I want to go on hormones or not, I don't want surgery at this point in time, and whatever path I choose, I want to do things *very* slowly." After a few sessions with a clinician, Alex was surprised by the response s/he received: 'she said I was clearly transsexual and suggested that she put me on the list to see the endocrinologist, since it took "a long time" to get in to see them – about three or four months. In reply, I told her that I wasn't interested in going that route right then, and she again suggested that I go on the waitlist.' What Alex had sought was some information and available options with the aim of becoming comfortable with his/herself, 'to sort things out.' He found instead that TG issues were not a part of that clinician's treatment repertoire:

> Having her 'diagnose' me as transsexual was a clear sign that she wasn't paying much attention to who I was and what I needed to look at. I certainly didn't think of myself as TS – and still don't – I identify as TG. This pressure to be TS really turned me off the clinic. So then I sort of ran away from the clinic for a few months. When more crises came up and I needed some support, I heard from some pals that there was a new psychiatrist there and she seemed to be really good, so I called her up to see if I could switch ... and saw her and that worked out really well for me.

Eventually, Alex did start taking low-dose hormones using transdermal patches, but with hesitations: 'you have to be okay to an extent with not knowing what to expect, or with being a bit of a guinea pig. There's a lot less known about the health risks of doing low-dose hormones, or hormones for long periods of time without removing gonads.' Overall, this example reveals a paradox in trans health care: of refusing service to some of those who desire SRS (e.g., TS applicants who are also sex-trade workers), while pushing others towards an undesired place of fixed-ness, such as Alex's experience of being wrongly classified as TS, conceived as 'solely male in a female body.'

Cromwell (1997) cites the medical establishment's repudiation of TG indeterminacy, a 'refusal to acknowledge individuals who maintain an intermediate status' (p. 133). This refusal extends to class discrimination, as Namaste (2000) points out. She found that trans refugees (who do not have access to Canada's health care system), sex-trade workers, and intravenous drug users[2] often encounter discrimination by the health care system, which tends to 'erase,' or to refuse to help, them. The effect is to frequently force these subjects into obtaining hormones from the street without medical supervision, a more dangerous proposition:

> Hormones can have serious side effects, including nausea, vomiting, headaches, mood swings, blood clots, liver damage, heart and lung complications, and problems with blood circulation and veins (phlebitis). For these reasons, it is important that individuals who take hormones be monitored regularly by a physician. (Ibid. p. 160)

Another notable paradox is evident with Canada's 'universal' health care system, that is, its frequent inaccessibility to low income transpeople. In the Province of British Columbia, the location where my interviews were conducted, there is no longer a gender clinic. Austerity cuts levied by provincial government cutbacks closed down the one that did exist in Vancouver. There are places where transpeople can go for advocacy or referrals, yet there is often ambiguity on which surgical procedures will be covered by the public health insurance program. This ambiguity is the source of much unnecessary anxiety for transpeople.

De-listing SRS as a procedure that can be publicly funded is a policy issue with concrete impacts on transpeople's everyday/night worlds and embodied lives. The neo-liberal favouring of private, consumer models of health care exacerbates class divisions that privilege those with the economic ability to pay for private services. In Ontario, the election of a neo-liberal government in 1995 led to a fairly swift delisting of SRS as a publicly funded procedure (Namaste, 2000). The closing of gender clinics in the United States, such as the Johns Hopkins Clinic, led to privatization, and the development of consumer niche markets for private plastic surgeons. For wealthy American transsexuals, Meyerowitz (2002) reports that it 'opened the gates' (p. 273), making it easier for those with economic means to obtain SRS in places such as Trinidad, Colorado, where many Americans (and those Canadians wishing to bypass the public system) travel to obtain SRS.

Burnham (1999) found in her research with MtFs that facial electrolysis was viewed as a slightly more important procedure than vaginoplasty. However, income was cited by respondents as a principal barrier in accessing it. She also found, in discussions with FtMs, that the cost of phalloplasty and metoidioplasty (genital procedures) was generally beyond reach. In 'liberal' British Columbia,[3] these surgeries are not covered under the public health insurance program, even though vaginoplasty is for MtFs. Burnham also found a broad discrepancy regarding breast and chest procedures for MtFs and FtMs. For MtFs, limited mammoplasty is listed as a publicly insurable health service in BC, but is dependent on the diagnostic determination of 'inadequate breast size' for those MtFs having taken sufficient estrogen therapy. Hence, sometimes MtFs can get breast augmentation surgery. FtMs, however, cannot access chest contouring or second stage mastectomy since it is not covered.

Trans repudiation in the health care system leaves lingering and often traumatic effects on transpeople. Yossi's comments summarize the outcome of this category of repudiation:

> When you experience [transphobia] over and over again, it makes you very reluctant to seek care, because you feel like you're crazy and then you're worried that they're writing in your chart that you're just malingering or making it up or that you're cracked basically ... I don't go for medical care unless I'm on my death bed.

Public gender clinics may be useful for introducing and referring patients to trans-positive physicians. However, the public gender clinic model, while addressing class issues of accessibility, is not a panacea. Namaste (2000) found that many loathed their experiences at the gender clinics, experiencing systematic sexism in the diagnostic process, based on heteronormative expectations and sexist stereotyping. Moreover, the requirement of many gender clinics, that participants complete a 'real life test' of performing as the desired gender for up to two years prior to being prescribed hormones, places transpeople in jeopardy of physical and verbal abuse owing to their prolonged incongruous status.

2. Lavatories and Change Rooms

The topic of lavatory use frequently emerged as questions arose spontaneously in my dialogue with transpeople. Especially for TG people and TS people in the midst of transition, lavatories often represent aspects of the sex/gender binary that foreclose in-between possibili-

Table 3
Various lavatory symbols

Men	Women	Unisex	Disability	Trans

ties. Public toilets labelled 'men' or 'women' force people into a choice and, for transpeople, into a situation where they may be seen as making the wrong choice. This appears either as ridiculous (embarrassing/funny to observers) or a threat (and therefore dangerous). Table 3 illustrates the familiarity and force of the gender binary as it expresses itself symbolically. Referring to 'Ladies/Gentlemen' labels on segregated spaces, Lacan (1977) speaks of the relationship between the signifier and the signified (S/s), using this example 'to show how in fact the signifier enters the signified, namely, in a form which, not being immaterial raises the question of its place in reality' (p. 151). From the perspective of some of my informants, the reality seems to be that the signified (man/woman) is supposed to enter the signifier (the right door). For some transpeople, this poses not inconsequential problems.

In regard to the possibility of a 'trans' signifier/symbol, which is appearing on washroom doors at university campuses across Canada, it may solve the issue of the lack of acceptable toilet space for TG people. It may also function to draw attention to the plight of those who do not pass and the not infrequent harassment they receive for seemingly violating the law of the binary. I wonder, however, how TS people feel about this option, since their aim is to disappear into the binary and not to draw attention to themselves. Entering the 'trans room' could inadvertently 'out' them to observers. As a third-space symbol, it seems we should support its use, especially as several of my informants have called specifically for it. However, I also remain concerned that it may be used to segregate all transpeople, de-legitimizing or even prohibiting those who want to use the regular binary lavatories (M/F), rooms constructed according to 'the laws of urinary segregation' (Lacan, ibid., p. 151). Should the trans signifier be forced to enter a new signified and vice versa?

For most gender congruent people, visiting a public toilet is an unproblematic exercise, but for transpeople, especially those who do not easily pass according to standard stereotypes, public lavatory use can be irksome, problematic, or even a nightmare. Kimberly recalled an incident several years ago. She went window-shopping in a mall as the facility was closing down for the evening, knowing that fewer people would be around. Needing to use the washroom and waiting for the room to be vacant, she went into the women's room and into a cubicle. She then heard some voices approaching, and a group of women came in. Since this was early on in Kimberly's transition, she felt nervous, thinking it would be best to wait for them to leave before she emerged from the cubicle. When she no longer heard voices, she opened the door only to discover that there was still one woman putting on her lipstick in the mirror. Here is what transpired in Kimberly's words:

> I looked at her and got kind of scared, so I turned around and went back in the cubicle. I thought, 'I'll wait 'til she goes,' so she did, and I thought I'd give it a couple more minutes. My heart was pounding, and I thought, 'I've got to get out of here' ... suddenly I hear all of these voices and walkie-talkies, I thought, 'Oh my god, my life is over.' So they come banging on the cubicle door ... [pause] ... it was a real tough decision to open that latch because I knew that as soon as I did there would be trouble. So I can remember sliding that latch and the door opening ... and they grabbed me. There must have been eleven security guards surrounding me and grabbing me. Then they tried to put me in handcuffs, but I resisted and then they started threatening me. They basically grabbed and dragged me to this room where I was questioned for about two hours. They ultimately decided that I wasn't doing anything wrong. I remember my shoes had come off, and I had a really nice expensive gold chain and that was lost in the struggle.

Nick (TG – 'FtM') recalled the problem of ambiguity around lavatories from childhood, somewhat accurately reflecting his transgender being:

> Yeah, my mom used to say that I was a tomboy all the time and for some reason she didn't seem to mind it and my brother was a guy kind of a boy,

and my sister was femmy. People would mistakenly buzz me into the boy's bathrooms in public malls and that kind of thing.

While the ambivalence surrounding washrooms in childhood was easier for Nick to manage, in adulthood it has become more problematic. Because Nick is publicly read as male more often than female, s/he tends to use the men's lavatory. When s/he has chosen to use the women's room, problems often ensue. Women will respond thus:

> I get all kinds of looks like, 'Are you in the right washroom?' They always look at the door again to make sure they're going into the right room. Sometimes I just take my jacket off and try to show whatever female contours I have, but also for years now I often just go in and let them deal with it. Sometimes they even say something or they'll just look like they're uncomfortable. They think I'm a guy and they feel uncomfortable and if I was [them] maybe I would too ... you don't know, this guy might be a creep.

Sometimes Nick encounters a different kind of problem when using the men's room:

> I usually go in the men's washrooms and sometimes that's hard too, because then I really get hit on by gay men ... I have a certain look and energy in my face that is often mistook as cruising, but what it is, is I'm checking out the scene, there's a security concern for me because I'm trans. I have to be aware of where everything is, so I just cruise the joint quickly and often ... (laughter) ... I could get lucky so much with men! ... Often they're there outside the door and I know how everything works and I just smile and keep going.

Public washrooms do not allow people like Nick to maintain ambivalence regarding their gender – there is no third space, other than the disability facility that may or may not be available. Nick mentioned that he often uses the disability washroom when it is available. It is ironic, as will be discussed later, that many transpeople are shunted into the disabled (i.e., 'abnormal') category, when they are striving for a semblance of 'normality.'

A transitioning FtM transsexual relayed his difficulty in this arena:

Jeb: I've looked this way [in-between] for years and I've had lots of stuff happen, especially around washrooms ... all the time. You walk into the women's room and they tell you, 'You're in the wrong one.' But I generally go into women's rooms because I don't feel as threatened by women as by men.

Chris: What happens when you go in the men's washroom?

Jeb: There's only been one time when I've been 'caught' and the guy just gave me a look and I turned around and walked right out, but every other time I usually wait until I think it's pretty dead in there and I go in and out as fast as I can ... In the women's room, people will actually stop and tell you, 'Get out.' They'll say, 'You're in the wrong room'; and then everybody stops to look you over. Stuff like that has happened more times than I can count. I've had people hold up a hand as I go in and I'll usually just ignore them, or else I've had people tell me I'm in the wrong room, and I say, 'No, I'm not' and just keep doing my thing.

Jeb also resorts to using the disability washroom, even if it is far away, and suggested that an unlabelled single occupancy facility should always be available.

Jeb: Some people really need to have a women's room and a men's room for their comfort and that's fine with me, but I think there needs to be some that are gender-neutral.

Yossi believes that washrooms are a bigger issue for MtFs:

I experienced the same things with a lot of transpeople around bathrooms, getting people staring at you in the bathroom, getting really nervous that you're in the bathroom. I think FtMs often have an easier time of it than trans women, because men often really don't care, quite frankly. They're not as attentive to other people and don't really pay attention to other people the same way women do, so like many trans men I had an easier time than trans women who I knew were going through the transition process at the same time as me.

Wynn (MtF) tries to avoid using lavatories outside of home altogether, if she can manage. Prior to transitioning, she admitted to always having felt uncomfortable using the men's room. Her strategy was to do what was necessary to avoid using washrooms altogether or to seek out a disability room. Failing this, she would go outside and discreetly use the alley. At the beginning of her transition, she had a job where using the women's room was strongly discouraged: 'I was not going to the bathroom, and it was really bad because one of the meds I'm on is a diuretic and you have to go to the bathroom all the time.'

Although fully transitioned, Patricia (MtF) still admitted to hesitancy around using public lavatories:

> The odd time if it's a really busy washroom I still get a little nervous because of my voice, and wonder what people are going to say, but I just do it anyway. For the longest time, when I first started transitioning, I would always find a bench outside the washroom and wait until I knew there was nobody in there and then go in and use the bathroom ... the one good thing about women's washrooms, everyone has their own stall, it's not like a men's washroom where you're standing at a urinal.

Alex (TG–'FtM') recounted using a women's washroom while dressed like a man:

> There've been lots of times that washrooms have been a challenge even before I started identifying as trans, much less when I was on T [testosterone]. One time I was in the department store downtown – this was before I'd started on hormones – I was wearing men's clothes all the time, and I'm five-foot-ten, so people often read me as a guy at first glance. At the store, the women's washroom on the fifth floor is down at the end of a long corridor. Usually that washroom isn't that busy, so it tended to be one that I headed for when I was downtown. One time as I was going in, this woman was coming out and she physically blocked my path – I moved from one side to the other, and she stepped right in front of me each time, until I said, 'Excuse me,' and as I wasn't on T, the voice matched the washroom, and then she apologized and got all flustered. But this kind of thing happened fairly regularly, that people would think or tell me that I was in the wrong washroom.

Keenan (FtM) assumed that he would be safer using the lavatory in a lesbian bar:

> When I used the men's washroom I was targeted and harassed by men. One time some male skinheads looked over the washroom stall while I

was in there and they demanded to know 'what I was.' I was also harassed by lesbians when I used the women's washroom – I wrongly thought at that time [early transition] that it would be easier to just go into the women's. After that, if I was out and had to use the washroom, I just avoided it altogether. It was easier to just go outside and relieve myself in the alley.

On another occasion, Keenan was assaulted while using a lavatory in a queer bar:

I was at a bar and I got sick, so I went to the woman's washroom and vomited. A woman came into the bathroom and started yelling at me and she kicked me. She went and got the manager and had me thrown out of the bar for one night.

Keenan's experience is not unique. In the case of Sheridan v. Sanctuary Investments Ltd (1998), a trans woman in the process of transition was barred entry to a gay and lesbian nightclub due to previous complaints about her use of that club's women's washroom. The British Columbia Human Rights Tribunal found in her favour:

... the woman had been discriminated against on the basis of sex and disability and that the owner of the club had failed in his duty to accommodate her needs ... the discomfort, or preference, of other patrons is not a defense for discrimination. (As cited in Darke and Cope, 2002, p. 58)

The potential violence that transpeople face in using lavatories was dramatized in the film *Better than Chocolate* (Wheeler and McGowan, 1999). The film portrays a trans woman who is brutally assaulted for using a lavatory in a lesbian bar. In the midst of the assault, two other lesbians intervene, stop the attack, and vigorously defend the injured trans woman's right to use the women's washroom. These stories of problems arising from lavatory use pinpoint the paradox/tension at the heart of TS/TG repudiation. Most of the time, transpeople cannot escape the binary: they have to choose. This situation extends to similar contexts, such as changing rooms. Frank recounted a difficult story that unsettled him and an FtM friend following a work-out at their local gym. Frank described his friend as a 'completely huge power lifter' who clearly passed as a man at the time of the incident, yet another power lifter remembered the friend as a 'former female':

This guy came into the change room and confronted my friend saying, 'What the "f" are you doing in here?' And my friend looked at him and said, 'You don't know what you're talking about.' He didn't escalate the situation, but we were both on the spot. I mean we were both looking up at this giant and he's angry. And he says, 'You're not supposed to be in here, you go to the other one.' And my friend said, 'No, you don't know what you're talking about.' My friend left the changing room and I finished putting my shoes on, and the guy said to me, 'That guy's a chick.' And I said, 'I think you got the wrong person.' Then the guy went yelling up the stairs to the proprietors of the gym: 'See that guy over there, he's not a guy, he's a chick, I know him from before.' I stayed quiet. I talked to my buddy later, and he said he would have done the same thing. But it was really rattling – he never went back to that gym.

Ultimately, it is about being perceived as the wrong person, with no right location, because trans-ness poses problems of re-cognition, of re-membering, producing an effect of categorical anxiety.

3. Family and Personal Relations

According to both sociology and psychology, the family (whether the Western nuclear family or other forms of collectivist family) undoubtedly has a powerful influence on identity formation and one's developing sense of self. Nuttbrock (2002) speaks of the role that parents play in affirming gender identity as 'critically important' (p. 5). In fact, in a society governed under the law of the binary, parents and siblings are usually the first of the many gender police to which we are generally subjected. Hence, it is unsurprising that transpeople often, though not universally, carry memories of unfortunate experiences with their families. In depth psychology, the temporal foundations of infancy and childhood create developmental features that are sedimented in the psyche. These dynamics are generally unconscious, with concepts such as repression being central in understanding some aspects of many transpeople's lives. Indeed, for some transpeople, the inter/intrapersonal bonds of loyalty that they may hold with their families are among the initial sources of repressing their trans-ness. Trevor (FtM) shared with me the rationale for waiting decades before embarking on his transition. Following his mother's funeral, he finally arranged a referral to the gender clinic: 'I had lived out my promise to myself that I had made in my twenties, that I'm not going to hurt my mother by openly being who I am.'

For families, there may be a sense of loss when their daughter or son, sister or brother, is no longer the person they thought they were – that person is gone. Trevor explained his father's reactions:

My father was actually in the early stages of Alzheimer's but didn't know it. And he was always somebody who never paid attention anyway. So I had no subtle messages with him. I said, 'Dad I have something to tell you and I want you to pay attention.' I told him straight out: 'I'm changing my sex, I'm going to be a man, this is my new name.' He wasn't too sure, it was a different Welsh name than what he had chosen – so, yes, that was fine. He was already slipping into dementia, so he would grasp any external cues to keep what he could together – he was talking to a man, so then I was a man. But on another level, he would sometimes ask where I was by my old name. Because he hadn't seen her for a while, where was she and why didn't she come to see him. And I would say, 'Well, I'm the person who comes now, and she really loves you and misses you, but she won't be able to come and visit, I'm the person who comes now.' Yet on another level he knew exactly who I was because he used my childhood nickname right up until the end. He went quite deeply into dementia and right up until the latest point would use my nickname, until he couldn't speak anymore. So I knew on some deep level he knew who I was and that he grasped it.[4]

Many of the transpeople interviewed disclosed the difficulties their families had with their trans-ness. Jamie-Lee mentioned that her father had 'really had his heart set that I was a male, right? And my sister too, she had difficulties because she'd always thought she'd had this brother, you know, so it was difficult, I think, for everyone.' The difficulty often lies in cohering the 'old' person with the 'new' and sufficiently re-gendering the relationship.

Roz (MtF) encountered persistent coercion throughout childhood to be the gender that she was assigned to at birth, yet she knew that she wasn't like the boys:

I was always most comfortable at school playing with the girls and doing all of that stuff, you know, I watched all of that rough and tumble and I wasn't [into] the guns and the cowboys and Indians and all of that. I was more into playing house and shop with the girls, and again at some point, age seven maybe, was strongly discouraged from that. I think that my folks suspected that I was a gay boy. And so I found that my life was a series of 'Oh well, we're sending you away to the Y camp' or 'We're sending you here, we've enrolled you in Cub Scouts. We've registered you in this.' And all of these things to make a man out of me, kind of thing, you know?

Roz also remembered her father's homophobic remarks:

And, of course, my dad was always making these comments – my father has a history in policing, and he was always saying, 'We got a call last night where somebody rolled another queer, those damn fags.' You know, so all these derogatory remarks about the LGBT community.

Roz recognized the impossibility of being who she was while living in her father's house. Her solution was to repress and sublimate her trans feelings into other activities:

It was just [because of] the tone and the language that he used that I thought, 'This is something he's not going to get, and my life will be a living hell if I ever try to do this now, so I'm just going to bottle it, push it away and deal with it later.' Then I found out years later that at that particular time [a person with] gender dysphoria was still classified as someone that would have to be committed to a mental institution and be treated with electroshock aversion therapy. So it was not the sort of thing I wanted to do as a sixteen-year-old, and I found my freedom at that time instead through swimming and playing water polo.

For some transpeople, adolescence is recalled as a particularly awful time. Some were no longer able to bear living with their families. Others found the whole experience, family, school, and so on, alienating. They did not see themselves or the pain of incongruency reflected in the world around them. While Frank did not disparage his family experiences, he nevertheless could not bear to be located in a milieu that consistently refused to confirm, mirror, or assist him in either validating or alleviating his pain. He left home at a very early age:

Back then there wasn't any language for it, but the other kids could tell I was 'different,' and I ended up just leaving school, I couldn't see myself in anyone else around me. Leaving my education and leaving my family, they weren't a bad family, there was just ... I was so buried in the shame. If nobody tells a child otherwise, I think it's very typical of the child to figure that it's all about them. That there really is something to be ashamed of, to be frightened of, and I started to act out in small ways, in very irritating ways, and I began to feel that I was more trouble than I was worth, so I just left. It was the sixties and I just left. I stuck my thumb out and I was gone for years and years and years. It's not like, as a twelve-year-old, I wanted to leave the security and the safety and the warmth of my family, but the angst inside was too great. If I had known, if anyone had known, that there could be something like gender dysphoria that may be going on ... I mean when I first saw that shrink's office [at the gender clinic] – there was a corner devoted to children's toys, he worked with kids that have got gender issues, to explore and observe and let the child express. You know, I can't help but believe that if something like that had been available to me that it would've given me a whole other life, and it certainly would have spared my parents a lot of agony.

Tami also left home, unable to bear the constant violence that she was subject to: 'I was abused a lot – [pause] – beat up by my brothers.'

Family relations may also become fragmented as a result of the decision to transition. In John's case, the fundamentalist Christian background of his family was not easy to reconcile with his transsexualism. He described his current relationship with his parents:

It's better now. I don't think they'll ever pronounce blessing on it, but they have come to a kind of acceptance. We have all moved to a different place with this, and I think it continues to evolve. We can talk and visit on holidays. Sometimes they even use my correct name, if not my correct pronoun. My mother is much more able to put things aside and relate as one human to another. She can express love and affection; she can hug me and we can talk. But my father and I are still a little bit uncomfortable. I think we're still working out our relationship. We're still in process.

John's comment resonates with Kristeva's (1982) idea of the subject in process / on trial. In this case, other family members are also on trial, and processing a new situation. The panoptic judgmental gaze is one that John and his family continue to negotiate and work on; their relationship is in process.

Transpeople also challenge the identities of family members, affecting their self-definition as parents, grandparents, aunts, uncles, siblings, sons and daughters. 'I am a father to a daughter' transitions to 'I am (now) a father to a son,' and so on. A deeper challenge is posed by TG people, since present language seems inadequate to the task. Moreover, family members may wonder if they are to blame for not detecting that their child was mis-sexed, and trying to prevent or solve it in some way.

Transpeople may also lose friends and social groups as a result of their coming out and transitioning. For some, especially those estranged or living far away from their families, losing social groups increases the probability of loneliness, alienation, or ostracism. Some will be able to make new friends; others may be too shy, or afraid of further rejection. I asked Trevor what happened to him after he came out as trans, and he mentioned how sad he felt after losing friends who were opposed to his transition:

> There were one or two lesbian friends – one said very clearly to me, 'You're not the way you used to be, I can't talk to you anymore,' and that was a loss. I really enjoyed her, we used to have really good talks.

There is a dearth of research into the extent of transpeople's loss of family, friends, intimate partners, and social groups, and the effects that these losses have on their lived experience and mental health. Questions regarding the production of new traumas and their effects on transpeople in the intimate social realm require better understandings on all sides, whether from the transpersons' or those of family and friends who also may, in a sense, lose someone too.

4. Employment

Darke and Cope (2002) reported that 40 per cent of 152 transpeople sampled were unemployed in Canada, despite 71 per cent having at least two years of post-secondary education. They also note that over 70 per cent had 'low' income as measured by standard Canadian indexes. Perhaps as a consequence, Goldberg (2002) points out that a significant number of transpeople (mostly, but not exclusively, MtFs) work full- or part-time in the sex trade. Many transpeople find their employment prospects curtailed by trans repudiation, with few career/work options available. One study Goldberg cites, for example, shows that 36 per cent of transpeople in Ontario were at one point employed in the sex trade. This can be a dangerous profession that places transpeople at (further) risk. Thus, in her account of having been a sex-trade worker over a twenty-year period in Canada, trans woman Alexandra Highcrest (1997) argues for the legalization of prostitution, a trade that helped pay her way through university. Other transpeople have had little or no work experience, which can be attributed to trans repudiation in the workplace (a factor that limits their ability to endure a job), or the refusal of employers to hire transpeople in the first place. Several narratives drawn from my interviews confirm the persistence of this problem and its concrete social and psychic effects.

Dean (FtM) described his former job and how it came to an end:

I worked at a drug and alcohol counselling centre for women, and my boss at the time was supposedly a really good friend of mine, and I told her that I wanted to get into the gender clinic to see if I could get on hormones, at which point she strongly encouraged me to leave my job. This was even before taking hormones ... I didn't want to make a big stink about it, so I just left ... That's discrimination, I don't care what you call it.

Roz also had a difficult time as a police officer but managed to retain her job while she transitioned. Her story draws attention to the struggles she endured:

The officer in charge called me into his office and said, 'Thanks for all the great work you've done and while you're here, there's this weird rumour going around the building.' At that point, I just said, 'Well the rumour is true, I'm transsexual, I'm waiting for a placement with the gender clinic' ... Immediately there were a couple of police officers who said, 'I refuse to work with the freak' ... [some] officers phoned me at home privately to offer their support but said, 'We cannot be seen publicly to be supporting you, we don't have a union and it would cost us a promotion or our jobs.' One officer even suggested that I should be relieved of my weapon and that I might be a danger to myself or to others, so I was ordered to go and have a psychiatric evaluation and I went and saw one of the police department psychiatrists and after about forty minutes she said, 'I'm going to send a report to the department letting them know that you're stable, you're fine, that there's nothing wrong with you here, that you're handling this well' ... and yet there was one police officer who came to me and said, 'Why don't you retire, why don't you resign, why don't you go and get a job in another part of the city somewhere because you're making people here really uncomfortable' ... [then] somebody leaked this to the press. People would see me, I would be on the elevator and they would be waiting to get on the elevator and see me and refuse to get on ('Oh I forgot something, or I forgot this or I forgot that') ... Or, if I got on the elevator, they would get off, or if I was walking down the hallway, they would be walking towards me and all of a sudden detour into a room or whatever. I mean, I just knew, once it was so obvious, a guy walked into a broom closet, saw an open door and walked into a broom closet ... there was ongoing stuff where I felt uncomfortable, alienated, and isolated.

Roz was subjected to an ostracism that, considering the nature of policing, potentially threatened her safety:

There were times where I was going to work or walking down to the parking lot with somebody ... people, other officers, would talk to whoever I was with, yet I was treated as if I wasn't there. So I just got to a place where I felt unsafe and concerned that in a jam there were certain people who wouldn't show up, or they would respond slowly to that complaint, and so I transferred out and worked instead at our Diversity Relations unit.

Roz began facilitating diversity trainings with other police officers. She recalled how difficult the work could be:

One of the members wanted to know if it was workplace harassment, if he could be charged under the discipline code for refusing to work with me or work around me because he found the whole thing disgusting and against God.

Roz's experiences are similar to those of a Toronto police officer who spent twenty-six years on the force. In a Human Rights complaint to the Province of Ontario, Bonnie Henderson (who went public with her experiences) alleges she endured taunts and bigotry, and in one case was stalked by another member of the force. Eventually she could no longer bear the common anti-trans attitudes within policing nor the associated harassment. Subsequently she opted for early retirement and filed a complaint of discrimination (Demara, 2004).

Wynn also described the difficulties she experienced while transitioning on one of her jobs:

> The boss guys would refuse to use my new name. They went out of their way to use masculine pronouns but did it in a way, like they were trying to be friendly, like they were trying to get me to be a guy or something. I think more than anything they were uncomfortable with it. I didn't stay at that job for long.

Like Wynn, Jeb found it difficult working while in the midst of transitioning. The ambiguity of gender presentation in this in-between state, and the difficulty coming out as trans to co-workers, prompted Jeb to quit his job at a supermarket:

> They knew I was queer but not trans and barely handled my being 'a lesbian.' There really was not a lot of understanding and not a lot of education and just the thought of having to go through it all over again as trans tired me out and I ended up leaving mostly because of that. There were too many people that I would have had to come out to and it would have been ongoing and never-ending; so I just got out of there. We had three or four trans customers that came in and I'd heard some pretty awful things employees said. A trans woman came in and asked for something and someone turned around and said, 'That's a man in a dress!' I tried to explain to them afterwards why that wasn't okay, and they didn't care. So I explained it all to management ... [then] a bunch of co-workers were going to have to go to diversity awareness training and they were mad about it. Everybody knew it was me that had complained about homophobia, so that ostracized me further, it was ugly.

The repression of the gendered self to suit work environments is also illustrated in Nick's job searches. He lamented what his barriers have been as a TG (wo)man: 'Well, every time I'd go for a job interview I'd have to feminize myself as much as possible, for years.'

Kimberly had accumulated many years of experience as an airline pilot. After she transitioned, however, she was unable to find work in her field:

I tried for many, many years, and I would get calls, interviews, instantly because of my experience and qualifications ... But because my history in flying had been under a male name, when I had to give a reference the new employer would always find out. Or I would tell them in advance, but usually they would find out by contacting the references. I remember I had an incident with a corporate charter company. They had actually hired me and then asked for my references to follow up the résumé ... I got my envelope and résumé torn up in, it must have been a hundred pieces, and then they stuffed it in another envelope and mailed it all back to me ... I've tried for eighteen years to get back into the field and the profession that I'm good at and should be doing.

Prejudice and discrimination directed towards transpeople is not limited to what are, or at least were traditionally perceived to be, chauvinistic professions such as policing or airline piloting. Aiyanna works as an artist and lamented the following:

I'm one of the only, globally, transsexual artists who has been working professionally, who has been able to successfully continue her career. It's a horrifying statistic, and I'm hardly proud of it, I'm ashamed of this on so many different levels.

Aiyanna speaks as a visual artist who has garnered considerable achievement in her career. She is a model to others of the possibility of success. Yet she is also quite aware of what a difficult struggle it is for one to succeed in their field when one is transparently trans. In another corner of the arts, the entertainment field, there is always the possibility of openly using one's trans-ness to make a living. Namaste's (2004) historical analysis of MtFs who worked in Montreal's popular cabaret and burlesque shows during the 1950s and 1960s demonstrates that these venues were among the only places to gain employment outside of the sex trade if one were MtF. Forty to fifty years later, little seems to have changed, and many transpeople find it difficult to secure and retain employment.

Patricia has had a hard time finding work and speculated on some of the reasons:

Yeah, I think some of the people I had interviews with would seriously consider hiring me, but they're not sure how everyone else would react.

They take the safe route. Instead of taking the chance of losing customers and clients, they would rather have someone who isn't trans.

5. Education

In 2001 the New York–based organization Human Rights Watch issued a report on lesbian, gay, bisexual, and transgender youth attending public (state) schools in the United States. The report notes that many students are wrongly perceived as transgender, yet such persons are similarly subject to persecution. Repudiation of any gender transgression is a systematic problem in schooling. The report states:

> If gay and lesbian people have received some modicum of acceptance in the United States over the past several decades, transgender people remain misunderstood at best and vilified at worst. ... Youth who identify or are perceived to be transgender face relentless harassment and live with overwhelming isolation. (P. 1)

Human Rights Watch notes that harassment of transpeople in schools is not limited to repudiations by fellow students, but also extends to repudiations from teachers, who often act to police gendered behaviours. The report concludes: '... peers enforce the rules through harassment, ostracism, and violence. School officials condone this cruel dynamic through inaction or in some cases because they, too, judge gay, lesbian, bisexual, and transgender youth to be undeserving of respect' (p. 1, concluding section).

The interviews that I conducted retrospectively narrate serious problems with primary, secondary, and post-secondary education. While these incidents may have occurred years ago, there is little persuasive evidence that much has changed or improved. Education as an institution is in need of being educated about transpeople. For example, Devor (1997) comments on the paucity of educational materials available to teens and teachers regarding trans issues in secondary schools. This is unfortunate considering that 'puberty is an especially horrendous time for many transsexuals' (Califia, 2003, p. xxxvi).

One of the interviewees, Alex (TG), recalled how he coped with the gender policing in his school. His reflections are evidence of the creative ways in which some transpeople manage to cope with the compulsory gender binary enshrined within schooling:

When I was in high school, I went to a girls' school where we had to wear uniforms which were kilts, and in the winter we got to wear ties. So I spent a lot of high school saying to myself, 'In Scotland, this is men's clothing, in Scotland, this is men's clothing.'

Alex also recalled that his 'all-girl' school at times made an unusual (and perhaps unthought) allowance for him to be cast as a male figure in school plays:

I think something about my gender identity probably came through to others, because in every single school play that I was in, I was cast as a male character – the one and only exception was the play that was all female characters.

At both primary[5] and secondary school levels, transpeople often face constant harassment. Robin recalled being taunted as a 'faggot and a queer.' Such taunting figured in some transpeople's decisions to drop out, as Jamie-Lee (MtF) recalled:

School was difficult because that's where I was finding I was different – I was teased because I was a very slight, effeminate boy. You know, there was the name calling and that kind of stuff, so I escaped into my little world ... I dropped out in grade ten [and it was] ... definitely due to the gender issues.

Frank recalled that puberty at school was a particularly difficult time:

Back then I didn't know I was a transperson ... I was in grade school in the early sixties and there wasn't any language for what was going on ... Nobody knew this existed, so looking back I remember how horrified I was in the changing rooms. I remember how things were mostly all right, and then I started to menstruate and it's something that none of the other kids talked about, so I didn't know that I was the only girl that was horrified. It wasn't just 'yuck, what's this?' I was absolutely mortified. I hid it from everyone for a good two years, as best as a child could hide it. But the changing rooms were horrifying too because it's the same kids that you're school with, and I had no idea what I was so ashamed about, what I was so frightened about; here were all these other kids so excited about all the changes with their bodies, comparing things, and I'm terri-

fied I'm going to 'get caught,' totally terrified even to be in there with
them, like I'm not supposed to be in there, in the girls' changing room ...
the other kids could tell I was 'different,' and I ended up just leaving
school – I couldn't see myself in anyone else around me.

Those who remained in school were frequently targeted for verbal
abuse. Dean confirmed that it can be a long ordeal. I asked him if he
had ever been beaten up at school, and he replied, 'Oh yeah, tons. All
through high school.'

Social isolation and ostracism is also a problem for many transpeople in school. Roz recalled feeling uncomfortable as a child at primary
and middle school. She wanted to play with the girls but was rejected
because she was a 'boy.' The boys bullied and harassed her, and Roz
generally spent her social time on her own. As Roz moved into secondary school, she continued to encounter systematic bullying:

My locker was down on the ground floor of the junior high school and
homeroom in the morning was up on the second floor. Everyday that I
climbed up those stairs with my books and papers under my arms, somebody in that stampede to go to classes would pull the binder from under
my arms, and it would scatter down the stairs and everybody would kick
the books all over the place and kick the papers everywhere. I was repeatedly targeted for really an extended period of time.

Jeb also recounted his experience of being targeted at school:

I wasn't openly trans, but I was definitely targeted because of the way I
walked and dressed, and it was all for very gender-related things even
though I was not out ... I had quite a few incidents where I was kind of
mobbed, where I would be surrounded by people.

In many cases, one's trans-ness is detectable by peers regardless if
one is out as trans or not. A sense of feeling different is a common
experience for trans youth. Wynn recalled finding some friends in secondary school, a small group comprised of others who 'didn't fit in'
and who 'watched out for each other.' She spoke about her experiences
of harassment and physical abuse:

This one good friend of mine was this kind of effeminate guy, and we
always hung out and everyone just assumed we were gay or whatever, so

we got lots of shit for being that way, and we dressed funny and so we got lots of comments and threats – 'fags,' etc., and plus I was always really tall and so a lot of the jock guys would want to fight me. I got jumped on my second week at my high school, knocked over and punched a bunch.

Aiyanna (MtF) recalled how her gender issues at school were tied-up with racism:

> When I started in school, it was back when the U.S. and Canada changed the law that allowed us [First Nations people] to go to public school. This was when I first found out that I was not a girl – I was quickly slapped with a reality that I was a boy, from this cute little child, tousled hair and dimpled cheek, 'What a cute little child,' to being this 'ugly little Indian boy.' And very quickly my neighbours who I had played with, this little girl, would no longer play with me once I started school ... now that 'I was a boy.'

Problems encountered in primary and secondary school often continue on at the post-secondary level of education. Robin told her story of trying to become a nurse, and how she eventually was forced to leave the program. In her statement, she summarized the intersectional dynamics of trans repudiation that often result in living a life of poverty:

> [crying] I'll tell you what hurts, is that instead of making fifty to sixty thousand dollars a year, I'm making nine or ten on welfare. That's what hurts. That's what I'm crying about, the money. And a place in the world, perhaps, but the money ... Marginalization. We all face it, all transpeople.

Jamie-Lee also tried training to become a nurse and found similar problems with trans repudiation. She filed a lawsuit against her school and won. However, that was not the end of the ordeal:

> I went to [a lawyer] and he sued the college and I won, but I remember this one instructor who didn't like me – she said to me, once I'd won, 'You may have won the battle but you won't win the war' ... it started happening again and I just thought, 'No.' You know, how can I study ... with this happening to me, right? So I dropped out.

In her research, Burnham (1999) found that pre-operative transsexuals were, on occasion, instructed by post-secondary teachers, advisors, or school counsellors to drop out and return to school only after their transitions were complete. Such advice often came with the proviso that it is best not to 'disturb or distract' other students from their studies. Other transpeople encounter financial barriers preventing them from paying tuition fees in the first place, and thereby closing the door to higher education. Namaste's (2000) analysis shows how applicants may be denied student loans. She cites institutional problems (in Quebec) that relate to barriers in having one's sex status changed on legal texts, official certificates, and so on. This makes it impossible for banks to process student loan applications.

Article 26 of the UN Declaration of Human Rights (United Nations, 1948) affirms that everyone has the right to an education. That many transpeople face persecution within the education system is both alarming and socially untenable. Clearly, there is a need for a cultural shift in schools and other institutional sites, so that gender-based discrimination can become a thing of the past.

6. Threat / Violence

The interviewees' stories confirm that transpeople are frequently exposed to threats and intimidation from others in their everyday/ night worlds. These acts represent an intersubjective aspect to the force of subjugation in transpeople's lives. Verbal threat/intimidation can in itself be traumatic and often escalates into physical assault. Physical assault is not an uncommon factor in transpeople's lives; 50 per cent of my interviewees reported having been physically assaulted.

Hank (FtM) told of his experience walking down the street:

I've never been beaten up, but I've had people do things that are threatening physically, like surround me while I'm walking down the street. Where there's eight young straight men around me, trying to bother me, usually throwing often transphobic, but also homophobic slurs. Getting in my space.

A perception of gender transgression is often the precursor to threat and intimidation. The interpellation of the gaze of repudiation is a constant risk, especially for those who are pre-transition or in the initial stages. Hank described one incident:

> I went on a date to a bar wearing a suit and these guys decided they were more of a man than I was and wanted to go outside and fight me. We went outside but their girlfriends pulled them off before they could hit me – they were like, 'You're not a man, we're going to show you you're not a man.' Stuff like that.

Perceptually, the sometimes narrow boundaries between queer and trans may perpetuate the superimposition of these two distinct categories under the gaze of a general homophobic/heterosexist repudiation. This problem is exemplified in Alex's experience:

> One time when I was twenty and had shaved my head but wasn't shaving my legs, I was wearing a hippie skirt and walking down a street in a small city in Ontario and a carload of guys drove by and yelled 'faggot' at me. I'm not sure if they honestly thought I was a guy or if they didn't know the word 'dyke.' Sometimes transphobia and homophobia can be pretty difficult to sort out.

For some transpeople, threat and harassment have been lived in the everyday/night world as a persistent ordeal, ever-present. Yossi told of his experience of having beer bottles thrown at him from passing car windows:

> That happened a lot, I mean, that was just a daily kind of thing. I just stopped going outside in that point of my transition where I was very visibly female bodied but had facial hair. People would yell, 'What are ya, a man or a woman? You fucking freak.' Blah, blah, blah. That happened all the time to me for a little while.

Sometimes these daily ordeals escalate in frightening ways. Roz shared her harrowing story:

> I'd gone out one morning for my run [in a park], and as I was finishing up and having my little cool-down walk when three teenaged boys went by me on bicycles. As they rode past me, one of them called out, 'Fucking faggot.' And I laughed for a couple of reasons thinking, 'Boy have you ever got it wrong,' ... So they came back and circled me and

threatened to hurt me and I just stayed there and stood my ground and looked at one of them that I considered to be the leader of the group and said, 'Okay which one of you wants to die first? I won't get all three of you, but I will get one and when the police arrive, they'll know which one it is because I'm going to rip your nuts off.' And we stood there in a stand-off stance for a few moments, then the leader of the group said, 'It's not worth it.' They rode away, my heart was pounding.

The matter of threat is more complicated for Roz, however, when it comes from her own colleagues. She told of the threats she received when she invited some trans friends to police headquarters, a gesture of thanks for assisting with her diversity training workshops. For doing this, a colleague 'quietly pulled me aside and said, "If you ever do that again, if you ever bring those people into our club again, there will be consequences and you won't like them."'

Intimidation as a dynamic can be subtler but nevertheless convey the message of repudiation. Jenny told of her experience on a city bus, noticing that

... when getting on the bus ... the kids move to the back of the bus because they don't want to sit near you ... once I overheard some girls start commenting, 'Oh you can never tell with those kind of people if they're guys or girls.' I think she couldn't tell if I was a guy or a girl ... She was in the seat behind me with one of her friends, so I heard every word.

Wynn has endured many experiences of threat and intimidation. She recounted a particularly frightening one:

My friend and I were walking home. It was about one in the morning, and a bunch of young men pulled up in a car and started screaming, 'Fucking faggot.' And screeched the car right up to me and a couple of them started getting out, so I basically took off – me and my friend ran to her apartment and got inside ... I was really scared with that one. There's been lots of times where people yelled from their cars or slowed down and said they're going to beat me up, but that one was really scary ... they were completely willing to attack me.

Jeb told me about some of the numerous experiences of threat and intimidation that he has suffered:

Growing up there were tons of things that happened. I used to walk to a coffee shop every night and almost every time there was someone – usually they were pretty wimpy about it – they'd wait until they were in their cars and then yell something. I've had cigarettes thrown at me, I've had full McDonald's pops thrown at me, I've had beer cans and beer bottles, I've had pennies, and they'll yell, 'Queer!' out the window as they do it. I've been spat on by someone driving by. This one kid and his friends, I would run into them everywhere and they would always say stuff like 'What, you think you're a man or something?' That started when I was twelve – that one kid was in one of my classes, and everyday he would lean into me and say, 'You've got a moustache, are you trying to be a man?' He would say stuff like that – and 'What are you?' – to try to intimidate me – that happened a lot. Since I've been in the city, it's been pretty tame though. I've had a couple of comments ... one guy, what did he call me? 'Faggot girl'? or something, like he didn't know what I was, so he said, 'What are you, a faggot or a girl?' And he followed me after we got off the bus. But that was the only sort of scary thing that happened in the city. I'm pretty careful what I do too, I'm pretty nervous and anxious, especially around younger people. I avoid them, I'll go over across the street or I'll wait 'til they're gone.

Jeb's statement, of feeling nervous and anxious around younger people especially, may point to teenagers' compliance to the law of the binary, the 'need' to solidify their gender identities in order to feel accepted. Teenagers may express less tolerance/restraint towards those who appear to transgress gender/sex boundaries, partly in fear that their stated defence of gender transgressors may lead to group expulsion or suspicions that they themselves might be, to use the British term, 'bent.' Those who are intoxicated may also have less capacity for restraint in regard to censoring unconscious impulses, and express their fear of Others with violence. Patricia, like Roz, has learned to use assertiveness in order to defuse potentially violent situations:

Patricia: I was walking home and this – I'll call him a gentleman – was drunk and he said, 'Get out of my way, you faggot.' He tried to push me, and I just turned around with my umbrella in my hand and I said, 'Come any closer and I'll smack you in the face with my umbrella.' But he didn't, he just kept on walking.

Nick, who lives with disabilities that entail chronic pain, needs to diffuse any potentially violent situation quickly. Any physical assault to his/her body could have dire consequences. Nick's TG status allows for fluidity, shifting when required in creative ways, to use the ambiguity of her/his body in order to avoid conflict:

> I sometimes feel like that's where I use some of my socialized female stuff to help resolve some of the situations I've been in and that's how I avoid a fight. I see it coming and prepare in physical ways – raise my voice, any breasts I can show, any female stuff I can show before it gets bad. Occasionally I've got, 'Are you a guy or are you a girl?' and I go, 'Why?' or, 'That's kind of a weird question.' And keep walking.

Nick exemplifies some of the advantages of a TG position by being able to draw on and exploit both ends of the binary when necessary, in finding ways to survive repudiations. Indeed, many of the excerpts presented above point to transpeople as objects for a potentially misplaced homophobia/heterosexism which perpetrators themselves struggle with, as reflected in statements such as 'what are you?' Perpetrators respond to perceptions of binary transgressions yet seem unable to nuance the differences that these transgressions entail. Being a butch dyke, a feminine gay man, a cross-dresser, or a drag King is quite different from transitioning into a liveable body as a result of having been mis-sexed. A poverty of language and lack of perceptual appreciation (understanding) of those who cross boundaries is unfortunately too common, whether the crossing is a temporary playful/parodic performance, or, as in the case of TS people, involves serious and permanent changes to the body. The performance element is useful when the need to defuse potentially violent situations arise. Yet it is not a foolproof strategy since transpeople often report experiences of violence regardless (Moran and Sharpe, 2004).

Physical Assault

Certainly among the most painful stories to emerge from this study were those accounts of having been physically and/or sexually assaulted. Goldberg (2002) points out that transpeople are vulnerable to an array of physical abuse from families, partners, johns (sex-trade clients), and unknown assailants. These acts often constitute hate crimes yet are generally not acknowledged by the authorities as such *specifically on the basis of one's trans status*. For example, when formal complaints are lodged by transpeople, they might be investigated under the category of sexual orientation. Perpetrators may not discern the differences between queer and trans anyway, even if this has the unintended effect of erasing or repudiating trans being-in-the-world.

Darke and Cope (2002) note that violence against transpeople is seriously under-reported. Goldberg (ibid.) also draws attention to the reluctance of transpeople to report violent incidents to police, due to prior negative experiences with law enforcement officials, a point which echoes the conclusions of Namaste's (2000, 2004) research. Indeed, in one of my interviews, a trans woman narrated a shocking account of sexual abuse that she claims she endured at the hands of a police officer who had, temporarily, forcibly confined her. This issue is undoubtedly linked to the woefully few studies that account for the actual numbers of transpeople who have experienced harassment and physical assault. In the UK transpeople report a 'lack of trust and confidence in policing' due to 'perceptions of hostility and discrimination coming from the police' (Moran and Sharpe, 2004, p. 396). However, without reporting attacks to the authorities, the opportunity to gather data – such as hate crime data – is lost, mitigating claims to accuracy and causing the incidence levels to appear low or even non-existent. Compounding the problem are questions regarding the motivation of an attack. While the victim might be certain that the motivation was solely based on their trans status, the hostility expressed could be filtered through a more complicated grid. The coexistence of other factors such as class, race, and sexuality can play a part in the attack. It is already clear from excerpts cited in this book that transpeople are frequently subject to homophobia and heterosexism, whether or not they themselves are heterosexual in orientation.

I have decided not to reproduce specific examples of narratives of physical abuse in this section since I find it too upsetting to select or to recount the *many* traumatic events of violence inflicted on transpeople. We live in a violent society. Images of war, terrorism, murder, gratuitous violence in the media, and so on, occur with stunning frequency. There is an ongoing danger that we will become collectively desensitized and dissociate ourselves from this frenetic array of violent images. I will assume that the reader can imagine the horror of these stories, and recognize the need to include transpeople among those against whom violence must be stopped.

7. Problems with Law Enforcement

Like other citizens, transpeople can be questioned, detained, and arrested by law enforcement agencies. And as the previous section noted, transpeople may themselves be in need of the services of the police, especially when they have been assaulted. How police interact with them, considering their authority and weaponry, is a matter of concern. For example, transpeople working in the sex trade are frequently targeted by police. In her study, Namaste (2000) found that all of the trans sex-trade workers whom she interviewed had encountered harassment by the police. This harassment was not just related, or limited, to the legal quagmires surrounding prostitution in Canada. The harassment, rather, frequently takes aim at the worker's trans embodiment. Some officers might ask MtFs for their former, masculine birth names, which they would then use instead of their correct names. Male terms would also be facetiously and insultingly used by police (directed to their patrol partner or the accosted trans woman), such as '"sir," "boy," "guy,"' or they would objectify and depersonalize trans women by referring to them as 'it' (ibid. p. 170). Namaste also found that verbal harassment sometimes escalated into physical beatings by police. These incidents of ridicule, humiliation, harassment, and physical violence led some trans women to refrain from accessing law enforcement services in other instances, such as following a beating from a pimp or lover. Harassment of trans women by police may be systemic. Meyerowitz (2002) outlines a persuasive case in her historical sketch of policing in San Francisco's Tenderloin district beginning in the early 1960s. She reports that police regularly beat transpeople with batons or 'demanded free sexual services' (p. 229).

Identifying a suspect in policing requires the establishment of the person's physical parameters (sex, 'race,' weight, height, and so on). Sex, like race, is a primary signifier of profiling that police use to categorize people. In recent years there have been multiple reports of 'racial profiling' of 'suspects' by police in Canada, a controversial practice that points to the problem of racism in our society. Roz's case, as recounted earlier, exemplifies the depth of transphobia that exists within the institution of policing. While not all officers of the law are transphobic, some clearly are. Establishing the extent of the problem requires that more research be conducted on interactions between police and transpeople. This will also entail the cooperation of the police, breaking codes of silence and allowing for a shift in policing culture. Education in gender issues certainly marks a good place to start in addition to LGBT liaison officers, who could help to build bridges for dialogue.

On a related matter, customs and immigration agents, too, can be concerned over a person's gender presentations. Califia (2003) raises the issue of *gender profiling*, a phenomena that seems to have increased under the seemingly interminable 'war against terrorism.' To what extent are transpeople unduly scrutinized at border crossings? Jeb spoke of his experience:

> [border agents] ... they've generally been decent to me but there have been times where they take a look at my ID and they're like, 'What's that about?' One night we got pulled aside and they searched the entire car, and they called me 'sir' – then they saw the F on my ID and their attitudes changed. They got more grumpy about the whole thing, like I'd purposefully tricked them.

8. Relations with (Other) Lesbians and Gays

Heterosexual transpeople can be mistaken as homosexual in their sexual orientation. Hence, like gay, lesbian, and bisexual transpeople, they too can experience homophobia and heterosexism in their everyday/night worlds. For transpeople, the LGBT alliance does not always vibrate the symbolic 'rainbow' that is supposed to signify inclusiveness. For example, Califia (2003) documents the fact that 'some of the most hateful journalism about transgendered people during the last five years has been written by gay men and lesbians' (p. xxxiii). This trend follows a long history of trans repudiation within gay and lesbian media, as Meyerowitz (2002) also notes in her social history of American transsexualism. While some transpeople identify as queer and feel a sense of community among lesbians, gays, and bisexuals, heterosexual transpeople may also associate themselves with the LGB(T) community, as they believe that they will find greater tolerance here than elsewhere (Califia, 2003).

In their report on human rights abuses in American schools towards gay, lesbian, bisexual, and transgender youth, Human Rights Watch (2001) states: 'During the course of our investigation, we had the opportunity to observe interactions between gay boys and transgender youth. In several cases, the gay boys behaved in ways that appeared to be sexually harassing' (p. 3).

Tami has experienced direct repudiations from gay men, especially at work:

Well, shocking news flash: some gay men and lesbian women have a hard time wrapping their heads around physically changing your body from one gender to the other or anywhere in between ... I worked at [organization X] primarily with gay men and it became very cliquish ... There was a complete lack of camaraderie, in fact, they were almost blatantly rude ... you know, a conversation is going on and I would try to enter it and everybody would just walk away, exclude me, regularly. Not just a couple of times and it wasn't just my imagination – I said, 'We're all trying to provide a service, you know?' I didn't want to make waves and make the service less comfortable for everybody else. So I thought I'd just let it go, but I still think it was the biggest beef I had in my transition. I've practically wanted to lodge a formal complaint and say to them, you know, 'You guys had better clean up your act in terms of how you're treating transsexual people.'

Hank, who likes to socialize at one of the gay nightclubs in the city, related some salient experiences:

Well, I was out on Thursday night at the nightclub. I walked in and went up to the bar past a table of men. And they were like, 'Is that a man or a woman?' Really loudly – the jukebox was loud and I could hear them. The whole line-up could hear them and they were discussing and evaluating my body, trying to figure out which one I was. When people are seen as being Other, people seem to forget that you can hear. They'll have a very loud conversation about you and don't seem to understand I can hear what they're saying.

Hank particularly lamented the difficulties he has encountered with gay men and lesbians:

I've had quite a bit of harassment and intense interactions with queer folk. And I think it's just like the rest of the world – they're not really educated on trans issues. Especially with FtM – since MtFs have been in the community a lot longer. So people are more used to it, not that they necessarily like it. I've had a lot of people, when I tell them I'm a tranny, think that I am MtF, that I'm a trans woman ... whereas a lot of straight people, especially in small towns, will be like, 'Oh yeah, whatever,' because they don't have so much weight on it. They don't really care – they're just like, 'Oh yeah,' moving on. They don't really want to talk about the differences – they don't have any language to process that through – so they're just like, 'Oh yeah.' Whereas queer people, especially queer women, want to talk about the whole ramifications of it: their lives, the community, the world, the struggle, all these sorts of things. So it becomes much more contentious, I think.

For Hank, interactions with other gay men have been, at times, difficult and upsetting:

I also had a waiter at [a gay restaurant] almost pick me up off my feet by the collar of my jacket into his face because he was not happy with me and not liking me. So I was right in his face and he was trying to tell me off while he was holding onto me ... we were there having drinks and there was a drag show going on, and someone who worked there, not him, like I was passing pretty well, wanted to talk to me or something. The waiter was passing a message that some boy there thought I was hot or whatever, and the waiter kept kind of, like knew I wasn't a bio male but also kept sort of flirting with me. He would touch my hand while he was talking to me, kind of flirtatiously bitchy. And then by the end of the evening he was like, 'Well, I don't understand you people, and I don't understand drag queens either.' And just started going off and I blocked out most of it, but then he pulled me up really close to his face so he could talk to me. And I was like, 'You need to put me down, you need to stop touching me, I'm going to get really angry if you don't stop touching me.' He said, 'I don't care about you people, I don't understand.' And I was like, 'Well, read a fucking book. If you don't understand it's not my problem, I'm just trying to leave. Maybe you need to do some learning for yourself.' He definitely scared me a bit – he was kind of jokingly being rude. It was kind of playful, but he was holding me really tightly. He wasn't screaming in my face, but it was kind of where the joke is not funny anymore. But he let go of me and I walked out.

In his first commentary, Hank points out a disturbing dynamic of depersonalization in his comment 'people seem to forget that you can hear.' This behaviour is part of a repudiation of transpeople that denies them self/personhood, something deeper than just a denial of subjectivity. In the second instance, he relates how some gay men make aggressive jokes about transpeople: 'I don't understand you people.'

Both comments point to lack of understanding and resulting repudiation as a problem in the LGBTQ 'community,' and to splits in be/longing, of fractures in this alliance.

On the morning of 28 June 1969, at the Stonewall Inn in New York City, a riot erupted that galvanized LGBTQ people to fight for their liberation. Transpeople were central to that event, yet too often it is mythologized as *the* 'gay liberation' moment. This both erases and repudiates transpeople and further marginalizes them. In the same way that feminists have been rewriting women back into the history (her-story) that men have erased them from, so too are transpeople such as Califia (2003) reinscribing trans back into their histories, their trans-stories. Aiyanna expressed her negative reaction to the erasure of transpeople from historically relevant events:

> Transpeople were instrumental, integral in instigating Stonewall and we have been erased from the movement from the very beginning. There have been numerous activists and numerous transsexual people since that time that have overtly or covertly continued to demand for inclusion ... White gay men still have a horrific time trying to accept the notion, because of what a penis means to a white gay man, gay men in general. For them to accept the notion that anyone with a penis would cut it off, or turn it inside out more appropriately – for gay men to accept the notion of transsexuals is just too, too hard. Too threatening. I'm certainly not saying all gay men, it's a broad brush.

Yossi is a gay man but has experienced trans repudiation from other gay men:

> And, you know, being a fag, a lot of the discomfort I get is from gay men. Once at a forum I facilitated around 'Coming Out' for gay and bi men – you know, people knew I was trans, but it wasn't a big whoop – at the break a drag queen came up to me and said, 'Oh it's really, you're so brave for facilitating this forum and I just want to say thank you and also to let you know that I would never have sex with you' (laughs). You know, it's like I get that a lot from gay men actually, that, you know, in theory they think it's very brave or heroic but, dear god, no flirting, no sexual anything. And, you know, it's that tension, right, within communities where they might want to pay lip service to being inclusive but they're so dis-, they're just so uncomfortable with you, you can tell, it's sometimes very obvious.

Trevor has also, at times, found some gays and lesbians to be very unsupportive of transpeople:

> I had been active in a queer group in the Church and [that was] the group that was least supportive, people I had loved, cared about, stood shoulder-to-shoulder in activism, worship, spiritual pursuits. I will still occasionally go back and join in an activity with that group of people. Last time I went there were still two or three people who didn't get the pronoun right, who still used my old name, who outed me to people who didn't know in the group. Hello! I mean these are people themselves who are struggling to be perceived as they are in a very conservative institution – the Church – and at the same time cannot see their own actions in terms of how they are treating somebody they see as Other ... some lesbian friends struggled but got it and they were able to come back a year – a year and a half – later and I really left the door open to anybody. If they want to talk, let's talk, I'm happy, wherever you want to go with this. And there were a couple of lesbian friends who sat down and said, 'I don't like this because ... it disgusts me because ... it frightens me because ...' We could really talk and engage with it. And they were able to shift, but it took them time.

Jamie-Lee related memories of her conflictual history with the gay community. It was a place that gave her refuge and at times employment, yet also sent her mixed messages:

> I first noticed it when some of my gay guy friends were going to [a gay club] and they wouldn't let me in looking like a girl. And so they just wanted this male club, gay club, so I noticed stereotypes like that ... I was disturbed by it, I was troubled because here I was already doing shows in the gay community; I was part of this community, that's where I found acceptance. But on the other hand I also found this barrier, it was confusing.

Dean demarcated sub-communities and suggested that there is a greater level of acceptance of transpeople in one group in particular:

> The way I see it is there's three communities. There's the gay community and the old-school guys: 'You're not a real guy until you have a dick.' And then there's the lesbian community: 'You're now becoming a traitor

because you're becoming a male.' And then there's the queer community, and the queer community I find is more accepting, more open.

In addition to conflicts with gay men and lesbians, transpeople also speak of tensions with radical cultural feminists, another equity-seeking group that represents the interests of the marginalized, yet is often implicated in repudiating transpeople.

9. Reactions from Radical Cultural Feminists

Most feminists are, I believe, tremendously supportive of transpeople and trans struggle. Historically, the former Danish justice Helga Pedersen helped to arrange the permission required for Christine Jorgensen to receive her famous SRS in 1950s Denmark. Today, feminists continue to produce scholarship that links feminist struggle with transpeople's struggles (Namaste, 2004; Scott-Dixon, 2006). However, many of those faithful to the doctrines of radical cultural feminism have steadfastly preserved a negative attitude towards transpeople. Others, who see the importance of supporting transpeople's rights, still in the end demarcate between 'women-born-women' and transwomen, arguing that 'women's spaces are not trans spaces' (Nicki, 2006, p. 154). This issue surfaced in the majority of the interviews that I conducted for this study. Robin identifies as a radical feminist and supports many of the political analyses and projects of local radical cultural feminists. However, as a trans woman, she has been negatively targeted by them. Robin told me her story of being heckled while giving a speech at a feminist event. The heckling was recorded and rebroadcast on local radio with accompanying 'feminist' analysis that repeatedly referred to her as 'a transgendered man.' Refusing to relinquish her identity as a radical feminist, Robin summarized her understanding of the problem:

> Segregation of trans women from feminist organizations mirrors patriarchal privilege and oppression against women, and reinforces the old idea that there are right women and wrong women, that there are right feminists and wrong feminists, and we need to be a lot more creative.

Dean lost friends and a job due to radical cultural feminist rejection of his transitioning, and lamented what one friend told him:

Oh yeah, like I've had friends – had – (pause) – let you know that: 'Men are rapists, if you become a man you will become a rapist. I don't have rapists in my life' ... and if it's about me as a person, I wasn't a rapist before, so I think it's pretty safe to assume I'm not going to become a rapist after testosterone, do you know what I mean? So that kind of thinking is not about a person, it's a stereotype.

Wynn also spoke of losing feminist friends as a result of transitioning:

I just want to say there's a woman in the feminist movement that I've known for a long time and that I used to be pretty close with, who now won't speak to me. It's like I'm not a person anymore ... She won't say 'hi' to me, like I've tried to talk to her and she'll just walk the other way ... I asked around to some that know her and a couple of people said that she has a real problem with it, especially with MtFs – she said it's like when men dress as women, this is just like white people wearing black face.

Frank, as a former radical cultural feminist, offered a personal perspective:

[Radical cultural] feminists are entitled to their opinion, but it wears thin real quick to have someone pontificating on what my reasons are for doing what I have to do. For me it was life and death – once I found out this avenue was available, I couldn't stay in that other cage any longer. And to have someone passing judgment ... like insisting on using the wrong pronouns – I mean, who the hell do they think they are? I think maybe I'll use the wrong pronouns with them from now on – see how they like it, see if maybe they can get even a dim emotional glimmer of how offensive that can be.

Jamie-Lee, a well-known trans activist and sex-trade worker advocate, recalled meeting feminist sociologist Professor Becki Ross at a public forum:

I remember attending a Vancouver Lesbian Connection forum and Becki Ross was on the panel. She had met me previously, so she had mentioned my name, and I'm sitting in the audience, right? About how much of a pleasure for her to meet me and the work I was doing. And this one lesbian woman was so angry at that, she got up and she yelled up to

Becki – at least she used the correct pronoun – she said: 'She's no lady! That's a man!' – (pause) – It was very hurtful.

Kimberly has devoted many years of her life to challenging the discriminatory practices of some radical cultural feminists in human rights tribunals and the law courts. As a feminist, Kimberly is moved by a core principle of feminist praxis:

> Feminism means working for all women, and that includes women of colour, lesbians, bisexual women, large, small women; it's addressing the systemic barriers together that all women face.

The vulnerability that many trans women experience, being targets for abuse, harassment, sexual assault, and in some cases severe violence leading to death, underscores the problem of trans repudiation and transphobia, as a very harmful and dangerous force. The issue of ending violence against women, as a central rallying point for the women's movement, is especially important for very marginalized women such as trans women. Yet, as we shall see, not all feminists wish to include trans women in the movement. Indeed, many have actively repudiated their status as 'real' women, excluding them from various social spaces defined as 'women only.'

This chapter has considered an array of social locations and interpersonal issues that transpeople contend with, issues that intersect interiority with exteriority. Dorothy Smith's (1999) sociological insistence that subjects are located in the social world as embodied beings is useful for considering the ways in which ruling relations pose institutionalized barriers for transpeople. However, the material or physical consequences of confronting barriers in the social world must be balanced with the potential for emotional trauma at the interiorized level of the psyche. Intersecting interiority with exteriority offers a more comprehensive account of the consequences of trans repudiation. The stories presented here remind us that transpeople are the experts on their own lives, and their narrative accounts clearly do not split the inner from the outer effects of repudiation. The expected solidarity from other marginalized groups such as gays, lesbians, and some feminists is sometimes surprisingly lacking. These gaps in solidarity also reiterate dominant ruling relations in ironic and paradoxical ways. Perhaps it is, once again, something that is parallel to Fanon's (1967) construct of the phobogenic object; could it be that non-trans people's reactions are based on their own defensive fictions, which lead them to interpret transpeople through the Other-ing lens of alterity? Since transpeople are, for some, abject objects, they are at risk of being viewed through the polarized optics of exoticism and hatred. Hook (2006) reminds us that 'abjection is always the flipside of desire' (p. 217). The next chapter explores the political dynamics that support the social repudiation of transpeople.

4 The Political Repudiations of Trans Subjectivity

Attitudes towards transpeople are complex and varied, as are the rationales behind transphobia and other forms of trans repudiation. In this sense, the political roots of the problem need to be acknowledged and better understood. Thus far we have considered trans repudiation in terms of affect (fear, desire) and considered the social barriers that transpeople tend to face. While fear appears to be a strong factor motivating many of these social barriers, it is not the universal cause. Another factor motivating various rejections and negations affecting transpeople can be found in faithfulness to political doctrines, whether overtly acknowledged or tacitly accepted. All points on the political spectrum are potentially capable of supporting trans repudiation, from the far right, through to the extreme left, from reactionary and conservative expressions of masculinity and machismo through to a radical feminist rejection of traditional gender roles.

The Conservative Repudiation

As Goodwin (1998) has pointed out, conservatism is not, in and of itself, a self-proclaimed ideology. Rather, it is a set of ideas that *reacts* to attempts to change the status quo in a progressive direction; hence, conservatism is prima facie a reactionary doctrine. In recent times, conservatism has espoused the defence of private property as an inviolable individual right based on an unrestrained free market. In this sense, conservatism has, over time, enjoined itself with some aspects of liberalism – rights, for example, being a liberal conception. Conservatives once believed that only aristocrats, or those of 'superior pedigree,' could own property. To preserve private property and its privilege, they generally defend those traditions that elevate private property and its inheritance: the nuclear family in its traditional representation, hierarchy, elitism, nationalism, patriotism, and law and order. Moreover, conservatives believe in the supposed integrity of nature, with 'her' selective bestowing of endowments. Nature is an inegalitarian force which 'naturally' ordains some to rule over others, given 'evident inferiority' or the 'natural submission' of these Others. Such is the 'law of the jungle,' by which those deemed to be lesser shall comply to follow the will of their 'superior leaders,' to submit in organic harmony.

Conservatives dislike and distrust change, and argue that the forces of tradition have naturally carried forward the good of the world. These forces are almost always conceptualized as metaphysical or God-given, the products of a preordained natural order, a selective favouring of evolution[1] that favours the 'strong' and keeps the 'weak' in their place. Conservatism is the doctrine of essentialism par excellence, since this fixed and immutable order should not be trifled with, lest chaos be unleashed. Conservatives reject, yet also fear, the possibility of a utopia of the workers, but seek, rather, the workers' ongoing submission to the preordained Will, in hierarchies that favour elite privilege. For them, this means renouncing woolly-minded conceptions of an unrealizable egalitarian state, and striving for an alternative utopia of the masters. Since the latter seems out of reach, the interim strategy is to maintain the (capitalist/neo-liberal) status quo. As Goodwin notes, 'If history is the record of change, and change is synonymous with decline, it follows that the best we can do is to resist change, halt mankind's decline and so – by implication – end history' (p. 151). Revolution threatens the organic integrity of society as Nature/God wills it. Hence, Burke opposed the French Revolution for its transgressions against the fruits of tradition and violating that which 'time refines' (ibid., p. 153), but does not essentially change.

Time will apparently refine institutions and reward the deserving through a natural, organic process, as exemplified in the metaphor 'the cream rises to the top.' In contrast, *human* nature, in general, is untrustworthy. People (the masses) are weak, susceptible to selfish acts, and prone to intractable irrationalism. They are unable to govern themselves and must be ruled, directly or by representation. The fallen nature of man mythologizes *his* untrustworthiness ('caused at root by Eve') and declares the inevitability of domination. People must, paradoxically, be ordered into the ways which nature intends; they must 'know their place,' and coercive institutions remind them of it should the temptation to go astray become too great to resist.

Inegalitarianism is construed as the 'common sense' of nature. Men are commonly assumed to be bigger and physically stronger than women and hence are thought by conservatives to be naturally superior in certain respects. Doreen Kimura (1999) argues that nature endows males with larger shoulders and bigger, more muscular arms, explaining their capacity to throw faster and farther than females. She dismisses claims to equality of endowment between the sexes since such arguments go against the measurements of empirical science. However, Kimura's conservative and 'common sense' arguments ignore how the historical division of labour comes to produce variations of the body, how bodies are coerced to materialize an approximation of social ideals, such as those based on the ideal aesthetics of masculinity and femininity. Her thesis is typical of how 'the end of history' argument entails the suppression of anything that challenges the official story, that confronts the limited and ahistorical empiricism of 'facts.'

If for merely a moment we were to accept the universality of Kimura's claims, it is nevertheless noteworthy that technology has made physical prowess between males and females a redundant 'fact.' More importantly, however, Kimura's position is not so much about science as it is about the moral positions that flow from conservative thinking. These positions make, by and large, moral appeals to the 'Truth of nature,' re-routing progressive, emancipatory strivings back into the conservative politics of location: woman and man must ultimately remain in their fixed stations in life, and any deviation is by definition deviant and therefore dangerous. For religious conservatives, the matter is simple: stray too far from God's intended plan for the sexes and you accumulate sin, which one apparently pays for upon death. Under this discourse, homosexuals and transpeople are to be 'saved' from themselves since their non-conformity has 'damned them.'

The conservative gay writer Andrew Sullivan (1996) reflexively argues that conservatism is in a 'deep etymological crisis' (p. 95), since the term has 'come to be used to describe a disposition, a political party, a theological faction, Christian fundamentalism, and, most oxymoronically of all, a "movement"' (p. 95). Like mainstream liberalism, conservatism does not acknowledge its own position as being ideological, opposing what it views as ideology and politics in favour of the cult of inevitability (there will always be poverty, there will always be war, there will always be crime, women are ... men are ... and so on). Efforts to read social phenomena such as crime or the control of market forces as political constructions are dismissed by conservatives as 'ideological,' a denial of the 'real.' Conservatives do not consider their objections as political in nature. Instead, they claim authority over the 'real' and utilize the findings of science when they are politically suitable. Their appeals to science are contradictory, as traditionally conservatives have been scornful towards science's ideal of progress, dismissing it as positivist utopianism, and viewing it as dangerous, solipsistically humanistic, and potentially undermining the will of God/Nature.

Conservatives believe in reward and punishment in doctrinaire ways. Man will always be at risk of criminality, violence, debauchery, and so on, due to his fallen nature. Sexuality must be strictly controlled, and state interference in the affairs of social life is desirable only to defend against the fallen nature of man, and to enforce the rules of hierarchy. Conservatives accept democracy so long as it favours them or concurs with the will of Nature. They prefer, however, a system that is static or regressive, espousing entrenched values based on sentimental myths of the 'lost golden age,' when the state of things was supposedly not questioned. This is especially so concerning gender roles, identities, and sexual orientation. This stance was famously satirized by the American popular culture character of the 1970s Archie Bunker (in *All in the Family*), who famously bellowed: '*Those were the days ... girls were girls and men were men.*' The widespread conservative condemnation of gay/lesbian marriage is a case in point.

All gender/sex transgressors threaten conservative social ideals, what Ahmed (2004) identifies as the fiction 'life as we know it' (p. 144). She contends that 'immigrants, queers, [and] other others' (p. 144) both structure a threat to 'life as we know it' and provide 'the normative subject with a utopian vision of what is lacking' (p. 162). The fascination towards transgressive sex/gender bodies becomes a justification for a tightening of the sex/gender binary. Border reinforcement is sought by demarcating 'we' (a false consensus) from those who do not belong within the consens-us, those who are 'foreign' and ought to be expelled, or those who require alignment and reform so as to conform to life as 'we' know it.

In regard to trans repudiation, the conservative justification is a simple one. Sex is a matter of substance, essence, and authoritarian inscription. One is a male or female because the doctor said so, because institutions that regulate the family said so, as evidenced through the appropriate documents, because one's mind *must* follow the rule of one's body, and because natural and immutable forces dictate that this is the way it is. Disciplines such as psychiatry, which often exhibit a conservative tendency, do not necessarily believe in the professed gender(s) of transpeople, but relent in the face of their own failure to alter the wayward mind from accepting concordance with the given body. Those with a 'gender identity disorder' are irretrievable in their intransigence, and psychiatry usually recognizes this. The obligation to help compels psychiatry to take the only available recourse and permit hormonal treatment and surgery.

Some psychiatrists and psychologists do accept that mind-body dualism itself has gone *naturally* astray in GID, and that the essence or substances of the body/mind split really are incongruent. In this instance there is no repudiation of trans subjectivity, but a begrudging pragmatism that accepts surgery as the only way to fix such an anomaly. Such persons are seen as victimized by a natural mistake not of their own doing, and deserving of the charity of congruent realignment along hormonal and surgical lines. This discourse suggests that transsexuals are to be pitied and can appeal to the expertise of medicine to do what is possible to correct an unsatisfactory state of affairs. In this instance, medical intervention is a justifiable practice, to restore what *should have been* in the first place, to rectify an error of nature.

There is a darker side of conservatism that expresses the reactionary stance of the doctrine in quite anti-scientific and anti-medical ways. This thread rejects the humanism that believes Nature can make a mistake, and refuses the claims of transpeople. It is aghast at medical interventions such as SRS, as an affront to the will of God. The Evangelical Alliance, an organization representing approximately one million evangelical British Christians, has condemned sex-change surgeries, claiming that transsexuals have succumbed to 'a fantasy and an illusion' (Southam, 2001, p. 1). This group believes that 'authentic change from a person's given sex is not possible and an ongoing transsexual lifestyle is incompatible with God's will' (ibid., p. 1). The group advocates that transpeople be blocked from any marriage that does not conform with their given sex and from holding positions of power in the church. Transsexuals should seek psychological counselling to accompany prayer, with the knowledge that 'God does not make mistakes' (ibid., p. 2). This position echoes conservative beliefs in the cult of inevitability. It is no surprise that in countries like Canada and the United States, right-wing Christian movements have been aligned with, or indeed central to, conservatism, since they hold many convergent points of view. These political movements are powerful and appear to be moving further to the political right. An example is the fairly recent demise of Canada's Progressive Conservative party, reconfigured plainly as the Conservative party. This shift came about as a result of a purge of so-called 'red Tories.'

In my interview with Frank the issue of conservative religion surfaced:

> Frank: Yeah I've come across the religious thing with a family member who is a Jehovah's Witness. He's been very accepting, but when I pressed him – you know, 'What does your church think of this?' – he said, 'Well, don't take hormones and let God sort it out.' And I asked him where you draw the line between what God creates and what he didn't create. I mean, if there is a God, then He created the hormones and the doctors and the gender clinic and the whole process, too, right, or didn't He? (pause) ... God made you this way ... I mean you just run into it, everybody's got an opinion.

Since leading threads of political conservatism (especially social/religious conservatives) openly support similar views, it is unsurprising that trans repudiation is commonly misperceived as exclusively aligned with right-wing ideas. This mis-association ignores those conservatives who support transpeople's need for SRS (for example, decades ago Progressive Conservatives in Ontario both permitted and publicly funded the practice) and the fact that trans repudiation exists across the political spectrum. The strongest, but certainly not the only, instance of trans repudiation among left-wing progressives can be found, as already stated, in radical cultural feminism. Before considering the problematics of this particular thread of feminism in relation to transpeople, a general discussion of liberalism as the dominant political force in the West, and in Canada, in particular, is warranted.

The Politics of Liberalism

L. Susan Brown's (2003) explication of Western individualism and her critical stance towards liberal feminism highlight one contradictory aspect of predominant liberalism: the irreconcilable tension between *existential individualism* and *instrumental individualism.* In celebrating the individual, liberalism, as currently expressed in the West, is a forced 'synthesis' between these two contradictory currents. In existential liberalism, the individual is prized as a free and autonomous being connected in voluntary association with others. Here, freedom is intrinsically expressed in the concept of self-determination, and valued as an *end* in itself through the honing of one's free will. However, Brown argues that the freedom to express oneself creatively, to become one's own person, and to celebrate uniqueness and individuality is often undermined by instrumental liberalism. This is especially so for the lower economic classes. Conservatism has become, over time, deeply entangled in the instrumental variant of liberalism.

Instrumental individualism conceptualizes the person as a competitor who desires ownership of private property, of both land and 'property in the person' (Brown, 2003, p. 3). Moreover, liberalism views individuals as owning their own bodies, with the right to individually sell their skills and labour power within the 'free' market. The selling of one's labour power, that is the use of one's body conceived as property in the person, corresponds with the inviolable right to 'buy and sell real property' (p. 3).

Instrumentalism, as deployed under liberal conditions, is construed as the freedom to pursue and accumulate unlimited material goods and assets. This core right is enshrined as a *means* to fulfil one's individual desires. It intrinsically includes the right to use others with less resources, as if they were an instrument, in fulfilling one's solipsistic goals. Those with less are usually compelled to sell their labour to an owner, with periods of domination ensuing. This arrangement is not necessarily freely chosen, as market forces produce an inequality which threatens material depravity. Many individuals are coerced to 'consent' to trading their property in the person. This is hardly a 'voluntary' state of affairs. For transpeople, who are deemed to own their body, the collision of the premise of existential individualism (the right to 'be') with the expectations of instrumentalism (property in the person – the conservative conception accommodated by liberalism) often produces high levels of unemployment.

The existential ideal is 'to be,' 'to become,' to enact freedom, which is predicated on 'the individual's capacity to be self-determining' (ibid., p. 33). Yet the hierarchical structure of instrumentalism places limits on striving to become and the exercise of freedom through self-determination. Many, especially in marginalized groups such as transpeople, do not necessarily feel 'free' under liberalism, regardless of the fact that it is a doctrine that paradoxically espouses 'freedom and democracy for all.'

This state of affairs, of often not feeling or being free, challenges the liberal rhetoric of absolute 'choice.' On the one hand, in choosing to transition, transpeople out themselves to employers as trans. They are then at risk of being deemed flawed or 'undesirable instruments.' Here, Brown rightly points to instrumental liberalism as a force that curtails and constrains the choices of many. Yet, on the other hand, she nevertheless defends the possibility of existential choice, claiming that 'individuals are free and responsible agents who are fit to determine their own development' (p. 2). This assertion is problematic as it assumes too much unfettered agency. When applied to TS people, it overlooks the fact that many did not initially choose to be TS but recognize that they have, in fact, no other choice. For many TS people, existence may precede essence, but it does not preclude essence. Whatever that essence might be, it too is preceded by a socio-political structure that affects TS existence. Choice is never unbounded. Importantly, while TS people may not have initially chosen to be TS, they can nevertheless choose to do something about it, to be who they really are and manifest this being through transitioning. Yet such transitioning is only possible to the extent that the macro political culture permits and provides both the technology and social support for it. Here the political culture also needs to provide the necessary knowledge transfer to those who misunderstand trans ontology so as to remedy the widespread problem of trans repudiation and phobia – because the contradiction is glaring: our culture permits transitioning to those deemed as genuinely mis-sexed but does not provide the requisite social support that transpeople need.

Existentialism is a Western philosophical ideal that presumes choice as both conscious and rational. Where an unconscious dynamic exists, its effect is to obscure an 'underlying authenticity.' Through self-insight this lack of clarity can dissipate. An authentic being-in-the-world allows genuineness to surface, maximizing one's agency, purifying real choice. However, many dispute the idea that choice is potentially unfettered. Poststructuralists, for example, view the existentialist position as one that mitigates the role of power in producing subjectivity and in producing existentialism itself. From a different perspective, radical cultural feminists argue that 'TS women' falsely 'choose' to be women, a 'choice' that is not open to them, since the discourse, which paradoxically argues for women's freedom and choice, basically purports that essence dictates existence.

TS/TG people should and could be free to make their own choices, to exercise a bounded agency, although they currently tend to experience obstacles to such freedom. For example, the unequal access to material resources based on class stratification, under instrumental liberalism, curtails the freedom of TS people: sex-change surgeries often remain financially beyond the means of many, even if they are technically available, especially in the United States and increasingly in Canada (Namaste, 2005). Furthermore, there are other barriers that go beyond material resources for transpeople. Political and ideological barriers exist that reject outright transpeople's claims to being missexed. This brings us to the politics of gender from another part of the political spectrum.

Radical Feminism and Liberalism

Rosemarie Putnam Tong (1998) outlines the ideological strata that differentiate the divergent radical libertarian, radical cultural, and liberal feminist threads. Liberal feminism is the oldest and arguably most influential thread, traced back to the eighteenth century and its spawning of first-wave feminism. The rise of second-wave radical libertarian and cultural feminisms[2] is generally traced to the 1960s, to groups such as the New York–based Redstockings. Unpacking the initial distinctions between these forms of feminist thought is complex. Yet the concept of 'rights' seems to be the common thread. Radical cultural feminism departs from the other two strands by insisting upon an overtly essentialist celebration of woman's 'femaleness' (ibid., p. 47). This position elevates the ontology of being female over that of being male, citing women's intrinsic virtues and values: 'interdependence, community, connection, sharing, emotion, body, trust, absence of hierarchy, nature, immanence, process, joy, peace and life' (ibid., p. 17). Extreme radical cultural feminists urge women to protect and cultivate these female values by segregating males from females. This entails excluding men from women's communities since males are said to be the biological creators and exponents of patriarchy. As Rudy (2001), a long-time radical cultural feminist who now locates herself in queer theory, writes:

> Radical feminism used an essentialist notion of identity to ground politics in what was thought to be the superior nature of women. Essentialism saw female identity as an ontological ground, a truth about nature itself and the virtuous nature of women specifically. The experience of being women, we argued, led to a unified identity that could ground politics. (P. 198)

This line of thinking contrasts with that of radical libertarian feminists, who do not see a value system or ethic essentially based on an assumed and immutable sex/gender difference. Hence the libertarians (Firestone, 1972; Millett, 1977) reject the biological differences that patriarchy promotes, whereas radical cultural feminists (such as Marilyn French and Mary Daly) ironically celebrate aspects of them. The aspects they reject are which end of the binary controls the other. Patriarchy is about man's desire to control the dyadic pairing of nature/woman, which inevitably leads to the triad of male destruction as expressed in war, rape, and genocide. The culturalists contend that if women were in control, that is if we lived under matriarchy, this triad would disappear. This reconceptualization is controversial, even among feminists. Monique Wittig (1988) counters that 'the category "woman" as well as the category "man" are political and economic categories, not eternal ones' (p. 443). She points out that matriarchy, like patriarchy, is similarly constructed along heterosexual lines; what changes is merely 'the sex of the oppressor still imprisoned in the categories of sex (woman and man)' (p. 440). A matriarchal doctrine (Mother-rule), moreover, continues to perpetuate the notion that a woman's capacity to give birth, predicated on given biological structures, is the fundamental aspect that defines woman, a position that Wittig rejects.

For radical cultural feminists, the nature of the debate is about sex, that is, which one of the 'two sexes' can claim the ethical high ground? And how can one defeat the reign of the opposite? Poststructuralist feminists disagree with this strategy since such a defeat would simply flip the existing binary, from one totality to another. Hence Chris Weedon (1987) speaks against the 'totalizing strategy of radical-feminist discourse' (p. 134), one that relies on transcendental woman guarding against its opponent, male patriarchy, with both signifying 'a fundamental organization of power on the basis of biological sex, an organization which, from a poststructuralist perspective, is not natural and inevitable, but socially produced' (p. 127).

Global and Third World feminists such as Chandra Mohanty (1991) also disagree with the evocation of this 'Transcendental Woman,' especially when wrongly represented in the plural form 'women,' insisting that 'such objectification (however benevolently motivated) needs to be both named and challenged' (p. 57). What emerged in radical cultural feminism's representations of woman, more often than not, was a white, middle-class, Western woman.[3] Hence, Mohanty alerts feminists to the dilemma of coexisting layers of oppression: 'beyond sisterhood there are still racism, colonialism, and imperialism' (p. 68). In addition, heterosexism, ableism, and trans repudiation all constitute important additional categories.

In contrast to the culturalists, the libertarian feminists seek to eradicate sexual repression as part of an overall strategy to undermine patriarchy. These feminists view the sexual repression of women, transpeople, practitioners of BDSM (bondage, domination, sadomasochism), sex-trade workers, and so on, as an insidious form of oppression. This contrasts with the position of radical cultural feminists, who view the libertarians as defending practices that are intrinsically sexist. The culturalists affirm egalitarian and monogamous lesbian relationships and non-sexist heterosexual unions. The libertarians countered the culturalists by pointing out the Puritanism of such views, accusing them of enforcing a new Victorian ethic dictating that the only proper sex is side-by-side and in love, to the exclusion of all else (Tong, 1998). Moreover, the libertarians challenge the separate spaces (excepting rape shelters and transition houses) that radical cultural feminists advocate as woman-only, seeing this segregation as misguided. Such exclusion ostensibly confuses all men with patriarchy, which in this perspective is a legal and institutional problem rather than a flesh-and-blood one. For the culturalists, women must untangle and eradicate the insidious forces of patriarchy with which all potentially violent male-bodied persons are contaminated. This essentialist view is based on a belief in males as the sole perpetrators of destruction: women engaging in destructive acts are male-identified, traitors to their sex.

Female victimization is at the heart of the culturalist doctrine, and the sexual binary must be maintained so that men remain clearly identifiable as the enemy. Hence, the culturalists' core thesis reinforces the fundamental binary upholding the sex/gender system that they claim, at least in rhetoric, to want to overthrow.

While the libertarians and the culturalists often engage in vexed disagreement, both variants are not without criticisms emanating from other feminist positions. In her critical analysis of radical cultural feminists, Elshtain (1981) suggests that they tend to split off their own masculine qualities and project them wholly onto men as a justification for building utopian, all *womyn* communities; whereas Ferguson (1984) unveils the fundamentally existentialist individualism that underpins the libertarian branch of feminism.

Both the radical cultural and libertarian positions have also been dismissed by Marxist feminists, denounced as not genuinely 'radical' but rather liberal variants with radical pretences. Charnie Guettel (1974) contends that 'most radical feminism, no matter how scathing its attack on existing institutions, is very much in the tradition of bourgeois liberalism' (p. 1). She outlines a classic Marxist analysis that views male dominance as having risen through *private property*, summarizing Friedrich Engels's (1845/1972) classic, historical analysis of how men as a group long ago seized the community surplus, an opportunistic move that was accomplished through the division of labour. By trading in herd animals, acquiring land and territory, and instituting patriarchy to ensure marital fidelity and sexual control over women's bodies, man tried to ensure that *his* children would receive *his* legacy. Conflicts over territory and interminable trade disputes led to the rise of the state to rule on ownership and facilitate the institutionalized seizure of more resources for even larger surpluses (imperialism and colonialism). Guettel, who mis-stepped by conflating all feminist thought with radical or liberal feminist varieties (a mistake often found amongst Marxists), was able, however, to connect both strands of radical feminism as distinctly liberal in aspects of their underlying ideology. It is my contention, however, that the libertarian thread is more liberal than the cultural. The cultural thread, ironically, is not radical in its view of gender plurality; rather, it is both conservative and staunchly metaphysical.

Radical libertarian and cultural feminists do agree that *patriarchal ideology* has facilitated women's oppression through various institutions such as the nuclear family, religion, education, law, the economic market, and so on. This oppression is said to precede other forms of oppression, including those based on race and class (French, 1985). Through being ruled under the auspices of these institutions, women have historically been subjugated, on both conscious and unconscious levels, to an institutional subordination to men. Patriarchal rule has been astonishingly – and unfortunately – effective in subordinating women to men, so much so that some women themselves internalize this subordination as normal, natural, inevitable, and desirable. Indeed, some anti-feminist women actively collude with patriarchal men in instilling and enforcing women's subjection as right and proper (as is illustrated by the policies of the conservative Canadian women's group R.E.A.L. Women).[4] How is such a widespread collusion possible? For example, one of the ways that patriarchy has been mystified, and rendered 'natural,' palatable, and even desirable, is through the romantic ideal of male-female love. Under this distorting influence, women are to be 'swept off their feet' whilst an underhanded subordination is instilled. The ideology of Romantic love is therefore something that radical feminism rejects (Kitzinger, 1987).

Socialist feminists such as Mitchell (1974) and Jaggar (2004) acknowledge a debt to radical feminism as a whole for generating insights, organizing, fighting for reproductive rights, including abortion, and raising the troublingly high incidence of everyday/night sexual objectification, battering, sexual harassment, and rape. Second-wave radical feminism has served a crucial role in the ups and downs of the women's movement over the past forty years. Indeed, I hold a deep sense of gratitude to radical cultural feminism, in particular, as it helped me in my formative intellectual years to comprehend what gender oppression is. Nevertheless, as a trans ally, I eventually had to renounce this political allegiance, because of the unwarranted hostility to transpeople that lies at the heart of much radical cultural feminist thought and its desire to retain the sex/gender binary. Radical cultural feminists have sustained some rather harsh attacks and criticisms over the decades, many of which were quite malicious and lacking in merit. Therefore, I think it prudent to carefully, yet candidly, proceed with my critique of the discourse, so as to demonstrate why I cannot support its theoretical position in relation to queer and transpeople.

The Radical Cultural Feminist Repudiation of Trans and Queer

Across the political spectrum, the repudiation of transpeople is a common phenomenon. I shall concentrate, to a certain degree, on the specific repudiation of transpeople unleashed by radical cultural feminism for two reasons: firstly, this doctrine consciously advocates for rejecting the legitimacy of trans claims to being mis-sexed or outside of the sex/gender binary, justifying its stance both in theory and practice;

secondly, many of the interviewees I consulted mentioned this activist discourse as a strong local source that generates 'transphobia.' Janice Raymond (1994) and Sheila Jeffreys (2003, 2005) are key figures in the promotion of trans repudiation, disavowing trans subjectivity, and inciting disrespectful behaviour towards transpeople, such as outcasting them where possible from woman-only spaces. They also, rather astonishingly, advocate for the abolition of sex reassignment surgeries on the contention that such medical practices are 'mutilation by proxy' and a 'human rights violation' (Jeffreys, 2003, p. 111).

Some proponents of radical cultural feminism promote the view that the 'creation' of transsexual people by the patriarchal medical establishment is a moneymaking scheme, one that serves the interest of male power. Patriarchal surgeons, for example, supposedly create mutilated 'pantomime dames' or 'men' who ostensibly masquerade as women (Greer, 1999, p. 81). 'Women are born women,' counter radical cultural feminists such as Lee Lakeman from Vancouver Rape Relief (as cited in findlay [sic], 2003). Germaine Greer (1999) argues that MtFs cannot be real women, suggesting that as a social phenomenon they would 'disappear overnight' if they were forced to have uterus and ovary transplants alongside vaginoplasty and breast implants (p. 81). Greer claims that the MtF simply wants access to woman-only spaces: 'he [sic] does as all rapists have always done ... he forces his way into the few private spaces women may enjoy' (p. 93). Greer is similarly scathing towards FtMs with her assertion that 'a thousand years from now the archaeologists who dig up their bones will know that [FtMs] were women' (p. 93).

Raymond (1994) condemns trans women for apparently reinforcing feminine stereotypes, while enhancing the economic power of drug manufacturers who allegedly push synthetic female hormones on misguided 'men.' These 'men' are said to 'rape women's bodies by reducing the real female form to an artefact ... Transsexuals merely cut off the most obvious means of invading women, so they seem non-invasive' (p. 104). Meanwhile, 'gay sado-masochists' like Michel Foucault, according to Jeffreys (2003), have spawned queer theory, which 'promotes sado-masochism' among lesbians and other gay men who go to 'cutting and piercing studios' (for tattoos, nipple, penile, and labial piercings), 'disappearing lesbians,' who are now identified as 'queer' (p. 55). Young lesbians are supposedly 'cutting-up' their bodies (p. 138), an act said to be inspired by queer theory. Worse, queer theory is seen as promoting transsexual surgeries, perceived once again as the cutting of bodies through the 'savage mutilations of transsexual surgery' (p. 46). Jeffreys, moreover, contends that FtM reconstruction is a process that represents a threat to the female body, its potential annihilation.

Queer theory, Jeffreys accuses, has made it more difficult for women to see violence against women – through the obfuscating lens of post-modernism – as violence against women. Rather, it promotes domina-tion of women by celebrating a supposedly dangerous performativity. For example, the butch/femme duality among lesbians is seen as a variation on the domination/submission theme espoused by patri-archy. This constitutes a distortion of sadism insidiously masked and reframed as transgressive. Queer theory and trans activists such as Patrick Califia (2003) are said to celebrate sadomasochism, which according to Jeffreys is neither egalitarian nor conducive to feminist aims to end violence against women. Yet from the perspective of trans-people, radical cultural feminists such as Jeffreys (2003) threaten them by insisting that SRS be outlawed as a 'violation of human rights' (p. 37).

Jeffreys (2003) also asserts that *all* transpeople are evading homo-sexuality, referring to a 'transsexualism with which young lesbians and gay men who are unable to accept homosexuality, or have reasons to hate and reject their bodies, can identify' (p. 47). As evidenced in my interviews with transpeople, Jeffreys, however, errs in assuming that all transpeople are 'gay men and lesbians who have been unable to cope with the idea of being homosexual' (p. 45). Conservative psycho-analysts have long made the identical repudiation, as will be discussed later. Both discourses misapprehend the subjectivity of transpeople, who evince a range of sexual orientations: straight, gay, bi, lesbian, queer, and asexual. Rather, Jeffreys erroneously and rather obtusely posits that queer theory, through a supposed affirmation of SRS surgery, is simply 'celebrating the castration of those who love the same sex' (p. 49). In regard to FtMs, Jeffreys similarly sees them *all* as lesbians, who submit to the 'destruction' of their bodies, and their 'les-bianism' with it (p. 122). According to this logic, one surmises that gay trans men are simply unable to cope with their 'heterosexuality.' But this is not the case; since Jeffreys cannot fathom the notion of gay trans men, she sees all FtMs as women.

Jeffreys deepens her sophism by declaring that *all* FtMs are 'victims of internalised homophobia' (p. 137). She accuses them of 'not reclaim-ing their female bodies, but cutting them up' (p. 138) by means of 'self-mutilation by proxy' (p. 139). Other factors she declares FtMs as succumbing to include 'the oppression of women, child sexual abuse, hatred of female body parts, fear of being socially despised as a woman and particularly an ageing woman, and the allure of male power which they believe can be attained by imitating a male body' (p. 143). Jeffreys therefore radically repudiates the FtM. Such 'crude analyses' are familiar to Butler (2004), analyses that 'don't ask whether it is easier to be *trans* than to be in a perceived bio-gender, that is, a gender that seems to "follow" from natural sex' (p. 94).

In a strange contradiction, Jeffreys also emphasizes the problems of a 'lesbian – and gay – hating culture' (p. 137), in which all queer people are embedded. This culture is ascertained to be at the root of internalized homophobia. Sometimes she is sympathetic towards gay men, yet at other times contemptuous, accusing them of succumbing to the misogynist 'ick factor' (p. 107), or hatred of female genitals. She reads gay men as universally disparaging lesbians, viewing them as 'disgusting' (p. 107). In faulting gay men for their misogynist male stratum, Jeffreys also simplifies the conflated identities that some gay 'men' hold. This position fails to consider the complexity of many gay men's identities: some gay men also simultaneously identify as queer; some only identify as queer; and others cannot fathom being 'men' yet retain, unlike transsexuals, bodily congruency. In faulting gay men as primarily men (essentially male), Jeffreys ignores the hegemonic masculinity of many heterosexual men who repudiate and subjugate queer men as not-men (Connell, 1995; Tacey, 1997).

I am not concerned with critiques of gay men that are levied in a manner that makes room for response/dialogue. However, I am concerned with universal and essentialist critiques that foreclose anything but irretrievable condemnation. Like other groups in society, gay men are located in a range of class positions and may be a part of the problem of class domination. For example, in the 1980s some gay men were key organizers in Vancouver's West End to push sex-trade workers, including some who are trans, out of their community and into unsafe, dark industrial areas (Namaste, 2000). In another example, the provincial MLA for Vancouver's West End is a gay man, Lorne Mayencourt, who has supported his government's austerity cuts to social, welfare, and medical programs, including the closing of the gender clinic at the Vancouver Hospital and Health Sciences Centre in 2001. He is what Goldstein (2002) characterizes as a 'homocon,' a gay conservative. Goldstein suggests that homocons are ashamed of being associated with queers: 'if you're gay its OK, if you're queer, disappear' (p. 3). For gay men, conformity to masculine gender norms brings prestige and wins them 'a place at the table' (in corporate boardrooms, exclusive country clubs, etc.). That some gay men both support and materialize phallic masculinity – including its misogynistic dynamics – is not the question. Fuss (1989) acknowledges that 'an oppressed subject can also, simultaneously, be an oppressing subject' (p. 99). To pontificate that *all* gay men are oppressing subjects is certainly cause for concern.

In her historical analysis, Meyerowitz (2002) argues that gender conservatives have been vocally a part of the gay and lesbian movement in America since the 1950s. The quintessential homocon, Andrew Sullivan (1996), wants gay men to adopt the status of being 'a gentleman jock' (Goldstein, 2002, p. 75), one that worships phallic masculinity and the 'real man' discourse. Proper gays are concerned with traditional institutions like marriage, or the right to serve in the military or to hold political office. The lesbian world has similar figures, like Camille Paglia, who also worships the cult of the masculine and, according to Goldstein, identifies with the aggressor. In this regard, Jeffreys's mistake is to conflate the homocons with queers in general, erasing *difference*. She asserts that 'queer politics ... [are] a move towards a gay consumer market rather than a community' (Jeffreys, 2003, p. 54), and blames queer theory for the nascent body fascism and gay profit-driven capitalism that has exploded in recent years. Her grand theory (as described below) rules out plurality and imposes a sameness on all male-bodied people whether homosexual or not. The subtext of Jeffreys's analysis is that queers should be ashamed of themselves; indeed, she remarks that many lesbians still find the term queer 'abhorrent' (p. 9).

Re-asserting the Power of the Binary

The narrow singularity that Jeffreys and like-minded radical cultural feminists promote is rooted in maintaining the essentialism at the core of the female/male binary. If one is born female or male, one has that status for life, whether or not one is straight or gay. This is one of the reasons that trans women have been denied access to some women-only spaces such as the Vancouver Rape Relief and Women's Shelter. Lee Lakeman, a founding member of Rape Relief (one of Canada's oldest feminist organizations), speaks of the historical events that mark women's lives, such as menstruation and getting their first bra, which apparently no trans woman can know (findlay, 2003). This assessment obviously assumes that all women wear bras, and that this garment serves as a compulsory element to womanhood, that all women menstruate, and so on. One wonders what happened to the radical women in the 1970s who burnt their bras? Or, what about women who take menses-suppressing drugs for non-medical reasons? Is any flat-chested female not a woman? And what about those with Turner's syndrome (chromosomal pattern XO), for whom menstruation is an impossibility? What about elderly women who suffer from dementia and lose their memories of these 'foundational' events? These questions are not posed in order to disavow the category of woman altogether, but to draw attention to problems raised by the essentialist construction at the core of radical cultural feminism.

The mirror position is that males, too, must have 'foundational' events that mark their manhood, a universal assumption that I disagree with. For example, in the Townships of South Africa, such as those in and around Cape Town, male Xhosa leave their families for a period of up to three months, living in tents, following their ritual circumcision. Before they can take their position as males in their tribal society, they must go through this experience. This is a cultural ritual ascribing 'maleness' and 'masculinity' that is valid for that cultural location. Cultural location and historical specificity are obviously important for understanding definitions and attitudes related to sex and gender. What is paradoxical in radical cultural feminism is its universal positing of biological essentialism as determinate of sex and gender, not culture, although Simone de Beauvoir already maintained in 1949 that 'one is not born, but rather becomes a woman' (1989/1952, p. vii), recognizing that male/female and man/woman are *cultural constructions*. Not only are women not born women, but many feminists maintain that the process of becoming a woman is painful. As Jacqueline Rose (1986) notes, 'Most women do not painlessly slip into their roles as women, if indeed they do at all' (p. 91). For de Beauvoir and perhaps Rose, existence precedes essence. Feminists remain divided on this central issue, as are transpeople, since TS people are more inclined to essentialism and TG people to constructivism.

Wittig (1988) maintains that for feminists the category of 'woman' exists *only* to be dismantled. When the category of 'man' is dissolved, so too is the category of woman – one cannot exist without the other. Here she reasons that there can be no slaves without ruling masters. In this context, Wittig asks, 'What does feminist mean?' She then provides her answer: '... for many of us it means someone who fights for women as a class and for the disappearance of this class. For many others it means someone who fights for woman and her defense – for the myth, then, and its reinforcement' (p. 443). The latter group refers undoubtedly to radical cultural feminists, who assuredly dispute – if not condemn – Wittig's radical cry: 'We are not women!' as exemplified in her classic essay 'One Is Not Born a Woman':

> ... our survival demands that we contribute all our strength to the destruction of the class of women within which men appropriate women. This can be accomplished only by the destruction of heterosexuality as a social system which is based on the oppression of women by men and which produces *the doctrine of the difference between the sexes to justify this oppression*. (Wittig, 1988, p. 447; italics added)

Radical cultural feminist groups like Vancouver Rape Relief and Women's Shelter and Michigan Womyn's Music Festival argue that trans women must be forever excluded, banished because they were not born women and can never become women. This exclusion is based on an essentialist reading of the body. Other radical cultural feminists such as John Stoltenberg (1989) argue against essentialism. Citing Andrea Dworkin, Stoltenberg's arguments go back to the days when radical cultural feminism was consonant with socialist feminism on the question of the origins of gender:

> *The discovery is, of course, that 'man' and 'woman' are fictions, caricatures, cultural constructs. As models they are reductive, totalitarian, inappropriate to human becoming. As roles they are static, demeaning to the female, dead-ended for the male and female both.* (Dworkin [1974], as cited in Stoltenberg, 1989, p. 28; italics in the original)

In building on Dworkin's analysis, Stoltenberg draws a stark parallel to underscore his point, suggesting that 'the idea of the male sex is like the idea of an Aryan race' (p. 29).

In the early years of radical culturalism, gender was conceptualized as a pervasive myth, and the binary was reconfigured as a continuum. This position now seems to have been abandoned by the culturalists, only to be picked up by queer theorists, who argue that the (fictive) sex binary is destructive. The binary's function is to socialize males and females in permanently opposing directions. Since queer theorists do not believe it is grounded in biology, it can be dismantled and cast aside through political action and rejected through personal awareness. These two irreconcilable views (essentialism and constructivism) are at the heart of all debates about trans issues. Diana Fuss (1989) argues that the essentialist/constructionist binary is irresolvable and that each, in fact, needs the other. Most feminists, however, employ the idea of nominal essence (e.g., woman as a class), based on John Locke's understanding (nominal = categorical convenience, in name only) rather than 'real' essence. This pertains to the notion that the 'phallus is prior to the penis' (ibid., p. 8), yet the phallus could not itself exist if not, even loosely, signifying some conceptual relationship to those with the flesh-and-blood organ.

Jeffreys (2003, 2005) is often inconsistent in her theorizing, asserting essentialism, on the one hand, and spuriously using social constructivism, on the other, juggling the two as it suits her argument. Unlike Fuss, however, she does not see the connection. Indeed, Jeffreys, Raymond, and Greer all refuse to acknowledge that socially constructed identity can be shed and people can become who they 'really are' as they see it and within reason. This implies that the individual can to some extent existentially self-determine. For some they can decide, in postmodern terms, which fictional identity to perform in accordance to how they feel inside. For others, they can shed what has been imposed on them (the wrong sex) and actualize who they consistently and temporally feel they are (the right sex). When it comes to transpeople, who wish to actualize how they feel inside, Jeffreys (2003) repudiates their claims and imposes identity on them:

> I will refer to FTMs with female pronouns and to MTFs with male pronouns in order to highlight their sex classes of origin. Use of the pronouns of the political class to which these people wish to be reassigned makes political analysis very difficult. (P. 123)

Sex class of origin points to a reading of the body that is essentialist, based on a determinist view of history (real essence). Jeffreys's position, once again, is contradictory, since she will at times conveniently conjure constructivism:

> Sexuality is *socially constructed* for men out of their position of dominance, and for women out of their position of subordination. Thus it is the eroti-

cized inequality of women which forms the excitement of sex under male supremacy. (P. 27; italics added)

Like other essentialists such as Kimura (1999), Jeffreys intentionally avoids the term *gender* in favour of *sex*, undermining her sparse foray into constructivism. In fact, she suggests that gender differences be abolished in favour of the dualism of domination and submission: 'I prefer to describe masculinity as "male-dominant behaviour" and femininity as "female-subordinate behaviour." No multiplicity of genders can emerge from this perspective' (pp. 43–4). Her hostility to multiple differences incites her to dismiss the work of Robert Connell (1995) and other pro-feminist men who have argued for the conceptual utility of terms such as *hegemonic masculinity*. This concept better accounts for the plurality of men's behaviour, especially around violence, than does the assumption that there is only one male variety of gender domination. Hegemonic masculinity is most clearly expressed when certain forms of masculinity rule others, where certain men regulate, dominate, violate, beat, rape, terrorize, or kill other men. The concept is outlined by Carrigan, Connell, and Lee (1987), who emphasize four of its dimensions: (1) hegemony as dominance and power, and as historically situated; (2) hegemony as persuasive; (3) hegemony as tied up with the division of labour; and (4) hegemony as negotiated and enforced by the state. In relation to masculinity, the authors note:

Hegemonic masculinity... [is] a question of how particular groups of men inhabit positions of power and wealth, and how they legitimate and reproduce the social relationships that generate their dominance... connected with the institutionalization of men's dominance over women. (P. 92)

Connell (1995) furthers this definition, noting the stratification of masculinities, with some forms held over others as more desirable, 'culturally exalted' (p. 76). This points to differing expressions of masculinity, transforming the term into the plural *masculinities*. Though the plural usage of 'masculinities' is a valuable contribution, and indeed conceptually more accurate than the singular 'masculinity,' this should not discourage the limited use of the singular where warranted. For example, in depth psychology, Horrocks (1994) suggests that a common denominator in the singular signifier 'masculinity' in male subjects configures an identity statement: 'I am not a woman' (p. 33).

A limited, singular use of 'masculinity' can analytically account for the phenomenon of men repudiating their own femininity. In depth psychology, when a forceful repression such as this occurs, it is thrown back out via projection, creating the sexed Other and defensively preventing what is thrown out from refracting back in. Jung identified the central problem of projection as follows:

> ... the cause of the emotion appears to lie, beyond all possibility of doubt, in the *other person*. No matter how obvious it may be to the neutral observer that it is a matter of projections, there is little hope that the subject will perceive this himself. He must be convinced that he throws a very long shadow before he is willing to withdraw his emotionally-toned projections from their object. (CW9ii, 1951, para. 4; italics added)

The power that constitutes hegemonic masculinity is evidenced, not just in oppressing femininity, but also in identifying and then dominating other competing forms of masculinity. Kimmel (1994) states that hegemonic masculinity is 'the standard against which all other masculinities are measured and against which individual men measure the success of their gender accomplishments' (p. 139, note 1). Hegemonic masculinity entails not only a dominance over women but also a coercive mode of dominance over other men that can take the form of violence. As Cartwright (2002) notes in psychodynamic terms, violence is a defensive manoeuvre that defends the ego so as to retain a coherent sense of identity, to 'uphold "phallic power"' (p. 47). Violence can be seen as defensive, as a means of dealing internally with ego dystonic states, such as the rancour of 'intolerable guilt,' as a way of defensively 'ridding the self of toxic mental states,' or of 'warding off attacking objects' (ibid., p. 53). Violence can also be roused in ego syntonic ways that are aligned with external political aims, such as violence used in theatres of war and other culturally sanctioned forms of attack. Violence, whether overtly enacted or threatened, is used to dominate and control; hence, it has a *hegemonic* aim.

Michael Kaufman (1987) outlines a triad of men's violence: (1) violence against women; (2) violence against other men; and (3) internalized violence towards men's selves. Feminism as a whole has profoundly illuminated the first corner of the triad. Men's movements, in their pro-feminist or mythopoetic forms, have drawn attention to the second corner by exploring and illuminating the tyranny and damage of violence between men themselves. Unfortunately, the 'illumination' offered by the mythopoetic strand (e.g., Bly, 1990) is conflated with a conservative and reactionary analysis primarily rooted in the backlash against feminism (Tacey, 1997). The third corner has often been of concern to depth psychology, the realm of interiority. For example, Kaufman (1987) argues, 'The failure to find safe avenues of emotional expression and discharge means that a whole range of emotions are transformed into anger and hostility' (p. 22). This internalised violence translates into some significant issues. For example, males of all age groups record the highest rates of successful suicide (in the United States in 2001, 81 per cent of suicides were committed by males) and of alcohol misuse (binge drinking is twice as common among males as among females) (Helgeson, 2005). Men also produce the most serious car wrecks, in which alcohol is often a factor, and men are also more likely to be admitted to hospital with chronic disease (ibid.). Paradoxically, other social analysts have noted that a hegemonic masculinity striving in working-class boys often functions to prevent or undermine upward mobility. In this case, boys are more likely to fail in academic achievement in primary and secondary school when compared to girls (Salisbury and Jackson, 1996). What I conclude from these points is that masculine hegemony does not necessarily translate into better lives for all men, and that a majority of men themselves have a stake in dismantling patriarchy.

Unfortunately, there is no room for a range of masculinities in analyses such as that of Jeffreys. For her, *all* men are the perpetrators of male dominance and *all* women the victims, and it is clear which side any individual is on. Queer theory and third-wave feminism disagree with the universality of this claim. Masculinity is not essentially grounded in sexed embodiment; it is not penile, but rather phallic. A plural understanding of masculinities is one that also seeks to unravel masculinities in women and femininities in men. Domination and submission, in Jeffreys's analysis, are essences rooted by implication in the sex chromosomes that predetermine men to dominate, including queer men, who, by virtue of being male, are assumed to be inescapable enemies of women. Hence Jeffreys does not conceptualize the difference between people and patriarchal institutions (historically contrived by men, but non-living conglomerate centres of power), which are gendered but cannot – I counter – have a sex. She also does not conceptualize unconscious dynamics that cause gender certainty to collapse (Samuels, 1989). Since queer theory disavows a ruling essentialism, arguing that human subjects can creatively mould their gender and perform identity, it comes under Jeffreys's attack for championing 'a cult of transsexualism' (Jeffreys, 2003, p. 1) and for promoting sado-masochistic practices (regardless of practitioners' negotiation of consent and limitations). Transgender is not allowed either, since it violates the *a priori* rules of nature: males are irretrievably bad; females are by nature good; and one cannot move from one realm to the other, or occupy a position of in-between-ness, two positions at once, or a sense of being outside of, or transcending, a binary of *two*.

In contrast to a hermeneutic approach, which is based on the to-and-fro of dialogue, Jeffreys prefers a monologue of condemnation. Nowhere in her writings does one find the voices of transpeople. Like the trans-repudiating work of evolutionary psychologist J. Michael Bailey (2003), such analyses are conducted by objectifying transpeople and silencing 'deviant' subjectivity, by eviscerating voice. One might also be concerned over the energy being spent on repudiating trans subjectivity, or inducing fragmentation between oppressed groups, rather than building solidarity. Instead of reaching out to a subjugated group who could be useful, for example, as volunteers at sexual assault centres, the culturalists further relegate transpeople to the margins. *Alienation* as an outcome of this ostracism inevitably follows, no matter how much radical cultural feminists claim to be campaigning against it as a whole on the assumption that only capitalism and patriarchy produce it (Jaggar, 1983).

The backlash against feminism has been particularly cruel to radical cultural feminism, which is a constant target for critics who use this discourse in order to attack the legitimacy of feminism, in general, and women's studies programs, in particular (e.g., Boyd, 2004). Ironically, attacks on trans women have had a positive effect in raising general awareness of the plight of transpeople, as the media have sensationalized the exclusion of these people by those who claim to be the champions of the oppressed. Since feminism more broadly is based on an ethic of care and social justice (Noddings, 2003), in the end the radical cultural feminist position on trans is paradoxically anti-feminist, reflecting a gender supremacist position, as Califia (2003) provocatively points out.

Dorothy Smith (2004/1974) maintains from her materialist feminist position that 'the world as it is constituted by men stands out in authority over that of women' (p. 22). Similarly, the world as it is constructed by men and women subjugated by a pervasive sex/gender binary, including left-wing radical cultural feminists, stands in authority over transpeople, judging and condemning them in ways that iron-ically resemble the repudiation expressed by right-wing conservative anti-feminists. The next chapter seeks to talk back to conservatives, radical cultural feminists, and the liberal status quo. The overlapping issues that trans/queer people face in terms of widespread repudia-tions and consequent subjugation[5] motivate me, as a queer though non-transperson, to take the risk of pursuing this attempt to talk back, to counter repudiations from a range of sources that seem, despite their different rationales, to have common elements. Whereas trans-people are often misread as queer and subject to heterosexism and homophobia, conversely non-trans queer people can also be misread as trans and subject to trans repudiation and transphobia. Hence, I am joining with them to protest and present a different perspective (theirs), which is also not homogenous, as 'queer' may not be an iden-tity that all transpeople can relate to. There is, however, enough common ground in these complex matters to generate substantial potential for solidarity.

5 Talking Back: Historicizing the Repudiation of Transsexualism

The Politics of Representation

The re-presentations of the trans body in contemporary (neo)liberal society carries with it a number of paradoxes. On the one hand, vital information about transpeople's lives and the possibility of medical help and treatment are conveyed through various media. For many trans and non-transpeople alike, this is the primary source of education and colloquial knowledge about trans issues. On the other hand, popular culture has often portrayed the trans body in both sensationalistic and exploitative forms. When the media depicts transpeople, they influence and affect common attitudes towards them. The entanglement of both positive and negative views mirrors the general ambivalence that (neo)liberalism exemplifies towards trans subjects. Under the status quo, one is permitted to *be* trans, with the potential to access medical help. And yet this consent exists within a social milieu that in tandem produces alarming levels of trans repudiation and phobia.

Meyerowitz (2002) analyses the impact of representations of the trans body through sensationalist journalism and other media such as film. Beginning in the United States in the 1930s, representations of trans bodies partly functioned to shore up the authority of science and medicine, and contributed to the strengthening of the concept of the modern self, 'a heightened value on self-expression, self-improvement, and self-transformation' (p. 9). Decades later, *'be all that you can be'* took root as an American cultural mantra, with the promises of medicine and science backing up this ideal of the 'self-made man.' Sensationally this self-made man could also become a non–self-made man, transforming into a woman.

Foucault (1984a) speaks of the self as a product of *bio-power*: bodies are useful to the degree that they become productive instruments. Under liberalism, the productive body is one that constantly self-improves, self-transforms, and self-locates. Dividing practices, which demarcate between healthy and sick bodies, differently sexed, classed, racialized, and abled bodies, demand that each fulfil a function, as would a machine. Market consumption based on productivity, and the associated exploitation of labour required to reinforce prevailing economic conditions, is dependent upon dividing practices. Markets target these divisions and the associated competitive effects of inequality, feeding upon internalized and subjective feelings of inadequacy (Salecl, 2003). Mass media representations of ideal bodies produce the internalized sense of having an imperfect body. The cosmetics, plastic surgery, and diet industries are successful to the extent that they play upon and exploit these widespread 'inadequacies,' perceived as deficiencies in one's body (Lorber and Moore, 2007). Within divided groups, normative expectations of what the body should be like are a part of the gendered, classed, and racialized construction of the body.

Medical science is challenged to heal broken bodies, bodies that are to be transformed from sick to healthy. Its task is to purge the body of disease, mend its joints, muscles, and bones, and to bring it back into direct productivity. Repetitive strain injuries, worn-out joints, industrial accidents, chronic back pain, stress-related diseases, and so on, must be healed in order for bodies to be useful, to produce. The healed and 'cleansed' body, subject to market forces and the conservative values rooted in what Foucault (1984b) calls the 'Christian ethic of the flesh' (p. 294), is highlighted in the puritan Protestant work ethic. Bodies must retain a modicum of health in order to do work, regardless of the fact that the work itself may be a factor in producing ill health.

The idealism intrinsic to the utopianism of science requires sustained faith in its power to cure. Medical science is essential to the functioning of the prevailing political economy, and to do its job, it requires widespread faith in its abilities to heal. That medical science can perform 'fantastic' procedures, such as sex changes through SRS, has the added effect of spawning admiration for its abilities, regardless of the controversies produced by SRS per se. SRS functions as a spectacle in and of itself, one that shores up the awe of medicine and health technologies.

The apparatuses that help to facilitate and construct faith in science as capable of ensuring a normative, productive body include an array of media – magazines, cinema, television, radio, newspaper articles, and so forth. Meyerowitz (2002) traces the representation of trans bodies in such media from the post–Second World War era, revealing concerted efforts that 'routinely expressed admiration for the power of science and the wizardry of technology' (p. 41). The sensationalized reports of MtF Christine Jorgensen in the 1950s had the effect of reinforcing the magic of science in the Cold War period, providing a distraction from the dangers and anxiety of atomic destruction by fascinating readers with science's ability to conquer even the most seemingly immutable realms, such as sex. That American transpeople of that period could not get SRS in the United States was beside the point. The person who 'changed sex' was exploited as a *spectacle*, regardless of the individual's psyche or social situation (Namaste, 2004). Spectacles are generated to inspire affect, desire, to entertain, and to promote on the peripheries – advertisement boards at football and hockey matches, commercials on television – material goods associated with these affect-generating spectacles.

Film, Television, and the Internet:
The Contradictory Influences of Media

Media, such as film, television, and the Internet, as sources of entertainment and information have a profound effect on questions of gender and identity. For example, Currie's (1999) study on the effects of media, particularly magazines or 'teen-zines' targeting adolescent girls, reveals that they carry ideological content. This content conveys what it means to be a girl and a woman in a liberal-capitalist society. These messages are cognitively internalized and affect the construction of a gendered identity. They also provide imagery of normative feminine ideals of beauty, depicting models for young women to emulate and to aspire towards. Women themselves often come to reproduce these ideologies under the liberal status quo, (re)perpetuating unthought masculinist images of ideal feminine forms that fuel various gendered niche markets (such as the fashion, cosmetics, and diet industries). Through media, girls and young women are socialized to participate in consumer markets that profit from the pursuit of these unattainable ideals. The paradox is that this consumer culture often incites young girls and women not to consume, that is, not to eat or to purge, in a maddening attempt to somehow embody these dangerous ideals. Moreover, these ideals, constituted through images of 'the feminine,' are often dangerously patriarchal in composition. Luce Irigaray (1985) outlined the problem in her concept of the *masculine-feminine* or *phallic feminine*, 'the feminine' as men have reproduced and represented it. The 'success' of the strategy is that these motives are often not consciously understood as exploitation through an underlying patriarchal structure, and this benefits those in power (Jaggar, 2004/1983).

Media images and representations have had a particularly contradictory (negative/positive) impact on transpeople's lives; on the negative side, they provide an exploitative spectacle ('freak show'). Here transpeople have been portrayed in extreme ways, sometimes as fiendish and frightening characters that conflate gender transgression with those who are sociopathic. A famous example is the classic 1960 film *Psycho*, in which a murderer (Norman Bates) cross-dresses in a delusional attempt to somehow become his dead mother. Transpeople (both TS and TG) have also been portrayed as avenging rapists, as in Rachel Welch's role as a trans woman in the 1970 film *Myra Breckinridge*, or as monstrous, such as in the cult classic *The Rocky Horror Picture Show*. The 1991 film *The Silence of the Lambs* depicts a trans woman as a serial killer. She is motivated to torture and then murder her female victims out of enmity/desire, subsequently harvesting the victim's skin in a deranged attempt to clothe herself in envied female flesh. Yet, on the positive side, we find the transmission of imperative information that healing of the mis-sexed body is possible. For those suffering in silence, this information can be life-saving.

Until recently, very few films have portrayed the sometimes extreme and violent repudiations that threaten the lives of transpeople. An exception is the 1999 film *Boys Don't Cry*, which dramatized the real-life, gruesome murder of trans man Brandon Teena. Other films, such as *The World According to Garp*, *The Crying Game*, *All about My Mother*, *Better than Chocolate*, *Transamerica*, and the documentaries *Southern Comfort* and *I Know That I Am*, all portray TG or TS characters as deserving of sympathy and as likeable people. These portrayals convey a much needed shift in representation that humanizes the difficulties and strengths that transpeople experience in their everyday/night lives.

Beyond cinema, trivializing television talk shows such as *Jerry Springer* have regularly featured fist-fighting transsexuals as spectacle. Moreover, erotic and pornographic images of trans bodies have likewise proliferated. In conducting Internet research using the term 'transsexual' on a standard search engine, I was stunned at the overwhelming amount of trans pornography that this search yielded.[1] For example, I found a notable prevalence of websites pertaining to pre-SRS or 'no-op' MtFs as exotic and eroticized others: 'lady with a penis,' 'she-males,' 'tranny babes,' 'chicks with dicks,' and so on. The contradictions that all these spectacles produce are complex. On the one hand, representations of trans bodies often convey derogatory messages, such as 'freak' and 'psycho,' expressing the fear and dread aspect of the 'phobogenic object,' while the erotic sexualization of transpeople conveys the representation of the exotic Other, of attraction, arousal, and desire. These media representations, nonetheless, are often important factors in assisting transpeople by providing initial information about the possibilities of sex change.

Peter Ringo (2002) interviewed nineteen FtMs on the role that the media play in the coming-out-to-oneself process and subsequent development of a trans and/or male identity.[2] He found that the media helped trans men to generate a new awareness of their embodied selves, facilitating their initial emergence as trans men and helping to either construct or consolidate their identity. Media depictions of transpeople and issues mirrored and roused often latent feelings, stirring up the viewer's deep sense of maleness or 'trans-ness,' as Ringo reports:

> Some indicated that they experienced their gender identities as generated from physical, mental, and/or psychic depths, using such expressions as 'boy inside,' 'emerging male within myself' and saying, 'something else deeper in my mind knew I was male.' Additionally, statements that pointed to media's triggering of an inner process or accessing a type of subconsciousness were quite common: 'clicked somewhere inside,' 'seemed to speak to something very deep inside of me,' and 'helped me to discover parts of myself that were hidden.' (P. 18)

The return of the repressed is embraced and incorporated into identity, an incorporation that is strong enough to 'pre-empt' a life of socialization along a contrary gender line. Ringo concludes his study by suggesting that the

... media's role can be understood as having encouraged its user's 'qualities of transness' to manifest and strengthen, to become organized under the purview of identity and to mature through the processes of physical, social, intellectual, emotional and spiritual transition. (P. 20)

My interviews with transpeople confirm that for some the media did help to incite a change of sex/gender consciousness. Prior to transition and his 'awakening,' John had lived a fundamentalist Christian lifestyle as a married heterosexual woman. Earlier, he had experienced feelings of being wrongly bodied but had learned to repress them. Television portrayals, books, and the Internet aided him eventually in becoming a man and adopting a gay male identity:

John: I was raised in a fundamentalist religion and that certainly figured into the 'wrongness' or absurdity of my feelings. As puberty arrived, I had to deal with the fact that I had a female body, I was a girl, and there was not a thing to be done about it. I remember sitting in the bedroom thinking, maybe it's not so bad, maybe it could be good to be a girl. This boy thing was just a fantasy that I had to put away. And so I continued into adolescence. I was definitely a tomboy, and I never did fully acclimate to female things such as wearing dresses. I always had to wear a dress to church. I remember some crying fights with my mother over this issue. Finally, when I was about sixteen, she allowed dress pants ... I never did master make-up; I remember trying it on the first day of junior high and I thought, 'Ugh! This is too much trouble.' I had such a sense of failure as a female. And I remember the other girls – they would be so excited about wearing a purse and they would come to church with their purses, and I didn't really understand that. So I just went along in my girl life and had crushes on boys – this, along with breasts and menstruation, forced me to be resigned to being a girl. I graduated high school and my parents sent me to a religious university. I met my now ex-husband there. That was the high point of my commitment to Christianity and being female. I had grown my hair very long, for example, and I had gradually begun to think that skirts might be okay. My mother gave me a purse at one point, and I used it for a short while. So married life continued more or less pleasantly, but there was still always this little thing that was following me. Many things were starting to emerge at this time; even though I continued to be involved in the church with my husband, yet being away from my parents and in my own home for the first time allowed me a certain independence of thought ... I began to question a lot of things. I used to be one of those people who was very homophobic; I really thought that being gay was a sin. It got to the point where I began to think: there is in fact nothing wrong with being gay, and I'm only thinking it's wrong because the Bible seems to say that it's wrong. So do I trust myself or do I trust the Bible? I began to trust myself.

Chris: And you had no understanding of yourself as being gay at that time?

John: No, although things certainly would come up from time to time. I would see something on television and it would stir up all these feelings inside and I would think, 'What does this mean, what's going on?' and I would write about it in my diary. Since I was sixteen, journaling has been important to me as kind of ongoing self-conversation.

Chris: So this sort of self-conversation kept you going?

John: Yes, and I've always been an avid reader, which probably helped counter the fundamentalist message. I was always exposed to all these new thoughts, and I was thinking about birth control, I was rethinking abortion, I was rethinking sex – I was rethinking so many things during my early to mid-twenties. And I was thinking about myself and what does this mean, and I was thinking about my childhood and thinking about my masculinity, which by then I was allowing to emerge. I was changing my style of dress and noticing how comfortable and natural it was for me to wear gender neutral or masculine styles. I was coming to accept myself as someone who didn't wear make-up or wasn't necessarily into all the accoutrements of femininity. And I was reading and seeing things on television. I remember once I saw a guy, a transgendered man, on TV; I think his name was Alex and he was going to Harvard. And I remember how it stirred up strong feelings, how alarming and weird and familiar this was. And I was writing about it – it was just such an intense time, and it did cross my mind sometimes, 'Am I transgendered? Am I a lesbian, or am I bisexual, what does this mean inside of me?' My orientation towards men was confusing; I had no idea at the time that gay FtMs existed.

Chris: So ... you simply didn't know that it was possible. And there had been all this stuff that you had to unpack over the years around religion and sinfulness?

John: Yeah, there were so many things being rearranged. I was flowering; I was starting to bloom inside. A pivotal moment occurred when I was twenty-five: I decided to stop going to church. I had been in church weekly since I was a baby. By the time I decided to stop going, I had become a very irritated Christian. I was writing things in my diary like 'I just don't get this, it doesn't make sense but I know that Jesus is the only way to salvation ... ' I was in a box and I couldn't get out. Finally, I said, 'I've had it, I've had it with this stifling, airless Christian subculture.' I stopped going to church and I stopped listening to Christian radio. There was a big bang inside and I started to expand, and I'm still expanding, seven, eight, nine years later. It was amazing – I felt like I could breathe. I'd left a very stifling atmosphere and I felt like I could breathe. It was frightening; it was like falling off a cliff. But my husband was amazingly supportive through all this. I continued to explore, read, and think, and then the Internet came into my life. And I began to explore a lot of things on the Internet, and I learned so much, particularly about transgender issues. It began to dawn upon me what I was. It was kind of slow going; I was still learning to trust my own sense of things, solidifying my self. I had even begun going to a therapist because I was wondering if I should even stay married. I married when I was twenty, and I was not an adult at the time – I was still very much a child inside. I was starting to expand, even to outgrow my marriage, and it was very chaotic and very painful. But it was also right; the old order had to die, and the new order had to come.

John's narrative exemplifies the *positive* impacts that various media have on transpeople's acceptance of their selves and the formation of their identities. In contrast, some of the reactions that radical cultural feminists proliferate are based on *negative* representations. Germaine Greer (1999), for example, makes direct comparisons of MtF transpeople with the character of Norman Bates in *Psycho* in an audacious attempt to discredit MtFs as similarly deranged. Moreover, her comparison and conflation of MtFs with 'pantomime dames' is an allusion to earlier vaudeville shows with spectacles of cross-dressing men. As with attention to drag queens, confusing the spectacle of congruent male-bodied comic actors with transsexuals distracts from the concrete, embodied problems that those with mis-sexed bodies seek to overcome.

Media representations that play on the transsexual theme as a means of entertainment do not generally consider that historically it has been extremely difficult for transpeople to access SRS. Contemporary neoliberalism, in its advocacy of the private market, is pressing for privatization of health care, which would include clinics that provide SRS. In Canada, the creeping privatization of an essential medical service risks making the procedure no different from elective practices such as cosmetic surgery. While paying privately for plastic surgery is acceptable to consumers who feel they have inadequate bodies – those prepared to pay for a rhinoplasty, breast augmentation, or liposuction for purely aesthetic reasons – such positions differ markedly from transpeople's requirement for plastic surgery, which is *essential* for their health. Moreover, privatization would force low-income transpeople into untenable positions.

The disjuncture between liberal representations of the possibility of SRS and the concrete, material limitations of access to the required services for transpeople is a constant reminder of unbridgeable gulfs that may loom within a privatized health care system. Under the status quo, SRS is reluctantly permitted for 'suitable' candidates, while it is denied outright in other cases. Those who are excluded include candidates with a recent criminal record, or a dual diagnosis (e.g., borderline personality disorder), and younger, pre-adolescent transpeople. Candidates who have any engagement with the sex trade are likewise excluded from accessing SRS (Namaste, 2000). Billings and Urban (1982) also note racial prejudice, such as American cases of disqualifying SRS applicants who are Puerto Rican, allegedly for defying representations of white heteronormativity (looking too much like 'fags' [p. 275]).

Stereotypical images of masculinity and femininity are often imposed on transpeople by gender identity clinics. Namaste (2000) found that MtFs carefully constructed their self-presentations when visiting clinic psychiatrists in order to meet normative expectations of femininity. Indeed, it has frequently been the case that 'doctors rejected candidates who would not conform after surgery to the dominant conventions of gender and sexuality' (Meyerowitz, 2002, p. 225). The conundrum that this double bind produces is exposed in McHugh's (2004) reflections as a psychiatrist who once 'served' those with GID. He dismisses MtF presentations, saying that these 'subjects struck me as caricatures of women' (p. 2). The 'caricatures' accusation recalls the attitude of radical cultural feminists, who fail to appreciate the double binds that have historically ruled transpeople's complex relations with psychiatry. MtFs' attempts to cross the gender binary can paradoxically be successful only if they reinforce it by emulating conservative portrayals of femininity.

Talking Back to Radical Cultural Feminism

Some of the claims that radical cultural feminists make in repudiating trans subjectivity concern the supposed 'production' of SRS as a scheme contrived to materially enrich the patriarchal medical establishment. This claim, proposed by two male sociologists, Billings and Urban (1982), was cited by radical cultural feminists like Greer (1999) to lend credence to their arguments. Billings and Urban contend that the post-surgical transsexual is solely produced through medical means that 'heal neither the body nor the mind, but perform a moral function instead' (p. 266). For them, the practice of SRS produces an 'identity category' (p. 266), one that legitimates, rationalizes and commodifies SRS. Through liberal choice, transpeople are said to 'buy a body,' as they would any other commodity.

In rebuttal, Billings and Urban's analysis elides the historical reasons for the development of SRS and also the reality of SRS as sought through gender identity clinics. In fact, SRS procedures such as vaginoplasty or phalloplasty were certainly not initiated or initially conceived to create a new market for surgeons to exploit. For example, the MtF procedure of vaginoplasty long pre-dates the 'identity category' of *transsexual*, the English term coined in the late 1940s by David Oliver Cauldwell, who was vigorously opposed to SRS. Rather, vaginoplasty began as a technology of the body that addressed the requests of nineteenth-century adult women who were born without a vagina. Mayer-Rokitansky-Kuster-Hauser syndrome (MRKH) is said to occur as a congenital intersex condition in some females. The syndrome usually includes the absence of vagina, uterus, fallopian tubes, and cervix. The incidence of MRKH is estimated at one in five thousand (Morris, 2005). Since there are no male organs present, the person is usually deemed at birth to be female.

It is not unreasonable that some born with MRKH may want a vagina, and it is not unreasonable that medical technologies can facilitate such a request. Furthermore, other procedures such as mastectomies, hysterectomies, penectomies, and so on, were developed for conditions such as cancer. Even the development of phalloplasty was not prompted by FtMs, but rather for other males who lost their penises due to accidents or war (a procedure developed after the First World War). All of these technologies of the body were eventually applied to those with GID. *These procedures were not in and of themselves created for transsexuals.*

Early twentieth-century medicine and biology inherited Darwin's view that humans gradually evolved from lower, hermaphroditic species. In their evolution, humans retained vestiges of this hermaphroditism, usually in undifferentiated form depending on their chromosomal status. Gonads, clitorises, penises, breasts, and nipples share a common embryonic origin that usually differentiates into the Wolfian (male) or Müllerian (female) ducts. The Austrian philosopher Otto Weininger (1880–1903) further popularized the theory of universal bisexualism (Meyerowitz, 2002). Freud, Adler, and Jung, as well as prominent sexologists such as Havelock Ellis, were certainly influenced by Weininger's theories. Alfred Adler (1998/1938) wrote:

> The fact is that all human beings carry traces of the other sex, just as there are also hormones of the other sex in the urine. This gives occasion for a surmise that seems rather bold; i.e. that there is a twin hidden in every one of us ... the hermaphroditism present in everyone. (Pp. 148–9)

Like Adler, Freud and Jung similarly espoused an inherent structural bisexualism[3] of the psyche, though each explained the phenomena differently. What was radical for these depth psychologists, writing as they did in the early twentieth century, was how their individual interpretations of the notion ran roughshod over traditional and metaphysical binary understandings of sex and gender. Hence, many were at the time aghast, particularly at Freud's (1905) proclamations of universal bisexualism alongside an all-pervasive (polymorphous) sexuality replete with discussions of infant and childhood sexuality.

Outside of psychoanalytic circles, the increasing acceptance of the theory of universal bisexualism was lent a boost with the discovery of the sex hormones in the 1910s. Subsequently, when testing practices evolved in ways that allowed their quantitative detection in humans (in the 1930s), the theoretical paradigm of universal bisexualism meant that eyebrows were not raised when males and females were found to house both male and female hormones (Bullough, 1994). Harry Benjamin (1885–1986), a German émigré to the United States, advocated for transsexuals on the basis of the universal bisexuality hypothesis. SRS poses fewer moral conundrums in terms of transsexual healing in the global medical scheme if the distinctions between male and female are not absolute. Medical technology cannot reverse the developmental favouring of one set of embryological ducts over another, yet surgically and hormonally intervening to match the potential of the suppressed set of features, however incomplete this might be, poses less of a problem under the doctrine of universal bisexualism.

Benjamin's task, to convince the medical establishment of the legitimacy of SRS, was nevertheless a daunting one. Contrary to profiteering claims made more recently by radical cultural feminists, the early practice of SRS was limited to a few rogue surgeons who faced tremendous opposition. Some doctors, Meyerowitz (2002) states, tried to stop the practice by arguing that 'sex change surgery, especially castration of males, was illegal in the United States. They referred to local mayhem statutes, based on English common law that outlawed the maiming of men who might serve as soldiers' (pp. 120–1). Although this legal strategy failed to succeed, the general prohibitions against SRS nevertheless incited desperate transpeople to seek these procedures in other countries if they could afford to do so.

Initially, transpeople actively pleaded for the medicalization of their incongruency as a means to legitimate surgical and hormonal interventions. As Prosser (1998) notes:

> Sexology provided the narrative setting for the transgendered subject to become medicalized. Without this medicalization of transgendered narratives, gender deviance would not have been hitched to the medical technology that 'cures' the transsexual through sex change. To become transsexual, to make that somatic transition from gender deviant to sex-changed, the transgender narrative needed to become diagnosable. (P. 139)

Through the efforts of Benjamin and other sexologists, transsexuals found allies to partially persuade a very reluctant medical establishment, primarily made up of men, to consent to a limited number of SRSs to be carried out in the United States. There were two reasons for this development. First, as discussed, the idea of sex change had been sensationalized in popular culture in American media beginning in the 1930s, culminating with Christine Jorgensen's return to America following her (in)famous SRS in Denmark in 1952. Such sensationalism gave the misleading impression that anyone might potentially do likewise. Second, with the knowledge that SRS was possible (yet paradoxically often impossible to get), physicians were being confronted with people, mostly MtFs, pleading for access to SRS. Almost all requests were declined. Unable to access SRS, some resorted to maiming themselves by attempting to remove their genitals with serious, if not mortal, consequences.

The medical establishment eventually conceded, and in 1966 the Johns Hopkins Hospital in Baltimore opened its gender identity clinic, the first in America. They accepted less than 2 per cent of all applicants for SRS, regardless of how desperate the requests were (Meyerowitz, 2002). In Canada, the situation is equally parsimonious. Out of hundreds of requests each year, Toronto's Centre for Addiction and Mental Health (formerly the Clarke Institute of Psychiatry) had recommended only six to seven SRSs per year (Namaste, 2000). The number of rejections promotes alternative black markets for hormones and the springing up of private SRS clinics, an inevitable outcome since the establishment, by and large, dissuades rather than promotes or permits, most requests for sexual reassignment surgery.

The thesis that the medical establishment is solely responsible for the production of transsexuality obviously collapses under historical analysis. When SRS was first applied to gender deviance there was no English term 'transsexual,' yet human subjects with a chronic sense of incongruity and a mis-sexed body certainly pre-date SRS technologies. Prosser (1998) outlines a case of an FtM who pleaded with the German sexologist Carl Westphal in 1864 for medical assistance. Cromwell (1997) draws on the work of René Grémaux, who found that there were scores of female-bodied men living as men in the Balkans from 1800 onwards. He also notes that among the Siberian Chukchi there have been female-bodied people living as men and openly acknowledged by their fellows as 'true men' (p. 132).

Finally, the thesis that the medical establishment creates sex-change as a feature consonant with Western, liberal, consumerist values elides the presence of transpeople who receive SRS in non-Western societies. Iran, for example, has permitted hundreds of MtF and FtM SRSs. Iran is hardly a society that is sympathetic to Western liberalism. Muslim judicial clerics under the Iranian Islamic government have permitted SRS and the legal change of birth certificates (Fathi, 2004). That this exists under an overtly patriarchal and religious system is very surprising, but illustrates the fact that transsexuality is not culture specific, though reactions to it are. However, as the Iranian/Canadian documentary *I Know That I Am* reveals, most Iranian transpeople cannot afford SRS (Khosravi and Yousefi, 2005). Transphobia and trans repudiation in Iran severely affect the majority of trans women who cannot access surgeries. Since homosexuality is illegal in Iran ('buggery' is punishable by death), and pre-operative trans women are not legally considered women, they are placed in precarious positions, frequently rejected by their families, often forced into prostitution, and subject to police oppression and abuse.

Case Vignette: Kimberly Nixon and Vancouver Rape Relief[4]

Vancouver Rape Relief, a feminist organization, entered into the trans debate when it refused to allow a trans woman to participate as a volunteer in 1995. The story begins in 1993, when Kimberly Nixon, who had suffered physical and emotional abuse from a former male partner, sought assistance from another battered women's support agency. The experience helped her to heal, and she decided to give back to her community by volunteering at Vancouver Rape Relief. In my interview with Kimberly (who did not wish to be anonymous), she recalls in vivid detail what transpired. I will cite her account at length because it is very significant:

> Kimberly: Vancouver Rape Relief was looking for volunteers for the Vancouver Rape Relief and Women's Shelter, and I thought that was the work I wanted to pursue. I did a telephone interview and then I was invited to do a one-on-one interview, and was invited to start attending the training. That was August 29th, 1995 and I went that night to Rape Relief's first training session. They took a break at about quarter to eight that evening and one of the women facilitators took me aside, and I thought, 'Uh-oh' ... She asked me to come out to the courtyard, and she sat down and started to question my gender, but then she said, 'Oh my God, am I making a big mistake?' At that time I sort of knew the road she was going down and I thought, well, if she has that prejudice it must reflect in her work. Being a transition house and operating a shelter and crisis line, I thought, does that mean transgendered people aren't welcome here and do they not provide services to transgendered women in crisis? Which seems, after hearing they do all this anti-oppression work, anti-racism work, homophobia work, and going down the list, and then they turn around and in this instance say I'm not welcome because I also happen to be transsexual? That didn't make much sense to me, it didn't seem right. I know that other groups historically have also experienced that from women's organizations, meaning lesbians, women of colour, bisexual women as well.

Chris: Excluded because they were lesbian, bisexual, or women of colour?

Kimberly: Yeah, and so that was it, it just floored me.

Chris: So she told you, 'You are not welcome?' – when you disclosed?

Kimberly: I didn't actually disclose – I said, 'What if I was and what if I wasn't?' I wasn't willing to enter into discussion, and then she said, 'Well, men aren't allowed here.' I said, 'I'm not a man.' She said, 'Gay men aren't allowed here.' I said, 'I'm not a gay man.' And she went down this list and none of them applied to me. I was there like any of the other women. It was a big shock, it was very distressing. I was pretty distraught, and one of the things around healing from emotional or physical abuse, the way to empower people and to help women heal, is believing them. Abusers constantly chip away at a person's self-esteem, and not being validated or believed definitely affects adversely a person's self-esteem, self-worth, their dignity. At that time I felt that I wasn't part of this world, it was pretty awful. I went away thinking that that was so wrong. That night they again said I wasn't welcome to return to the group. There were about thirty-five women in the room and they were all wondering what was happening. I went back to see if the other facilitators agreed with what was happening, and they said they agreed with her, so I said that I would leave on one condition: that I would be able to say good-bye to the other women in the group. I went into the other room where the women were sitting and waiting and I told them that I was not welcome in the group but that I was there for the same reasons that they were and that I felt that was very wrong. Then I said good-bye and was silent for a moment, waiting, and I was deep down wondering if someone would say, 'What's the matter?' or someone would stand up and say, 'This is very wrong, what's happening here?' There was a woman who spoke out and said, 'Good-bye Kimberly,' and then I left. The next morning, I was so upset. I called two of my friends and they were so aghast at what had just happened and so disgusted with part of the community that they shared. They supported me that evening because it made me feel so like not wanting to be here anymore, the humiliation in front of all those women. Then the next morning, I thought my only recourse was to make things different or try to change things for the right, so I filed a human rights complaint. That has been in litigation basically for the last ten years.

Initially Kimberly won her case in 2003 against Vancouver Rape Relief at the BC Human Rights Tribunal, which found that Kimberly Nixon had been discriminated against. Vancouver Rape Relief immediately appealed the decision to the Supreme Court of BC. They argued that Kimberly Nixon is not a real woman because, according to them, she does not have the history of living as a girl or a woman. Rape Relief insists that it has a woman-only policy (which Kimberly agrees with) and is entitled to define who is a woman. They disregard Kimberly's legal and medical status as a woman, and discriminate against her 'justifiably' by recourse to legislative loopholes, by excluding her from their organization. Counsel for Rape Relief did not dispute Chief Justice Mr E.R.A. Edwards's (2003) characterization of Rape Relief's political position as 'an article of faith which I believe we both understood to mean matters of received or accepted wisdom akin to religious beliefs, intuitively correct and not requiring logical or scientific demonstration for their validity' (p. 9).

Kimberly Nixon disputes Rape Relief's claim that her history is a 'male' history:

> Kimberly: I would say from a very early age, when I was four years old, I realized that I was female and I would take every opportunity that I could [to dress as a girl], come home from school and come home at lunch hour ... when my family went away on holidays, sometimes I would stay home so I could be me and that was basically lifelong, through my adolescence and into adulthood. I've lived this way since my mid-twenties –
>
> Chris: So you mean full-time?
>
> Kimberly: Yeah, the so-called full-time was from when I was in my mid-twenties and I had applied to the gender clinic in 1986, but I had been living this way long before that.

Kimberly could not live with a masculine veneer, to meet society's expectations of a boy and then a man. She sought and achieved medical interventions that allow her to live a congruently embodied and social life as a woman. Vancouver Rape Relief nevertheless repudiated Kimberly's subjectivity and legal identity by imposing the signifier of 'male' on her as a mark of disqualification. In this sense, Rape Relief's attitude coincides with that of conservatives, like the Evangelical Fellowship of Britain mentioned in chapter 4, who, to reiterate, view trans-embodiment claims and associated subjectivity as a 'fantasy and an illusion.'

In 2003 the BC Supreme Court overturned the BC Human Rights Tribunal decision in favour of Rape Relief. Chief Justice Edwards, in justifying his decision, notes: 'Rape Relief's exclusion of Ms. Nixon was private. That does not mean it was subjectively less hurtful to her, but it was not a public indignity' (p. 30). The judge was evidently persuaded by a clause of exemption in the Human Rights Code of BC that permits organizations the right to give preferential exclusion to certain organizations who, in their not-for-profit status, seek to assist marginalized groups. Moreover, the judge also claimed: 'No objective male to female transsexual, standing in Ms. Nixon's shoes, could plausibly say: "Rape Relief has excluded me. I can no longer participate fully in the economic, social and cultural life of the province"' (p. 31). While Rape Relief rejoiced in Justice Edwards's ruling, he further wrote, in his scathing judgments, a statement that must give them less satisfaction:

> By reason of Rape Relief's self-definition, perhaps reflected in its small number of members, exclusion from its programs is quite evidently exclusion from a backwater, not from the mainstream of the economic, social and cultural life of the province. It may be an important backwater to its members and to Ms. Nixon, but that is a subjective assessment. (P. 32)

Edwards's judgment is not only prejudicial towards transpeople like Kimberly, but also derisive of feminist groups such as Rape Relief. Like many feminist organizations in BC, Rape Relief struggles with the social fallout of policies initiated under a neo-liberal provincial government that has cut essential public funding to social services and women's centres. While Rape Relief has adopted a particularly negative attitude towards transpeople, it has also helped many women to heal from physical and sexual assault at the hands of men. Edwards's judgment also sets a bad precedent, as the solicitor for Kimberly Nixon, barbara findlay [sic] (2003) notes, since 'disability organizations could refuse people with HIV/AIDS on the grounds that its members agreed that members must have been disabled from birth' (p. 24).

Kimberly Nixon appealed the Supreme Court of BC ruling to the BC Court of Appeal. A subsequent decision, one that upheld Justice Edwards's ruling, was issued in December 2005. This decision, although favouring Rape Relief, nevertheless acknowledges Kimberly's legal status as a woman and that Rape Relief had discriminated against her. barbara findlay argues that the core issue is the extent to which groups that provide a public service can exclude or discriminate against those who are broadly included within that group's defined membership: 'The unfortunate consequence of this decision is that now other organizations created to serve marginalised groups will also be able to discriminate against sub-groups they don't like and get away with it' (as cited in Hainsworth, 2005, p. 9). Kimberly's next step was to appeal to the Supreme Court of Canada.

On 1 February 2007 the Supreme Court of Canada announced that it would not hear Nixon's appeal, ending a twelve-year legal battle. The Supreme Court generally agrees to hear about 11 per cent of those cases that it receives. Since the Court does not make its rationale for declining cases public, we will probably never know their reasons for not hearing Nixon's case. When asked by a reporter if the case was 'worth it,' barbara findlay (as cited in Perelle, 2007), Nixon's lawyer, had this response:

> It was absolutely worth it because of the impact this case [has had] on feminism and women's groups in Canada. We have been able to serve as a catalyst for the Women's movement. Almost all of the Women's Centres in Canada are now trans-inclusive. I think Kimberly is a hero. (P. 9)

Caroline White (2002) examined the issue of trans accessibility to sexual assault and transition houses. She notes that 72.5 per cent of the 62 organizations in British Columbia who responded to her survey were accessible to trans women. She further notes that 22.5 per cent were not accessible, while 4.8 per cent did not give their position either way. Clearly, the majority of sexual assault and transition houses in BC accept the potential vulnerability of trans women to men's potential physical and sexual violence. Vancouver Rape Relief is among a dwindling number of feminist groups who retain the faulty view that trans women are still 'really men,' having had a 'male' history. Such a view is rooted in the wish to preserve the Western commitment to a sexual binary that 'cannot be transgressed,' which preserves the sacred notion of Transcendental Woman. In elevating Western conceptions of the sex/gender binary to universal status, this view also conceals an un-thought racism. Many non-Western (e.g., Indigenous) ontologies recognize Two-Spirit and gender liminal persons, whose colonial subjugation is further sustained by those who accept and perpetuate the imposition of a Western sexed binary. Namaste's (2005) sociological analyses, similarly, express concern with the elevation of sex as a category over other aspects of subjugation.

Becki Ross (1995) argues that exclusionary feminist politics have a harmful effect on marginalized women:

> Exclusionary parameters police populations and operate to compartmentalize constituencies as acceptable or unacceptable. I argue that no movement for gender and sexual liberation can afford the evacuation of a male-to-female lesbian transsexual, a leather dyke into s/m fantasy, a lesbian (or any woman) who is HIV+, a softball-playing and factory-working gay woman, a rural lesbian who has never heard of Susie Sexpert, or a lesbian of colour who refuses to slice her self into identity-pieces with lesbian on top. (P. 228)

Califia (2003) discusses the dogmatic tendencies of trans exclusion, describing them as based on a 'fundamentalist' variety of feminism, which mirrors the 'religious cast' of 'the New Christian Right' (p. 89). A former radical cultural feminist and an FtM, Califia notes that one of the false attractions of fundamentalism lies in its strategy of initial digestibility and plausibility, its common-sense appeal. These dogmatic tendencies appear, however, to be increasingly rare, as most feminisms are neither dogmatic nor fundamentalist, eschewing such forms of thought.

Non-fundamentalist feminists, some of whom formerly produced 'transphobic' analyses, illustrate a self-correcting ethos, premised on an ethic of care (Noddings, 2003). Newitz (2004) recalls how she had previously analysed the 'predominance of MtF transsexualism,' having assumed that there are more MtFs than FtMs. Essentially, she argued that MtFs are engaging in *gender slumming*: 'Slumming can mean going into ethnic ghettos to experience "authentic" – and usually cheap – food, music and crafts produced by disadvantaged minority groups' (p. 14). Slumming can also mean wealthy First World people travelling to more impoverished parts of the world, where they may *choose* to live in poor districts and 'enjoy slum culture' (p. 14). Similarly, she argued that MtFs 'choose' to identify with and fantasize about being a part of a disadvantaged group: women. 'When they dress up in other people's bodies and clothes, transgendered people and slummers play at living in a world where social mobility is possible for everyone' (p. 17). Six years after writing that article, Newitz apologized: 'While there is no excuse for my ignorance ... I would nevertheless plead with my readers to consider how much more information exists in the public sphere about transgendered identity now than in 1993' (p. 3). She evidences a willingness to learn from her experience by naming what underlies her initial, flawed analysis: 'Like many phobias, my transphobia here, I believe, came from discomfort with my own gender role, and an unacknowledged identification with FtM transgendered people' (p. 4).

Greer (1999) and Jeffreys (2003) make similar arguments to what Newitz had made; however, unlike Newitz, they have not recanted. The suggestion that MtFs have succumbed to consumerism by 'buying a body' they just happen to prefer is a political sleight of hand. It is a refusal to consider the facts in order to protect the doctrinaire qualities of a thesis, no matter how attractive or persuasive other aspects of the thesis may be (e.g., how to end violence against women).

The Double-Edged Scalpel:
Psychiatric and Psychoanalytic Repudiations

In order to shed further light on why trans repudiation is so widespread and has evolved in right, 'centre,' and left political realms, it is useful now to turn to a different but related set of discourses, depth psychology. Depth psychology is sometimes viewed as an impractical, dogmatic, and oppressive class of ideas and associated practices (Popper, 1976; Webster, 1996). In 1968, 'The New Left' denounced psychoanalysis as both elitist and conservative (Macey, 2000). However, such condemnations overlooked the syntheses that dialectical theorists such as Reich (1946) and Marcuse (1955), for example, put forward. Indeed, psychoanalysis has been reclaimed and theorized in innovative ways by socialist feminists and others (e.g., Mitchell, 1974; Rose, 1986; Kurzweil, 1995; and Elliot and Roen, 1998).

Why is depth psychology relevant to transpeople? Conservative, clinical psychoanalysis, often conflated with psychiatry, has had much to say about the alleged causes of gender identity disorder, providing explanations based on a fundamental repudiation of trans claims to being mis-sexed. These repudiating proclamations call for: (1) *a return of the gaze*; and (2) a *talking-back*. In the first instance, a return of the gaze refuses the visual objectification of the body by those in positions of power who wish to preserve the normativity of the sex/gender binary. For example, those who do not 'pass' (or are not expected to, following hormone treatment and SRS) are seen by some clinicians, as we shall see, as especially deviant. Those who refuse to pass or adopt a stable sexed/gendered position have also been subject to a judgmental gaze of deviance/disorder and are classically refused requests for partial surgeries. In the second instance, transpeople and their allies, in the act of 'talking back,' exert a necessary agency in resisting those who dismiss, ignore, or diminish transpeople's voices through the discourses of psychopathology.

Transpeople who seek surgical and hormonal intervention usually require the initial services of a psychiatrist or clinical psychologist. Psychiatry especially becomes, under status quo conditions, a necessary practice to 'help' transpeople over the hurdles they need to jump in order to be reassigned. Through referrals, psychiatry authorizes or denies transpeople access to medical specialists who can address their mis-sexed embodiment. Psychiatry and clinical psychology have control over the diagnostic referents of 'mental illness,' as listed in *DSM*-IV-TR (APA, 2000), and like medicine more broadly, they claim authority over the treatment of non-normative bodies/minds. Hence, in Canada, a justification for healing the mis-sexed body can be made that permits, in most cases, the publicly funded coverage of medical services (where available) such as psychiatry, endocrinology, and surgery.

In proceeding with a critique of psychiatric and psychological theory and practice towards transpeople, I am cognizant of a need for caution. At present, if the binary of the abnormal/normal body disappeared, making transpeople no longer the clear subjects of psychiatry, matters could practically be made worse for them. For example, there might be no further justification for public money to be spent on transpeople's healing. This could have the effect of completely casting transpeople out into the inequity of the private market, a situation where those experiencing material poverty would be prevented from accessing medical services. Nevertheless, the conundrum of transpeople's 'need' for psychiatric assessment in order to obtain treatment remains problematic, since they do not necessarily want to see a psychiatrist, whose role as gatekeeper either grants or denies access to hormones and surgery.

In Canada, depending on the province of residence and the patient's citizenship status, transpeople are usually insured for most psychiatric and medical services under the public health-care system. Yet Canada is also a class-based society where materially poor or debt-burdened middle-class transpeople might very well fear losing their qualification for publicly funded health services should their diagnostic referents, *DSM*-IV-TR diagnoses numbers 302.6, 302.85, and 302.6,[5] be lost. Inequities still exist, with non-resident status patients (e.g., refugees), those without proper documents, and those in provinces that do not fund various procedures, being denied services that would otherwise heal the mis-sexed body. Those who do qualify are placed, nevertheless, in another double bind, a dysfunctional relationship that forces most transpeople to acquiesce, to submit to the psychiatric gaze. The catch-22 for many transpeople in Canada is that they need psychiatry, yet largely dislike and disdain it (Namaste, 2000). This issue frequently surfaced in my interviews; for example, with Dean:

> Yeah, I had to go to the clinic, the gatekeepers. I had to see two shrinks there – both I found kind of condescending. You know, for people that were the gatekeepers to life-changing decisions, they weren't very personable. They should have been surgeons that just dealt with people that were asleep.

Diagnostic Repudiations in DSM-IV-TR

The *Diagnostic and Statistical Manual of Mental Disorders* (APA, 2000) represents embodied gender incongruity, under the guise of gender identity disorder, as a 'disturbance' that is 'strong,' 'persistent,' and based on 'identification' (p. 576). The individual experiences 'distress' or 'impairment' and exemplifies 'marked preoccupations.' In children, disorderly behaviours such as playing with the wrong gendered toys, refusing to urinate in the proper posture/position, or pretending that one's genitals are or will eventually become otherwise, are all indicative of a 'mental disorder.' Under the general heading of 'Associated Descriptive Features and Mental Disorders' (p. 578), GID is said to correspond in 'many' transpeople with social isolation and low self-esteem, and in 'boys' with 'marked feminine mannerisms,' a 'preoccupation with appearance,' and the risk of 'impaired' relations with parents. In 'males' (*DSM* authors are speaking of the sex assigned at birth) there is a risk of MtF 'prostitution' and hence of 'HIV/AIDS.' Drug misuse is also commonly noted as a feature of the 'disorder.' Worse, GIDs place transpeople at risk of 'suicide' (p. 578).

In the *DSM*, adult MtF 'males' are broken down into two clinical categories. The first syndrome is termed *autogynephilia*. This sub-type is characterized by marked fetishes; for example, masturbating while visualizing the self as engaged in stereotypical feminine activities 'such as knitting' (p. 579). Such 'males' are viewed on a spectrum of perversion, including a kind of frozen or permanent version of 'transvestic fetishism.' Whereas the transvestite usually reverts to the proper social role as a man after orgasm, the autogynephile remains irretrievably fixated on the incongruent body, 'the thought or image of oneself as a woman' (p. 578). These 'males' 'pathologically' fail to revert, to allow the fantasy of femininity to be released with orgasm. The inference is that the autogynephile is basically a heterosexual male stranded within a permanent fetish, a frozen fetish that has blanketed the whole body and made the self an objectified sexual object (which is what Freud saw women as anyway). Bailey (2003) repudiates the mis-sexed claim: 'No, autogynephiles are not women trapped in men's bodies. They are men who desperately want to become women' (p. 169).

The other sub-type of MtF is defined as sexually attracted to 'other males.' These MtFs are gazed upon and repudiated by psychiatry as 'homosexual males,' those who wish to alter their bodies in order to mystify the straight male partner 'he' desires. The inference is that 'he' wishes to trick a 'normal' heterosexual and potential male partner into believing that 'he' is a biological female. This sub-type is not a 'real woman' either, but a 'male' who cannot fathom/accept his own maleness. 'He' is like the flower that has a colour scheme matching the stripes of the bumblebee, and thereby tricks the bumblebee into a sexual act; hence, the 'homosexual male' MtF is out to attract a 'real male' by a pathologically situated means of self/other deception. Bailey (2003) repudiates their status as trans: 'homosexual transsexuals are a type of gay man' (p. 178).

The *DSM* characterizations of both types of MtF constitute representations of mental illness. The psychiatric establishment is generally unconvinced of the realness of transsexual claims yet, importantly, convinced of their persistence and associated suffering. The claim of being mis-sexed points to an acknowledged reification of the trans self, manifest as not pathological in body but pathological in *identity*. The swing of the psychiatric pendulum will not un-convince trans-embodied minds to relinquish the 'fantasy' of their intransigent identities. Psychiatric chemotherapeutic alliances have also failed to invent a drug to cure such mismatched defiance, to force the gendered mind to acquiesce to its sexed body, to construct a concordant and normalized gender identity.

The *DSM* subsection 'Associated Physical Examination Findings and General Medical Conditions' provides evidence of psychiatry's fixated gaze on trans embodiment. Transpeople diagnosed with GID apparently exhibit 'normal' genitalia. This gaze also sets up an implicit comparison with the 'abnormality' of IS genitals, exposing psychiatry's concurrence with paediatric surgeons, who generally refuse to relinquish the justifications for modifying the genitals of IS babies (Chase, 2000, 2002). When the psychiatric gaze shifts to FtM embodiment, the gaze of repudiation follows: FtMs are described as often having 'distorted breasts' or 'breast rashes' from associated binding. This psychiatric gaze also laments post-surgical complications in both MtFs and FtMs:

> ... in genetic females [these] include prominent chest wall scars, and in genetic males, vaginal strictures, recto-vaginal fistulas, urethra stenoses, and misdirected urinary streams. Adult females with Gender Identity Disorder may have a higher-than-expected likelihood of polycystic disease. (Ibid., p. 579)

Psychiatry views the mis-sexed body as unruly. Bona fide transsexuals, those who meet diagnostic criteria of having a faulty identity, are recognized, however, as chronically suffering people who need psychiatric and possibly other medical interventions for alleviation. The *DSM* conclusion posits the phenomenon of GID as evidence of a 'profound disturbance' (p. 580). Butler (2004) notes the effect of this clinical lens on transpeople:

> The diagnosis makes many assumptions that undercut transautonomy. It subscribes to forms of psychological assessment which assume that the diagnosed person is affected by forces he or she does not understand. It assumes that there is delusion or dysphoria in such people. It assumes that certain gender norms have not been properly embodied, and that an error and a failure have taken place. (P. 77).

Other notable aspects of *DSM* nomenclature include the supposed social dynamics and demographics of the phenomenon. 'Females' or FtMs are said to experience less social ostracism, less peer rejection, than 'male' MtFs. The *DSM* also states that the 'disorder' is more prevalent in 'males,' citing 1 per 30,000, as opposed to 'females,' ostensibly occurring in 1 per 100,000 births. Those who meet the 'chronic' outcome of a GID diagnosis justify the surgical and hormonal interventions to which psychiatry reluctantly, but by no means universally, consents. The disorder 'represents a profound disturbance of the individual's sense of identity with regard to maleness or femaleness' (p. 580). Any critical reading of psychiatry, a discipline that is, like psychology, part of what Foucault (1984b) conceptualizes as the *psy-complex*, needs to take into account the double-edged scalpel that psychiatry represents for transpeople: necessary ally / unnecessary foe that mis/serves this population. Within this pairing, there is no overarching consensus among psychiatrists on causes or representations of GID, independent of *DSM* nomenclature. As partial allies, psychiatry/psychology aid some transpeople to realize their transition goals. Yet the diagnosis itself has other negative effects, which Butler (2004) argues constitute, on the whole, 'paternalistic forms of power.' She further tabulates the diagnosis as having the capacity to

(a) instil a sense of mental disorder on those whom it diagnoses, (b) entrench the power of the diagnosis to conceptualize transsexuality as a pathology, and (c) be used as a rationale by those who are in well-funded research institutes whose aim is to keep transsexuality within the sphere of mental pathology. (P. 83)

Importantly, Butler also considers the effects that the stigma of carrying a diagnosable mental disorder can have on transpeople. These include the potential of losing rights and liberties, including custody of children, and barriers around employment and housing. This stigma operates in tandem with the social power that the psy-complex has amassed since its formalization in the late nineteenth century.

In *Beyond Good and Evil*, Nietzsche[6] (1886/1972, aphorism 1, part 3) describes psychology as 'the great hunt.' Its hunting grounds are the terrain of the human mind and the body it purports to control. Empirical psychology contends that the mind is knowable – it can be subject to capture. This type of psychology is committed to sensing and then displaying by means of description what it claims to have captured. It often succumbs to unthought-out moral polarities, especially the binary of true/false (Cadello, 1999). Nietzsche points out that this binary has repeatedly entrapped metaphysicians. In contrast, he argues for a psychology that engages 'dangerous maybes' (ibid., p. 28). Psychology's faith in moral oppositions (good/evil, true/false, sane/insane, normal/abnormal) constitutes a prejudice that produces 'the shipwreck of psychology' (Nietzsche, ibid., p. 28), a hunt steered naïvely in the direction of 'crusades for ... truths' (ibid., p. 34). Such a psychology buries 'much of the full range of human inner experience in silence' (ibid., p. 29).

The 'dangerous maybes' within contested theorizing on GID aetiology provide evidence of theoretical splits in psychiatry and between psychiatry and other branches of medicine. Not all psychiatrists accept the pathological postulates of 'perversion,' such as Bailey's (2003), or like inferences represented in *DSM* diagnostic descriptions. Rather, some psychiatrists and sexologists lean towards an exclusively essentialist explanation: GID may be caused in the prenatal brain, which is sexed in the wrong direction from the body (Zhou et al., 1997). This thesis argues that prenatal womb baths cause mind/body incongruity along sexual lines, which exonerates the transperson from environmental psychopathology. Others posit an exclusively environmental explanation, as put forward by Money (1986). In this case, gender identity is environmentally configured and irreversibly fixed, forming and subsequently freezing in early childhood (usually around the age of three). This aetiological thesis also exonerates the transperson from a 'curable' psychopathology. Some psychiatric theorists evoke hybridity in theorizing the cause, drawing on the interplay between biology and environmental factors (Gooren, 1993). Finally, those with a conservative psychoanalytic training tend to favour an explanation rooted in poor mothering, as is the case with Stoller (1968).

Psychoanalytic theorizing on transpeople warrants particular consideration, especially as I maintain that depth psychology is useful in understanding trans repudiation. All theories of aetiology, however, attribute little agency to transpeople, pointing out things that have pathologically run astray in ways that cannot be considered the transperson's fault (either biologically or environmentally in early childhood). In most psychiatric discourses, transpeople are not considered responsible for their disorderly identities, and this rationale contributes to the reluctant permission to authorize consent for radical, corporeal interventions.

Conservative Psychoanalysis

Clinical psychoanalysis has often been used to repudiate trans subjectivity through an imposed relationship whereby transpeople are often forced to confer with clinical professionals, some of whom hold psychoanalytic views. A psychoanalytic project of repudiation re-authors transpeople's narratives in order to pathologize them (Prosser, 1998). Under the conservative psychoanalyst's gaze, the 'mis-sexed' body is not really mis-sexed but is, rather, a mis-interpreted and mis-experienced body that has succumbed to infant or childhood psychopathology.

In orthodox psychoanalysis, the central and universally posited importance of the Oedipal phase (ages 3–4 years) rests on broader Freudian assertions of psychosexual development. The proper navigation of the psychosexual crises peculiar to infancy and childhood is said to form the basis for both mental health and any subsequent psychopathology. The mechanism of *identification* (that is, an unconscious investment in parental objects) facilitates all the important aspects of ego development, based on gender and sexual identity. Adult psychopathology, of which orthodox analysts broadly include the perversions, homosexuality, gender identity disorders, narcissism, paranoia, anxiety disorders, neurotic depression, and so on, is traced at root to problems navigating or resolving crises in the phases of psychosexual development.

Suffering from a 'gender identity disorder,' transpeople are not seen as ontologically constituted by an intrinsic integrity, but rather their grievance is seen as the product of environmental pathology traced to improper object relations during these crucial psychosexual phases. This pathology is apparent, supposedly, when the 'male' child exemplifies inappropriate levels of femininity, or the reverse situation for 'female' children. These arguments were notably consolidated in the work of Robert Stoller (1925–1991). Though he is certainly not the only psychoanalytic theorist to have discoursed on trans subjectivity, it is Stoller's ideas that are usually recapitulated in other conservative psychoanalytic accounts. His 1968 text, *Sex and Gender: The Development of Masculinity and Femininity*, is a psychoanalytic repudiation of trans integrity, a monograph of mother-blaming and a pessimistic account of gender deviance. That Stoller advocated for adult transsexual surgeries is not due to his endorsement of transpeople's mis-sexed claims, but to a resigned acknowledgment that these individuals are, essentially, lost souls for whom nothing else will work. Stoller argues that a nascent trans identity can be halted in childhood through early and sustained psychoanalytic intervention, but that even an intense analysis is of little use to adult subjects.

Stoller credits D.O. Cauldwell's 1949 book *Psychopathia Transsexualis* as the modern source where transsexualism was first named and documented as a 'mental disease.' Following John Money's usage of the term 'gender,' a term Money had borrowed from linguistics, Stoller began his discourse of utilizing a Freudian lens to explain the aetiology of transsexualism. At the time, 'gender' was not a commonly used term, and this gave Stoller the opportunity to insert psychological dynamics into subjectivity that differed from the more deterministic category of 'sex.' While this could have been a revolutionary start, for transpeople it marked their further condemnation. In outlining the genesis of GID, Stoller was clear in his judgment: in adulthood, it constitutes 'a malignant condition irreversible by psychological methods' (p. 140). In MtFs, he blames an over-loving mother who affords too much bodily contact with her male infant and encourages, indeed seduces, his identification with her.

Stoller tends to universalize trans experience as MtF, assuming that it leads, or certainly ought to lead, to post-surgical heterosexuality. Notably, the FtM subject is virtually absent from his theorizing in *Sex and Gender*. In reference to the pre-operative MtF, Stoller contends that 'his [*sic*] day is completely spent immersed in fantasies of becoming a normal woman who is married to a normal man' (ibid., p. 190). Stoller views the healthy, 'normal' person as having a congruent, traditional, and heteronormative life. His work is one of the influences that, for decades, have normalized anticipation of a heterosexual outcome as a criterion for referral for SRS.

For Stoller, GID is always traced to an excessive and symbiotic bond between mother and child, and ending this kind of relational dynamic between mother and son is the essential and universal treatment aim. He writes that 'since the boy's father has failed to do this, the therapist must. First, one must convince the family that the condition is pathological' (p. 253). This sets up the task of indoctrinating the family, if necessary, on the deviance of the child, and assigning blame: 'by the time such boys are four or five, their mothers can recognise the damage they have done when an authority clearly points it out to them' (p. 253). By tracing GIDs to faulty mothering, Stoller locates the 'pathology' as something that she inadvertently causes. Mothers are seen as having failed to reproduce the proper gender identity, and accused of having breached the rule of the binary, of failing to conduct their parenting in accordance with the Law of the Father.

Stoller advocated for the normative gendering of children and the policing of deviant gender expressions: 'the goal of treatment should be to make the child feel that he is a male and wants to be a masculine boy' (p. 252). Overall, transpeople are basically exhibited as examples of what could happen if a child's gender deviance is not nipped in the bud. And consistently, effeminate male-bodied children are the prime suspects. His treatment aims for offending children are exemplary of conservative political views in regard to the appropriateness of conformity to the sex/gender binary, especially for males. The intent is to obstruct gender deviations and reproduce gendered subjects that obey the rules/Law. The goal is

(1) to help complete the process of separation between mother and son; (2) to support the mother as she goes through this traumatic separation, and to change her character structure sufficiently so that she can not only survive the separation but also salvage her own sense of identity; (3) to have the therapist of the child serve as a model for masculine identification; (4) to support the child during the process of separation and to treat the ensuing anxiety states; (5) to involve the father in the family's life so that he will become a source of masculinity for his son. (Stoller, 1968, p. 253)

After reading Stoller's text, I couldn't help but wonder how many mothers must have left his office in despair, feeling that they had messed up their children? How many mothers and fathers adopted the uncomfortable role of becoming the gender police, on the 'good' doctor's orders?

Stoller's unthought aim reflects the ideology of reinforcing the traditional nuclear family, and proposing gender conformity as a marker of sanity. His more than forty years of influence endures within psychoanalytic accounts of GID. Myra Hird (2003), a feminist, recounts her experience at the conference titled 'Atypical Gender Identity Development: Therapeutic Models, Philosophical and Ethical Issues,' sponsored by the eminent London Tavistock Clinic. Her report indicates that little has changed since the days of Robert Stoller. She comments that explanations of gender deviance (childhood/adult) persist under the intense clinical gaze of presumed pathology. The binary is preserved as the only marker of gender sanity. This is in defiance (or ignorance) of scholars such as Fausto-Sterling (2003), who outlines Western society's fallacy of rewriting history in the act of sanctifying only two True sexes, denying the potential multiplicity of sexes which the Western binary suppresses. This is also in defiance of the fact that Plato spoke of three sexes (the third is the androgynous, or what is now understood under the inter-sex designation); that the Talmud and the Tosefta – the Jewish books of law – acknowledge three sexes; and that Fausto-Sterling excavates five sexes; and so on. Hird (ibid.) reports that speakers at the Tavis-tock conference continue to be faithful to Western penchants for reifying sexual dimorphism, stating that 'none of the presenters acknowledged the long-standing feminist critiques in psychology of concepts such as "gender role"' (p. 186). She concludes that clinicians continue to subscribe to 'the assumption that gender identity devel-ops from a stable morphological base [which] allows therapists to delineate between a majority "normally" gendered population, and a minority "deviant" population suffering from a gender identity "dysphoria"' (p. 189). That many transpeople must consult clinicians who hold such views, in order to obtain surgical consent forms, is a cause for heightened concern.

The influence of conservative psychoanalysis on the lives of trans-people has been immense. In his account of transpeople whom he saw as the psychiatrist-in-chief at Johns Hopkins Hospital, Paul McHugh (2004) points to the psychoanalytic research of Jon Meyer as crucial in the eventual closing of the Hopkins Gender Identity Clinic. McHugh's acceptance of the 'autogynephile' and 'homosexuality' theses, syn-dromes that are said to be the underlying pathological reasons for MtF requests for SRS, led him and other psychiatrists at Hopkins to stop recommending SRS for transpeople. This effectively closed down the gender clinic at Hopkins and led to a ripple effect, with other univer-sity gender clinic closures elsewhere in the United States (Meyerowitz, 2002). In their stead, private SRS clinics are now the main option for SRS in America. McHugh (2004) condemns the practice of SRS: 'we have wasted scientific and technical resources and damaged our pro-fessional credibility by collaborating with madness rather than trying to study, cure, and ultimately prevent [GID]' (p. 9). He also implicitly derides the private clinics: 'we at Hopkins hold that official psychiatry has good evidence ... to close down the practice [of SRS] everywhere' (p. 7).

In the case of the 'autogynephile,' McHugh concentrates on finding evidence of perversion in the 'paraphilic' (perverse) histories of these particular trans women. His puritan gaze searches for 'aberrant' sexual expression, which forecloses the possibility of MtFs being genuinely mis-sexed subjects who express erotic desire that finds creative forms of expression, considering mis-sexed limitations. McHugh assumes that *all* MtFs who desire other women (as lesbians/bisexuals) are perverse, rejecting the assistance that cross-dressing might play (using 'transitional objects') to facilitate a narrative of emergence. Curiously, in pursuing a thesis of perverse psychopathology in MtFs, he ignores the S/M practices of some trans men (e.g., Califia, 2003), solely discrediting trans women, revealing a fixated interest in this group. This begs the question: can transpeople not engage in non-normative sexual practices without disrupting the integrity of their claims to (mis)embodied subjectivity? Why is gender congruent people's embodied integrity not questioned when they engage in similar practices?

McHugh's repudiation of trans subjectivity concurs with the psychoanalytic work of Charles W. Socarides (1969). Socarides, up until his death in 2005, was a vocal opponent of SRS, which he views as a request rooted in a deeper, more pathological homosexuality: 'only the most ill homosexuals resort to the desperate course of offering their bodies for mutilative processes' (p. 173). For Socarides, sex is an essential fact of life that cannot be altered. The fact of sex is decided upon conception, a genetic determination that cannot be amended. He argues that GID can only be eradicated if homosexuality is treated to reconfigure a 'sane heterosexuality.' Socarides contends that there is no fundamental distinction between transgender/transsexual/homosexual – all are aberrations that demand a psychoanalytic cure. Hird (2000) points out that views such as these constitute a moral exercise. These positions, moreover, defy the fact that no credible evidence for a psychoanalytic cure has emerged, and that the psychoanalytic success rate for 'curing' bona fide GID is zero (Meyerowitz, 2002).

In France, a similar psychoanalytic gaze of repudiation has appeared more recently with only minimal improvements over that of McHugh or Socarides. Colette Chiland (2005), psychiatrist-in-chief at the Alfred Binet Centre and a training analyst at the Paris Psychoanalytical Society, also repudiates trans subjectivity. She notes, however, that

... some transsexuals who have had the operation do request psychotherapy or even psychoanalysis – sometimes several years after the operation
– and are indeed capable of deriving some benefit from it. They still maintain, all the same, that they could not have done without the operation
itself. (P. 37)

Chiland is not pleased with those pre-operative transsexuals who
consult her for analysis:

Once their complaint and their request is expressed, they have nothing
else to say. They protect themselves against engaging in a transference
relationship. They feel that the person sitting opposite them wants to
entrap them and make them abandon their project; they are ready to take
to their heels. (Ibid., p. 41)

Chiland argues that transsexuals are in a state of denial regarding their
real sex and suffering from a 'narcissistic disorder' (p. 45). She claims,
nevertheless, that she has managed to 'dialogue with them on equal
terms' (p. 47). This does not, however, modify her opinion that 'the
very idea of changing one's sex is a mad idea' (p. 47). Chiland declares
that 'transsexuals put us [psychoanalysts] to the test ... at every
moment our counter-transference is mobilized' (p. 73). Her compromise to transsexuals is to acknowledge that 'compassion justifies to
some extent the practice of hormonal and surgical reassignment' even
though, she counters, 'nobody can change his or her sex – sex is not an
opinion, it is a reality' (p. 76).
   Conservative psychoanalysis is intolerant of the transperson's narrative claims. Rather than accepting these accounts, they analyse them
away, revealing 'psychoanalysis's mode of reading – its tendency to
reauthor the patient's personal narrative' (Prosser, 1998, p. 151). Such
an attitude is noted by Namaste (2000), who argues that the psychoanalysts' position amounts to 'condescension, disrespect, and contempt for transgendered people' (p. 192). Hence, the double-edged
scalpel. Thankfully, not all (perhaps not most) psychiatrists follow a
conservative psychoanalytic discourse. This is evidenced by the existence of psychiatrists who do not repudiate transpeople, or try not to.
Rather, they aim to heal the mis-sexed body by being helpful and affirmative to those who meet the diagnostic criteria. Regardless, psychoanalysts, even those who suppose that they will positively support a

trans patient, may unconsciously hold transphobic feelings and project these feelings onto the patient through counter-transferential feelings. St Claire (1999) suggests that those analysts who work with transpeople need to become aware of their internalized transphobia, so that it does not adversely affect the patient.

Psychiatry and Psychoanalysis

As my interview with Kimberly revealed, some transpeople readily endorse the psychiatric assistance they have received. Nevertheless, psychiatry has represented transpeople, as textual documents such as the *DSM* exhibit, through an overall discourse that pathologizes them by recourse to the concept of *disturbance*. Transpeople's body/mind incongruity will not yield to the talking cure, the straight jacket, the wide array of tranquillizers, anti-depressant/anxiety medications, and so on. Psychiatry cannot cure the trans incongruency that it details in the *DSM*.

The meaning of 'disturbance' starts with *dis* or negation. A population that disturbs is bent upon negating something. The Oxford dictionary definitions of disturbance include: 'an interruption,' 'agitation,' 'worry,' 'a tumult; an uproar,' and, finally, 'the process of being disturbed, of disturbing.' Psychiatry, I contend, has been disturbed by the intransigence of the trans body, because such a body will not convince/allow the mind to adopt a 'proper identity.' This has led psychiatry to project disturbance onto trans-embodied people, to repudiate the actuality of the mis-sexed claim. The agitation, interruption, tumult, and uproar psychiatry cites convey the threat that trans embodiment holds for society as a whole. As an institution, and a largely conservative one at that, psychiatry has been empowered to regulate the collision provoked by the *dis* that transpeople present for the sexual binary. Psychiatry will not ultimately permit transpeople to contest the legitimacy of the naturalized sex and gender binary; rather, it ultimately blocks such wayward individuals from being socially sanctioned (as being valuable in their own right) by pathologizing them. It misinterprets the 'truth of symptoms,' rejecting the pain that the binary inflicts and preferring causal explanations for gender deviance as based on an individualized mental disorder. Psychiatry, hence, is not a depth psychology in the Nietzschean sense, since, as Cadello (1999) writes, 'a psychology that is able to descend to the depths is so because it does not mistake symptomatology for truth' (p.

33), that is, it does not take the expression of psychic pain as the end location of 'aberrance.'

Psychiatry is empowered by the state to act as a referee with considerable authority to regulate the body through which 'sexual difference is enforced' (Hird, 2000, p. 359). On the whole, it is disturbed by transpeople, for trans-ness represents a monumental break from one of the key assumptions that Western civilization rests upon, the infallibility of the binary myth of woman/female and man/male. That embodiment can break with the historical force of this institution is indeed disturbing for conservatives, who can only view such waywardness as a profound disturbance/deviation. Psychiatry's limited compromise with transpeople is to permit them to engage in SRS, to consent to allow movement – a movement that is limited to shifts between the poles of the binary itself.

Transpeople often speak of their disdain towards psychiatry. One of my interviewees was forced to deal with a psychiatrist who was also Freudian in approach:

Aiyanna: I knew enough about psychology to know the difference between Jungians and Freudians. The Freudian, every time he would start with his mother fucking father obsessing shit, I refused to answer and would just throw back at him some aspect of my cultural being ... he might ask an interesting question and then he'd go back to his Freudian shit. By the third session, he quit asking me any of his questions, and we continued with me expounding on Indigenous Culture 101 and that's how I made my way through the [gender] clinic.

In this example, psychoanalysis, in its universalizing status as a master theory, is also complicit with colonial repudiations that negate more than the sex/gender status of transpeople. Aiyanna's success, as a First Nations woman, is that she was able to insert her non-Western being into the clinic and make her way through the process. Aiyanna returned the gaze. This was not easy, pointing to the difficulties that many transpeople face and negotiate in dealing with intersected subjugations that are more complex than sex/gender alone.

Appropriating the Master's Tools

Paradoxically, depth psychology – including psychoanalysis – has the potential to dispute and theoretically undermine the conservative moral, common-sense, and rational 'understandings' of sex and gender that it, too, is guilty of producing. Emphasis on the force of guiding fictions and emotive, conflictual irrationality in the context of the unknown, the not-understood, destabilizes the ground upon which gendered convictions are erected. Hence, those interested in radical change have often engaged with psychoanalytic ideas.

For example, the refashioning of psychoanalysis to suit a quest for better understandings of marginalized people's gendered lives has been undertaken by a number of feminists. Juliet Mitchell (1974) proposed a feminist appropriation of psychoanalytic ideas in order to illuminate women's oppression on the level of interiority. Since Mitchell's influential study, psychoanalytic and gender feminism have probed the psyche as the repository of coercive inscription, of patriarchally induced trauma, and of internalized oppression. Such probing seeks to disavow the conservative psychoanalytic gaze, providing a means to understand the complexities of women's interiority and the unconscious effects of patriarchy on identity. Mitchell not only returns the gaze to the conservatives, but she also outlines the necessity of feminist involvement in depth psychology, so that the sedimented interiority of the psyche, like the oppression experienced in the external social world, may also be understood and liberated.

Not all practitioners of depth psychology use a model of pathology in their clinical work with transpeople. Carl G. Jung's (1931) school of *analytical psychology* in its traditional form is quite conservative towards matters of sex and gender, but contemporary Jungians have redeployed his ideas to assist transpeople in healing the mis-sexed body. The work of Rachael St Claire (1999) is an example of how Jungian conceptions can be utilized to understand the mental health needs of transpeople[7] in ways that do not see their status as an expression of psychopathology.

In returning the gaze to the orthodox psychoanalysts, I suggest that the psychoanalytic project of trying to clinically understand transpeople be abandoned. Rather, some core psychoanalytic concepts can be reharnessed in an attempt to understand the perpetrators of trans repudiation. This was my aim in chapter 2, where I discussed trans alterity and repudiation at length. Similarly, Butler (2004) also argues that

psychoanalysis can work in the service of a conception of humans as bearing an irreversible humility in their relations to others and to themselves. There is always a dimension of ourselves and our relation to others that we cannot know, and this not-knowing persists with us as a condition of existence and, indeed of survivability. We are, to an extent, driven by what we do not know, and cannot know, and this 'drive' (*Trieb*) is precisely what is neither exclusively biological nor cultural, but always the site of their dense convergence. (P. 15)

A further comment in talking back to those who claim clinical mastery over transpeople: It seems perfectly plausible that misogyny – the hatred of women – is operating here with the aim of defending and protecting masculinity. Masculinity acts as a defence against infantile fears rooted in the mother-infant relationship (Kurzweil, 1995). This standpoint is consistent with Frosh's (1994) contention that 'mother is terrifying to the man ... the threat of fusion, of being sucked back into her narcissistic womb' (p. 111). Here, Mother is an ambivalent figure, for in the Kleinian discourse she has a good and a bad breast. Klein's mother-object, what McDougall (1995) calls the *smother-mother-lover*, is a figure consumed, taken in – mother as the 'whole' world. In introjecting the mother, the child also ingests the constructed sanctity of the sexual binary, which, for Western subjects, often reverberates with the Judeo/Christian mythology of original sin. In totalizing the mother, the social conditions that produce her are, in the Kleinian discourse, smothered by the breast. This over-emphasis, regrettably, led psychoanalysis into infamous mother-blaming as a means to explain the aetiology of many forms of psy-chopathology, including gender dysphoria as discussed in this chapter. These attempts at assigning culpability conjure the persecut-ing and threatening breast, while eliding the surrounding phallic culture that loves/hates it.

Finally, Winnicott's (1958) outlining of infantile fears, such as the baby's fear of 'falling forever,' may be useful in returning the repudi-ating gaze of psychiatrists like Paul McHugh, or psychoanalysts such as Charles W. Socarides. As with violent physical attackers, their trans repudiation may point more to their own unconscious, sedimented fears of a collapse of their deeply held, conservative views of the immutable and essentialist nature of sex, especially the male sex. They may fear castration, or be frightened of growing female breasts. If transsexuals *really* are what they claim to be, McHugh and Socarides may – to their horror – fall forever.

6 Adlerian Theory

In trans studies, the socially oriented depth psychology of Alfred Adler (1870–1937) has not yet been considered. Instead, many of the conversations taking place engage alternate debates between various modern, postmodern, and poststructuralist theories on society, the body, and identity as well as literary and theoretical aspects to trans' being-in-the-world. Those who do engage with the depth psychologies tend towards psychoanalytic theory as a means to both probe and enrich sober, critical engagements with issues pertinent to transpeople (Prosser, 1998). Scholars in trans studies who work outside of psychoanalytic theory tend to engage in sociological questions, in which the location of subjects in the social world takes precedence and the sphere of exteriority serves as a starting point rather than the interiority of the psyche (Devor, 1997). Adler is relevant to these debates since he emphasized both spheres as equally important. Indeed, as the first of the great dissenters from psychoanalysis, it is notable that his departure centred on a dispute that began with a concept he introduced to his Freudian colleagues, *psychic hermaphroditism*, which was rejected by Freud. In this chapter, I shall cover the ground of Adler's break from psychoanalysis, centring as it did on a topic pertinent to trans issues, and throughout discuss his relevance to trans studies. As an Adlerian, I have taken care to be critically reflexive; in introducing this discussion, I am well aware that orthodox Adlerian conceptions of gender transgression are among the school's weakest points (Shelley, 1998). The founding figures of depth psychology (Freud, Adler, and Jung) were essentially gender conformists and held moral convictions and clinical views on appropriate gendered behaviours, setting a precedent that carries on in debates, discussions, and revisions to this day.

Adler made significant contributions to understanding the dynamics of subjectivity. His school of depth psychology, while traditionally conformist to sex/gender normativity, provides insights into the phenomenon of repudiation. Though preceding poststructuralism, some of his insights foreshadow later developments, while others are in direct opposition to them. French psychoanalysis, with its disdain for ego psychology's conceptions of the 'self,' demonstrates almost total disregard for Adler's contributions. This oversight is worthy of analysis, since poststructuralist psychoanalysis actually has several points in common with Adler. For example, it was Adler, and not Lacan, who first reread Freud's tendency to biodeterminism as based on symbolic constructions, or 'fictions' (Lehrer, 1999). Adler's humanism and faith in holism, expressed more directly in his later period, may have caused poststructuralists to overlook earlier nuances in Adlerian theory that are precursors to their own deconstructive rereadings. This issue pertains most saliently to the subject/self debate and the relative centrality of language, the body, and society/culture in the formation of individual persons.

The Adlerian turn to the self in depth psychology occupies a position consistent with Prosser's (1998) work. He evoked Didier Anzieu's psychoanalytic reclamation of selfhood, a construct that is not only useful but integral to understanding trans (especially TS) embodiment. Similarly, for Adler the implicit self is responsible for the task of repairing fracture – of making an integrity emerge from fragmentation, establishing healing, or mending, as a useful fiction. The Adlerian constructivist position posits the self as *striving* for the integration of an unconscious fracture. The pre-eminence of poststructural psychoanalytic theorizing in (trans)gender debates (e.g., Butler, 1990) elides Adler's earlier contributions in this area. Hence, the present discussion aims to reconsider Adler's separation from Freud as the first attempt to build a constructivist depth psychology, and to draw attention to its relevance to trans theorizing. It also reviews the controversy around 'ego psychology' as central to one of the paradoxes of the trans condition: that the self is obviously split, as poststructuralists claim, but transpeople nevertheless seek a new, rather than original/lost, wholeness, one that evokes this affective nostalgia for a 'lost home,' the desire to actualize what should have been.

Adler's Break with Psychoanalysis

Adler established an influential system of psychotherapy, a personality theory, and a social/context psychology paradoxically known as *individual psychology*. His life and work are recalled in biographical detail by Bottome (1957), Ellenberger (1970), and Hoffman (1994), who emphasize the general, yet often unheralded, impact that Adler's school has had on twentieth-century psychology. He was a physician practising in Vienna at the time when Freud began the formalization of psychoanalysis. The two first became acquainted in 1899, Freud having responded to a letter by Adler, the content of which distinguished the differential diagnosis between hysteria and epilepsy (Fiebert, 1997; Handlbauer, 1998).

In 1902, Freud invited Adler and a couple of other colleagues to his home for informal discussion on the topic of psychoanalysis. This small nucleus, which grew over time, became known as the famous Wednesday Society. These members were responsible for co-founding the psychoanalytic movement under Freud's leadership. Adler remained a part of the group for nine years. With Freud's endorsement, Adler was installed as the first president of the subsequent Vienna Psychoanalytic Society and became the first editor of the associated journal *Zentralblatt für Psychoanalyse*. However, disagreements emerged and became more common as the tension between the two men intensified. Eventually, their cordiality ceased when Adler's views began to compromise the core sexual tenets of Freudian psychoanalysis, and Freud came to regard him with utter contempt (Fiebert, 1997). Adler, in turn, rejected Freud's fatalistic tendencies, adopting a more optimistic view of people's potential for healing. In his later clinical work, he imparted this positive attitude in therapy, discarding the psychoanalytic stance of neutrality that Freudians insist upon. Both therapeutic attitudes, however, have their separate clinical merits. Presently there is little discernible sectarianism between the two schools, with much of it having rightly dissipated. They remain theoretically distinct, both shining differing lights on the complexity of the human condition.

Over the years of his association with psychoanalysis, Adler became increasingly impatient with what he viewed as Freud's dogmatic style. Jung (1961), too, would later note the same characteristic, recalling how Freud desired to fix the libidinal hypothesis as though it were the firmament: 'I can recall vividly how Freud said to me, "My dear Jung, promise me never to abandon the sexual theory. That is the most essential thing of all. You see, we must make a dogma of it, an unshakeable bulwark"' (p. 147). Disagreement over the absolute status of the libido was a factor in Adler's eventual split from Freud in 1911 and Jung's subsequent split in 1913. Both Adler and Jung believed that instinctual sexuality could be an important element in the neuroses, but was not the exclusive one.

Adler's early views were also shaped by his adherence to Marx's social theory, though his critics note that he was not an orthodox Marxist (Jacoby, 1975). In his first publication, *Das Gesundheitsbuch für das Schneidergewerbe* [1898],[1] Adler argued for the prevention of illness through the application of social medicine, preventative education, and a rethinking of exploitative working conditions in the tailor trade, acknowledging socio-economic factors that Freud ignored. Freud tended to focus on internalized, reductive fragmentation, whereas Adler always insisted on a figure/ground lens, contextualizing subjects in a social field (Collier, 1964).

During Adler's association with Freud he was deemed 'the social-ist,'[2] and indeed one can see the accuracy of this portrayal in the *Minutes of the Vienna Psychoanalytic Society* (Nunberg and Federn, 1962–74), which indicate that Adler frequently offered a Marxist inter-pretation of various issues under discussion. An example is high-lighted by Kurzweil (1995), who discusses Adler's criticisms of Fritz Wittels's questionable thesis on 'the unconscious meaning of menstru-ation.' Wittels opposed the admission of women into the Wednesday Society and held anti-feminist views, believing that feminists were women who actually wanted to be men. Adler rebuked Wittels and in retort argued that 'the fate' of women is determined by patriarchal arrangements and the control of private property, relations that histor-ically come to disadvantage women. It is noteworthy that Adler and his wife, Raissa Epstein (who was a lifelong socialist feminist), were personal friends of Leon Trotsky, often entertaining him at their home during the years when Trotsky lived in Vienna (1907–14). Also, Adler was the first to propose a synthesis between psychoanalysis and Marxism, though his paper on this topic is lost (Ellenberger, 1970). He was also the first to argue a psychoanalytic position in support of fem-inism, as the sociologist Connell (1995) and feminists like Kurzweil (1995) and Tong (1998) have all correctly noted.

Following his break from Freud, Adler formed the Society for Free Psychoanalysis, which later evolved into the school of *individual psy-chology*, a somewhat confusing reference to the Latin *individuus*, meaning indivisibility. This obscure reference to 'indivisibility' – perhaps due to inappropriate translation into English where its intended meaning is not at all obvious – was consistent with Adler's insistence upon the fictional unity of the neuroses and indeed the fictional (yet useful) unity of the self. His position contrasts with Freudian psychoanalysis and its counter-insistence upon permanent, compartmentalized conflict, an un-mendable fracture. The American adoption of Adler's school favoured the retention of the colloquially understood term 'individual' as referring to one person, rather than collective issues. However, Adler's meaning, while pertaining to his theorizing on the *unique* and creative power of the individual psyche, did not ignore contextual and collective aspects. It is paradoxical that Adler's 'individual psychology' is actually a social psychology (King and Shelley, 2008).

Ansbacher and Ansbacher (as cited in Adler, 1956) argue that the conflict between Adler and Freud essentially pitted 'psychology with a soul [Adler] against a psychology where the soul or self was eclipsed [Freud].' The Ansbachers further conclude that 'the self or the soul[3] must remain the focal point if psychology is to provide satisfactory explanations' (p. 62). Indeed, both Adler and Jung shared a holistic regard for the psyche, and did not ignore its spiritual dimensions (whether religious or existential), remaining faithful to the root meaning of psyche as the prefix of *psych-ology* (soul-logic).

The noted Jungian scholar James Hillman (1983) argues that 'if there are Freudian parallels with Jung, even more so are there Adlerian ones ... meaning, individuality, collective consciousness and kinship feeling, opposites and compensation, and psychic bisexuality' (p. 96). While there are Adlerians (Oberst and Stewart, 2003) and post-Jungians (Kulkarni, 1997) who emphasize constructivism rather than metaphysics in their clinical approaches, both Jung and Adler themselves shared an unwavering endorsement of metaphysics. Adler's later writings (1998/1938) turn towards 'the meaning of life,' as he courts metaphysical ideas on spirituality, such as the social ideal he posits as constituted 'sub specie aeternitatis' (under the aspect or light of eternity) (p. 271). Adler was also an early adherent of phenomenology in psychology, well before existential and humanistic therapies came into vogue. However, Adlerians dispute the Cartesian dualism of classical phenomenology, as evidenced in the concept of 'organ jargon' (Griffith, 2006; Linden, 1997), which resonates in part with Kristeva's much later positing of the 'speaking body' (Oliver, 1993). Adler contends that the body speaks what the un/conscious forbids, what conflicts with the 'fictional final goal,' a term to be discussed shortly. Organ jargon and compensation are aspects of an ideal, an embodied striving for holism. In psychotherapy, cognitive change goes hand in hand with shifts in the unconscious, which are in turn reflected in the ways in which the body speaks. Adler's retention of a dynamic unconscious further differentiates his school from those that are Cartesian in their phenomenological or cognitive views (Shelley, 2006).

Adler was contradictory in his 'turn to the ego'[4] in ways that separate him from the tenets of 'cognitive therapy,' a modality that classically extols an exclusive focus on consciousness. Hillman and Ventura (1992) problematize phenomenologically based cognitive and associated 'behaviouralisms,' contending that these approaches are based on a puritanical ideology, one that attempts to impose the Protestant ethic of self-control. Their argument echoes the scorn that Lacan held for North American variants of ego psychology, because of what he insisted was their denial of rupture, and the undoing of the radical potential of a psychoanalytic unconscious (Horrocks, 1998). Karen Horney also accused Adler of shifting too much to the ego, of failing to take a proper journey into the depths (Paris, 1994). Curiously, historians of psychiatry nevertheless describe Horney herself as more of a neo-Adlerian than a neo-Freudian (Ehrenwald, 1991).

Ellenberger (1970) characterizes Adler as the 'father of ego psychology,' but in some ways this is a faulty representation. In ego psychology, the self-contained ego, as the centre of consciousness and experience, seems to stand outside of time and space, unconnected to relational contexts. Rather, Adler's psychology is much less an 'ego' psychology than a context psychology, in which strict and bordered demarcations between interiority and exteriority are broken down. He emphasized that 'no psychologist can determine the meaning of any expression if [they] fail to consider it in its social context' (Adler, 1998/1938, p. 118). Ansbacher and Ansbacher (as cited in Adler, 1956) conclude that even though Adler's psychology is known as one of the depth psychology models, which search for deep 'unconscious phenomena,' 'one can better speak of Adler's psychology as "context psychology"' (p. 3) in which the figure/ground constantly waxes and wanes. His so-called turn to the ego requires further explication, as theoretically it is a complex turn that may actually point to something else altogether.

The Guiding Fiction: The Un/Conscious as a *Mise-en-abîme*[5]

Following his break with Freud, Adler drew upon the work of two philosophers to strengthen his ideas, both of whom accepted the notion of an unconscious: (1) the neo-Kantian and post-Nietzschean philosopher Hans Vaihinger (1965/1911); and (2) the South African statesman Jan C. Smuts (1926). In the first instance, Adler adopted Vaihinger's concept of *fictionalism* (*fictio*). Ansbacher and Ansbacher (as cited in Adler, 1956) describe the concept as 'ideas, including unconscious notions, which have no counterpart in reality which serve the useful function of enabling us to deal with [reality] better than we could otherwise' (p. 77). In the spirit of Kant, Vaihinger emphasizes the subjectivity of fictions, which work on the principle of 'as – if.' For example, gendered constructs are fictional, functioning *as if* gendered material were pre-given, *apriori*, a reified set of facts, or 'objective reality.' Gendered subjects unconsciously construct and creatively rework gendered fictions, often through early internalization of available material (existence precedes essence), to produce their own images, fantasies, dreams, ideas, ideals, and beliefs about masculinity and femininity. By unknowingly fashioning their fictions, subjects create hidden goals to strive for and a biased apperception with which to view others and the world in relation to these fictive goals.

Adlerians argue that these fictions are tangled with notions of *private logic*, that is, a logic that is not shared or consensual. Dreikurs (1973) suggests that private logic is opposed to the *sensus communis*, the striving for reason as expressed in 'common sense.' Adler used the private logic and common sense polarity in the manner which Kant had intended (Ansbacher, 1965). Kant spoke of the *sensus privatus* as *Eigensin*, which means 'one's own sense/meaning,' that is, stubbornness or unreasonableness in holding a divergent interpretation. This understanding of *common* sense (as opposed to individual idiosyncrasy) differs markedly from the liberal-empirical, anti-Hegelian common-sense discourse that dialectical materialists such as Jacoby (1975) and Parker (1997) discuss. Poststructuralists also refute the claims of a 'naturalistic' common sense. Derrida's writings on deconstruction as a whole instruct analysts to resist the naturalization of that which is not natural, no matter how 'natural' the gesture may appear.

Some of Adler's German concepts were translated into English terms such as 'common sense' and 'lifestyle' (e.g., *Lebens-Schablone*), which are now easily misconstrued, sometimes approximating too closely to contemporary right-wing rhetoric. Neo-conservatism, which spawns 'common sense' political movements, coincidentally uses 'lifestyle' as a marker of a hedonistic, liberal society (as in 'the homosexual lifestyle'). Adler did not intend these meanings in his use of the concepts. As an Adlerian, I am very careful to avoid these terms and use clearer translations (e.g., a dialogic *communal sense*, and, following Ansbacher, 1999, *style of life*).

Combining Vaihinger's concept of the 'fiction' with a (constructed) 'teleological' orientation, Adler created the concept of a 'guiding fiction' or 'fictional finalism.' The unconscious is constituted by an unknown *creative* force, producing fictions spontaneously to aid in the child's development. Adler used creativity in the Aristotelian sense (*poiesis*), as 'the creative force of the human being' (Oberst and Stewart, 2003, p. 10). The Ansbachers (as cited in Adler, 1956) sum up the meaning of Adler's conjunction of fictionalism and teleology thus: 'by now describing goals and the future as fictional, he expressed in effect that this future was not the objective future but a subjective future as experienced in the present' (p. 88). Hence, Adler's depth psychology differs from psychoanalysis by looking into the past (early childhood recollections) in order to uncover and interpret the prospective function of the body/psyche, to reveal unconscious goals, or the 'future.' Some Adlerians conflate Adler's later reading of metaphysical teleology (*sub specie aeternitatis*) with his earlier constructivist fictional finalism. I am careful not to, preferring the earlier theorizing without the notion of eternity.

The unconscious nature of an individual's guiding fiction is summarized by Adler (1956):

> Every individual acts and suffers in accordance with his peculiar teleology, which has all the inevitability of fate, so long as he does not understand it, that is so long as it remains unconscious. Its springs may be traced to his earliest childhood, and nearly always we find that they have been diverted into false channels by the pressure of the earliest situations in the child's life. (P. 93)

The fictional final goal is used interchangeably with the 'guiding self-ideal,' a term Adler introduced in 1912, following his break with Freud. This concept preceded Freud's usage of 'ego ideal' (1914), a forerunner to Freud's superego. The terms differ significantly. Adler's concept was structured as an original creation of the child consistent with their unique and stylized creative power. In contrast, Freud's ego ideal and superego are reactive constructs, formed as a result of parental criticisms and Oedipal relations, as a 'substitution for the lost narcissism of childhood' (Ansbacher and Ansbacher, as cited in Adler, 1956, p. 95). For Adler, the uniquely created fictional final goal produces directionality with regard to movement and psychic development. Since this is seen as a largely unconscious construct, posited at the centre of one's style of life, Adler's psychology should be classified as an embedded modality of depth psychology and not a superficial 'surface psychology' as Jacoby (1975), Robinson (1993), and Kaufmann (2003) have charged.

People are not always aware of their intentions; the 'knowing subject' is only a 'partially knowing subject.' The limits of agency circulate within the (not wholly) conscious ego, or 'consciousness.' According to Adler, 'the uncovering of the neurotic system of the style of life is the most important component of therapy because [it] can only be preserved when a patient successfully withdraws it from his/her own criticisms and understanding' (Adler, as cited in Datler, 1999, p. 36). This analysis is consistent with Vaihinger's understanding and formulation of the fiction, which he saw as 'carried on in the darkness of the unconscious' (Vaihinger, as cited in Adler, 1956, p. 88). Dreikurs (1973) also accepts this understanding of the unconscious, claiming that 'our goals are always hidden and unconscious' (p. 89). In the Adlerian reading, gender is fictional. *Fictional final goals of masculinity and femininity* are constructed gender ideals, 'purposeful,' partly phenomenological constructions, tempered by an ever-present and circulating unconscious. The *mise-en-abîme* of gender (a story within a story) is constituted by fictions that one strives for on the basis of 'as – if.' Gender is never achievable yet always pursued. We are gendered as if there were such a thing as gender. In trans studies and queer theory, Halberstam (1994) writes about gender as a fiction in her analysis of 'female masculinity,' taking up a similar theme.

Adler also synthesized the holistic philosophy of J.C. Smuts (1926) with his adoption of ideas from Vaihinger. Smuts, whose work also philosophically underpins Gestalt therapy (Gorten, 1987), likewise supports the notion of an unconscious that is conceptualized holistically. For Smuts,

the field of Mind then comes to mean that area of its functions and activities which falls below the 'threshold' of consciousness, which remains unilluminated and dark, which cannot, therefore, be known by direct inspection and which, as in the cases of the other fields, can only be ascertained by its indirect effects. (P. 254)

Adler and Smuts shared Kant's concept of the *realm of ends*, believing that through sensation and apperception the subjective mind moves towards various ideals and that all perception is relegated through a synthetic judgment, what Kant referred to as the *synthetic unity of apperception*. This unity of apperception is at the core of Adler's conception of personality, which he referred to as the *style of life* (life style; life pattern). Style of life is a more comprehensive term than personality, as it includes the idea of movement, the degree of community feeling (*Gemeinschaftsgefühl*), and a greater striving towards this ideal (social interest) than the more limited concept of personality otherwise permits.

Adlerians do not deny that conflict exists within the psyche; indeed, Adler claims that 'nothing at all can take place without conflict' (Adler, 1998/1938, p. 120). However, he also argues that once the primary unconscious goal has been revealed, it will demonstrate the synthetic tendency, the attempt to lend coherence and unity to an otherwise incoherent fracturing of the psyche, the battleground of conflict. Adler disputes the psychoanalytic claim of an inherent conflict between the conscious and the unconscious, 'even the so-called conscious, or the ego, is chock full of the unconscious, or, as I have called it, the "not understood"' (p. 150).[6] Smuts's (1926) view of the unconscious was no doubt consistent with Adler's, as he contends that

even the unremembered past experience is not dead, but alive and active below the level of consciousness. In the debating chamber of the present it may not speak, but it votes, and its silent vote is often decisive ... remembered or unremembered the past exerts its full force on the present experience. (P. 254)

I shall return to Smuts in the next chapter, pointing out his contributions to the idea of the holistic self as well as the problematic nature of holistic grand narratives more broadly. Holism is an important issue for many transpeople; hence, analysis of the concept is warranted in trans studies.

The Contested Realm of the Ego

There was a demographic difference between Adler's and Freud's patient populations, one that drew Adler in the direction of the 'ego' as the point of entry in therapy: Adler saw more patients from the lower classes, whereas Freud saw more upper-class patients, who could well afford a long analysis. In contrast to Freud's insistence upon an analysis protracted by, for example, the use of regression and sustained transferences, Adler's therapy was consistently shorter. He certainly did not deny the transference phenomenon and utilized it in therapy as a means to transform the style of life when practical to do so. However, due to the often shorter nature of the relationship, transferences would be identified for their capacity to reveal unconscious fictions and then extinguished rather than protracted. Moreover, counter-transferential feelings in Adlerian supervision are crucial analytic tools, providing a rich source for the development of the therapist's reflexive maturation and crucial clues to the evolution of the therapy itself.

Handlbauer (1998) points out that 'the background of his patients brought Adler nearer than Freud to the effects of social misery' (p. 179). Adler was often consulted by patients who suffered from severe problems that, under the circumstances, prioritized the strengthening of rational capacities. He was therefore compelled to devise a quick and effective treatment approach for such patients in order to help alleviate their symptoms. Perhaps critical theorists and therapy critics alike could cite this as an example of social control, in the sense that Adler adjusted such patients so that they could go back to their exploitative social conditions (Jacoby, 1975; Kitzinger, 1987).[7] The evident catch-22 is that of providing help or leaving suffering subjects to languish. Adlerians, however, argue for both prevention and treatment, and in the process avoid one-sided 'solutions' (King and Shelley, 2008).

In order to avoid the problematics of ego conceptualization, Heinz and Rowena Ansbacher, who were responsible for some of the organization and translations of Adler's German writings into English, translated the German 'Ich' (ego or I) into the English 'self,' a more holistic conceptualization that includes both conscious and unconscious dimensions. Adler's writing was so imbued with the idea of the 'self' that Hoffman (1994) titled his biography of Adler *The Drive for Self*. The ego as discrete consciousness is not what Adler conceptualized; rather, the *mise-en-abîme* of the ego in Adler's scheme reflects the *unconscious as 'present' in the conscious.* The phenomenological self is not, in this schema, synonymous with 'ego'; it is not pure consciousness, or unfettered awareness (Shelley, 2006).[8] This point resonates with Gadamer's (1960) idea that perception is clouded by the blinding forces of 'tradition,' what is carried forward, shading temporality. The risk of choice is dependent upon the extent of consciousness and is never completely free (as humanistic and existentialist psychotherapy theory seems to imply) of the uncertainty of fallacy or delusion. No one can be purely authentic in the real sense, but one can be authentic in the nominal. An Adlerian turn to the ego is one that retains some agency, while recognizing its limits.

Oberst and Stewart (2003) note that Adler's school of depth psychology began by stressing Vaihinger's constructivist insights, which support his relevance to both cognitive psychology and what is now referred to as poststructuralism. Adler's late period (from 1925 onwards) marked a more pronounced humanism and existentialism, a 'step backwards' from the direction of postmodernity (ibid., p. 163). Adler turned towards 'romantic humanism' (such as the ideal of community) as a response to the escalating crises that led to the rise of fascism and the Second World War. This period witnessed Adler emerging as a more messianic figure, who wanted his Individual Psychology to rescue mankind. Though I am loath to distance myself from Adler's idealistic humanism, I nevertheless recognize the discursively revealed, critical problems within the humanist discourse (Weedon, 1987; Hook, 2006).

Oberst and Stewart (2003) contend that constructivism is a key epistemological framework that supports postmodern analyses. Interestingly, they also argue that Adler is of historical importance as an early constructivist in psychology: 'Adler's view of the human being and human conditions, his refusal of determinism and of physicalist viewpoints in psychology, his agreement with Vaihinger's ideas, make Individual Psychology a first project of constructivism in psychology' (p. 163). I would add that Adler's view of the unconscious as 'present' in the conscious, and his roots in aspects of Nietzsche's philosophy (Lehrer, 1999), further support Oberst and Stewart's claim. The relevance of constructivism to trans studies has been central to debates raised by Butler (1990, 1993, 2004) and Hird (2000) as well as those trans theorists who are sceptical towards the discourses of postmodernity in relation to transsexuals (Namaste, 2005), and critics of transness more broadly (Jeffreys, 2003). Moreover, I would be remiss if I did not state the fact that a great number of Adlerians do not consider themselves postmodernists, preferring to retain Adler's later emphasis on existentialism and humanism, both of which have strong links to modernity.

Masculine Protest

In retrospect, Freud and Adler's dispute was at root a conflict between conceptions of sex and gender and the relationship between them. Freud subsumed gendered material (produced by social conditions) under the grand category of 'sex,' yet his privileging of the instincts gave rise to a biologistic discourse, which is what Freud intended (Freud, 1933; Frosh, 1994). Adler, in contrast, argued for concepts derived from the unique and creative utilization of socially constructed material – reworked into an individual's personal set of fictions – underlying behaviour or performance. This is the stuff of gender. Tied into this are power dynamics and various compensations based on the subjective inferiority/superiority dynamic, a dynamic that reflects socio-political inequality and the fact of human imperfection. Safeguarding strategies (e.g., repression, denial, projection) are often used by gendered subjects to defend their un/conscious gender fictions. However, Freud confused the issue in an antithetical sense by accusing Adler of arguing mere biology rather than psychology, whereas the reverse has proved to be the case (Freud, 1933). In a presentation to the Wednesday Society in 1909, Adler began to speak of a subjective 'feeling of inferiority,' in contrast to his earlier biologistic references to 'organ inferiority,' for which compensation for weak constitutional elements was seen as the key to understanding neurosis. Adler's turn to subjective feelings and interpretations of embodiment amounted to a paradigm shift in his thinking, away from biology and towards a constrained 'phenomenology' (Handlbauer, 1998). In this sense, he moved the unconscious from the confines of the mind's shrouded vestiges and spread it all over the body.

In cementing his paradigm shift away from Freud, Adler moved towards a limited phenomenology, in which the un/conscious could also be deciphered. This shift was evidenced when Adler again addressed the Wednesday Society. This time he proposed that the notion of 'psychic hermaphroditism,' predicated on an interior interpretation effecting a gendered sense of felt inferiority, was at the root of neurosis. This new conceptualization, entailing gendered value judgments based upon subjective appraisals of 'strength' and 'weakness,' hypothesized that individuals possess both the masculine and feminine, based on their association with aggressive and passive feelings. Adler purposely invoked 'hermaphroditism,' avoiding the term 'bisexuality,' drawing a new theoretical direction away from the core drive tenets of psychoanalysis. Freud's 'bisexuality' was, as far as Adler was concerned, mired in an inescapable instinctual paradigm.[9]

Adler's concluding remarks foreshadowed his later move to the construction of the fiction: 'the child's infantile understanding compels him to look upon everything inferior as unmanly and to conceive of it as feminine' (as cited in Nunberg and Federn, 1967, p. 428). His presentation, however, left the Society somewhat confused, and indeed his initial outlining of the thesis of 'psychic hermaphroditism' was, at least initially, rather bewildering.

Many decades later, in his discussion of Adler's term, Hillman (1983) provides an interpretation:

> Hermaphroditus is the archetypal figure of healing, the psychic healing of imagination, the healing fiction, the fictional healer for whom no personal pronoun fits ... That figure, concealed in 'the opposites' (which are as a defense against it), is also the figure embodied as goal by therapy. (Pp. 102–3)

For the Jungian Hillman, Adler's 'psychic hermaphroditism' provides depth psychology as a whole, whether Freudian, Adlerian, or Jungian, with one of its most important metaphors, that of healing. Yet Adler's original presentation of the concept to the Wednesday Society lacked clarity. He attempted to clarify matters at a Scientific Meeting of the Society (1 February 1911), when he presented his paper 'The Masculine Protest as the Central Problem of Neurosis.' In this presentation, he argued that one of the driving features of Western civilization is its devaluation of women, which he described as 'the carcinoma of our culture' (as cited in Oberst and Stewart, 2003, p. 10). The outcome, in psychic terms, is that women were provoked to express a 'masculine protest,' that is, a protest against masculinity, that can be deciphered from both 'normal' and 'neurotic' 'female' symptomatology. In men, a counterpart is exhibited to this protest, such as the unconscious fear of losing social and personal power (virility).

The neurotic culprit underpinning it all is the binary and its antithetical expressions internalized and then counter-expressed in psychopathology. For example, Adler argued that an unconscious fear of woman's 'superiority' can be found in the dreams of neurotic men. He cites situational castration anxiety, birth fantasies, and the unconscious wish to be a girl as evidence of the impossibility of achieving the masculine ideal. He proposed that a boy's Oedipal desire to have intercourse with his mother was not based on gratification of sexual drives. Rather it is a safeguarding fantasy, a desire to elevate himself above the mother, to 'debase' her as expressed in a compensation strategy revealed in the 'desire to be on top.' This idea of masculine superiority, as a defence mechanism to ward off feelings of inferiority (interpreted as 'feminine'), implies that historically constructed power dynamics, including the power of parental authority, are deeper than biological sexuality. Adler contends that these power dynamics profoundly affect human psychology.

Following Adler's presentation, most in attendance expressed criticism and disapproval. Freud was particularly annoyed with Adler's use of new terminology. For example, the minutes record Freud's objection that these ideas constitute nothing new: 'Even our old friend bisexuality he calls "psychic hermaphroditism," as if it were something else' (p. 145). Commenting on Adler's recent publications, Freud concluded: 'Adler's writings are not a continuation upward, nor are they a foundation underneath; they are something else entirely. This is not Psychoanalysis' (p. 146). Adler's proposals were dismissed as a denial of the unconscious, a traitorous compromise of the sexual libido that Freud uncompromisingly exalted. In a later reflection on Adler's 'heresy,' Freud wrote to Jung in 1911: 'I now feel that I must avenge the offended goddess Libido and I mean to be more careful from now on ... I would never have expected a psychoanalyst to be so taken in by the ego' (as cited in Fiebert, 1997, p. 253).

Some of the criticisms levied against Adler's concept of the 'masculine protest' were warranted. The notion itself, though correctly identified as a feature of many neuroses, failed to foreground the importance of power that underlies any such protest and tended to reduce the analysis to stereotypical sex-role traits. Moreover, the masculine protest was conceptualized on the basis of the child's (m/f) immature value judgments, whereby all so-called masculine attributes were elevated as more powerful than feminine attributes. The child's perception of women, whom Adler saw as generally embodying constructions of femininity, conceptually demanded that they be seen as masculine whenever power and authority were exercised, as in punishment. Indeed, Kleinians have demonstrated that the *feminine* mother is frequently experienced as a power to be reckoned with; hence, the infamous splitting into the good and bad breast.

Another pervasive problem in Adler's subsequent theorizing on gender is that he tended to frame masculinity and femininity as synonymous with one's embodied sex and the normatively expected 'sex role' expected to flow from it. He proposed a fiction of gender and yet usually failed to apply this insight, frequently resorting to stereotypical moral judgments that privilege a sexed and gendered normativity. Picking up on Adler's mistaken tendency to slip into normative judgments, Jacoby (1975) retorts that 'psychoanalysis pulls the shrouds off the ideology of values, norms, and ethics which is the stuff of Adler and the post-Freudians' (p. 33). On the one hand, Adler's (1978) gaze, exemplified in discussion of non-normative gender presentations, did pathologize a child's revolt against expected sex-concordant gender roles. He expected boys to behave as boys and girls as girls, for them to conform to the social will insofar as gender was concerned. For transsexuals, the implication is that they cannot be allowed to belong to the other sex; for transgenderists, they cannot engage in fluidity or in-between-ness; and for both groups, clinical adjustment to comply with normativity must be prescribed. In supporting gender/sex normativity, he rather stunningly ignored his own caution: 'this apperception according to the masculine-feminine pattern, however, ... introduces a sexual jargon into the neuroses that should be regarded *symbolically*' (Adler, 2002/1927, p. 16; italics added).

Theoretically, the masculine protest was originally formulated as a universal concept to rival Freud's libido theory. Yet following his departure from the Freudians, Adler somewhat abandoned the concept, especially as a universal principle. When he did invoke the term, it was limited to a specific clinical dynamic found to underlie symptoms of sexual neuroses in women, such as the unconscious wish to become a man deciphered from their dreams and fantasies. In this more restricted sense, a masculine protest constitutes, perhaps, a seeming unconscious identification with the aggressor. Its deeper meaning, though, is a social one since it is symptomatically and symbolically a 'masculine protest' against patriarchy, spoken by the organ jargon of the body. Adler found evidence of this in various psychosexual disturbances like 'vaginismus' and 'sexual anaesthesia,' and in certain 'character disorders.'[10] In this regard, he can be credited with explicating the significance of gendered material in the aetiology of neurosis and developmental personality pathology.[11] These observations were verified in a contemporary (non-Adlerian) analysis of gender and psychopathology. Busfield (1996) argues that 'the linkages between gender and type of mental disorder are some of the most consistent findings of psychiatric epidemiology' (p. 15).

In discarding the universal masculine protest as the central driving force in *all* neuroses, Adler adopted a new universal and dynamic factor in neurosis: superiority striving as a compensatory mechanism for feelings of inferiority. This shift gave rise to Adler's most famous concepts, the *inferiority* and *superiority complexes*. In formulating these principles, Adler was influenced by Nietzsche's concept of the 'will to power,' especially in arguing for superiority striving (Lehrer, 1999). Adler (1956) explains it thus:

> We all wish to overcome difficulties. We all strive to reach a goal by the attainment of which we shall feel strong, superior, and complete ... this great line of activity – this struggle to rise from an inferior to a superior position, from defeat to victory, from below to above. It begins in earliest childhood and continues to the end of our lives. (P. 104)

This striving to overcome is synonymous with a universal striving for fictive and 'teleological' perfection, for example, in the desire to obtain a perfect body. In eating disorders, the complex becomes extreme – the individual must become 'perfectly thin'; or in the taking of anabolic steroids, the subject desires a very muscular physique combined with 'omnipotent power.' These guiding fictions are tyrannical; they can never be real-ized since the end consequences always undermine the subject and damage community. These perfectionist strivings may be revealed in the un/conscious private logic within the style of life. For example, in masculinity fictions, one might come upon the fictive goal of mastery, with associated themes such as absolute triumph, rule, and domination. Although such imperial goals are associated with men and masculinity, Adler did not want to read the replacement concepts of inferiority and superiority in exclusively gendered terms. Rather, he introduced a grand guiding principle evoked to 'rescue' humankind, which erased gender/sex difference. The grand ideal principle of *Gemeinschaftsgefühl* (community feeling) became the new pinnacle of his psychology, whereby social equality and the resolution of power imbalances would produce mentally healthy subjects.

Community Feeling: The Problem of Be/longing

Ansbacher (1999) has drawn attention to the significance of community feeling in Adlerian psychology. The term loosely connotes a *feeling* of belonging (an affective sense of social connection) under the guiding fiction of a perfect community. If such an ideal were realized, all would ostensibly feel spiritually at one with/in the universe. Community feeling entails a highly developed empathy towards other people, nature / the Earth, and a holistic 'oneness' with the cosmos. Community feeling is said to reflect a spiritual and metaphysical development in Adler's psychology, a partial turning away from Marx, retaining Marx's social idealism but rejecting his economics. Ansbacher (1999) translated the German *Gemeinschaftsgefühl* into the English 'social interest,' avoiding the Romanticism of the German conception by adopting a term better adapted to pragmatic and operational use.

Adler (1938), however, maintained that there is 'no reason to be afraid of metaphysics; it has had a great influence on human life and development. We are not blessed with the possession of absolute truth; on that account we are compelled to form theories for ourselves about our future, about the results of our actions, etc.' (pp. 275–6). However, the problem with the theory as it developed is that it ignores the prevalence of here-and-now fracture such as the perpetually divided subject that the Lacanians speak of. Moreover, the premise assumes that *all* human subjects strive for a utopia of the whole (common/unity). This is not so since there are those who live with and accept a sense of fracture, who do not concur with the necessity of 'oneness,' who fear being subsumed under a 'community' that makes difference disappear. Such a utopianism does not reflect the interests of those who do not seek mending or merging but the right to non-conform freely.

Social interest was subsequently developed by Adlerians in Anglo-American contexts as the pragmatic application of the striving towards an ideal community (such as emphasizing the social psychological conception of cooperation). It entails the ability to act co-operatively for the good of the community in a way that potentially transcends self-boundedness (*Ichgebundenheit*). It requires that one face the 'three great task complexes of life' (work, friendship, and love and intimacy) with courage and social responsibility (Adler, 1956), and is activated when one strives for the good of oneself within the context of creating a better community. This attitude, when developed, is perceived as a *sign* of mental health. The definition of mental health conflated with community feeling is a crucial issue in Adlerian theorizing. Unfortunately, an intemperate 'community feeling,' one that disallows dissent, could point to a new fiction of superiority that repudiates the subjectivity of others and forces them to conform. This is most strongly evidenced in Adler's writings on gender conformity, homosexuality, and criminality. In all three cases, he abandoned a constructivist position and slipped into reactionary judgments that were aligned with an ahistorical liberalism. In Adler's (1956) discourse, those who did not conform were condemned as 'moral failures' rather than symptomatic (in whole or in part) of historic injustice based on social exclusion, displacement, anomie, imperialism/colonialism, racism, class oppression, inability to integrate the Law of the Father, and so on.

In my interviews with transpeople, I repeatedly heard a subtext to reports and disclosures of transphobia and repudiation: perpetrators convey that transpeople do not belong either in their sex/gender presentation or in the communities in which they live. Gay men and lesbians who harass transpeople, or feminists who expel trans women from women-only spaces, signal their convictions that transpeople do not belong. Employers and co-workers who refuse to accept a transperson's decision to transition, or threaten and harass them on the job, transmit a message that they are unwelcome, that they do not belong. Children who harass and bully trans youth (or other gender outlaws) in schools convey an attitude that they do not belong, an attitude that I believe contributes to common experiences of alienation and ostracism. Hence, the issue of belonging, which Adlerians highlight in their theory of mental health, is paramount to transpeople. To what extent do transpeople belong, or want to belong? I shall return to this issue of belonging, as it is one that is not confined to transpeople but relates to postmodern conditions more broadly, as we shall see.

A Repudiating Gaze: Homosexuality and Gender Identity Disorders

What little exists in Adlerian writings on transpeople points to the dangers of a totalizing 'community feeling' and associated sense of 'belonging' as the 'measure' of mental health. Adlerians have failed to ask, 'Whose community?' (Shelley, 1998). Who decides the criteria for membership? Moreover, are those who are forced or choose not to 'belong' at fault? This problem is extremely relevant to the traditional pathologization of homosexuality and other sexual 'perversions' or 'deviancies.' Some Adlerians have written about gender incongruency as a problem that is rooted in a deeper, pathological homosexuality.[12] Dorothy Pevin (1996), for example, reiterates Adler's position:

> ... throughout history, whenever an increase has occurred in the emancipation of women (as in Greek culture), an increase also has occurred in homosexual trends. Adler believed that men, in an escape from feelings of insecurity, attempt to put distance between themselves and women; they take flight from females into exclusively male society. (P. 406)

The problem with the position is that it is superficially historical; Pevin fails to consider the construction of homosexuality as a medicalized deviance traced to sexological writings of the late nineteenth century. Moreover, there is no need to go all the way back to ancient Greece in order to discover patterns pertaining to same-sex love and the governing social ethos. The more recent colonial imposition of Western morality, one that pathologized same-sex relations in Indigenous communities, can provide us with more sober knowledge on the topic of claims to cultural superiority. The problem is not equality somehow producing homosexuality, but rather superiority and subjugation of all those considered 'savage,' 'bestial,' 'buggers,' and 'sodomites.' The elevation of heteronormativity and Eurocentric norms over other forms of sexual desire and eroticism has long been tied to the racial subjugation of non-white others, as Fanon (1967) and Hook (2006) have also pointed out. Furthermore, the theory, which claims that a rise in male homosexuality is a pathological outcome of women's liberation in the West, elides lesbianism and bisexuality but does infer these practices as likewise perverse. The paradox here is that women's liberation allows for women to choose their sexual partners, including the right to reject men in favour of female erotic love. Patriarchy has always been threatened by women's sexual autonomy, which is why some radical cultural feminists encourage women to adopt exclusive lesbian practice as a revolutionary strategy.

Pevin does not see 'gender identity disorders' as differing substantially from homosexuality; both are presented as psychopathological syndromes. In arguing her point, she ignores the fact that transpeople themselves hold a range of differing sexual orientations. The conflated thesis that gay men (and perhaps lesbians) are in 'flight' from the opposite sex, that they 'lack courage,' is a prejudice that rationalizes the still pervasive binaries and associated moral beliefs on the sole rightness of heterosexuality, and heteronormativity constituted as the rational foundation of the 'natural family.' This view is based on Adler's prevailing and contingent tradition, that is, early twentieth-century Western morality, not his core theory of gender/sex as constructed on the basis of both salient and potent fictions. It is also a view that erases Adler's early familiarity with Marxist texts, such as Friedrich Engels's (1972/1845) *The Origin of the Family, Private Property, and the State*, which argue that the structure of the family as a social unit is not natural, but historically determined.

Adler's dubious speculations on sex, gender, sexuality, and criminality were often grossly distorted by the rigid conformity of his time. In seeking to spread Individual Psychology amongst the masses, Adler (1930/1993, 1978) tapped into populist sentiments, encouraging lay understandings of his psychology, and many of his more than three hundred books and articles were intended for lay readers. He moralized freely on the 'cowardice' of those engaged in criminality, accepting that homosexual behaviour was a criminal offence, and failed to make arguments for the social construction of criminality that would have resonated with his prior constructivism. This is the price he paid for relinquishing too much to the 'ego,' at times in the name of class pragmatism, at other times to capture popular attention, a slippage from *sensus communis* into a problematic 'common-sense' (Jacoby, 1975).

The danger of an unthought 'community feeling' lies precisely in the repudiation of individual subjectivity and subjugation of those who challenge heteronormativity or other hegemonies. Under Adler's gaze, the repudiation of homosexuality, and by extension of transpeople, is part of a 'perfect community,' which everyone is supposed to belong to after they have been 'cured.' Without a consensual view of community there is no community, there is no 'belonging.'[13] Hence, psychopathology creates the idea of psychiatric and psychological rescue as a disguise for law enforcement and coercion. In a letter to Albert Einstein on the question Why war?[14] Freud commented that 'the only real difference lies in the fact that what prevails is no longer the violence of an individual, but that of community' (p. 275). Freud (1930/1985) held a basic mistrust of community since it requires a substantial amount of repression in order to function and is always the site of tension between Eros and Thanatos.

Sneja Gunew, in an interview with Yiu-nam Leung (2004), speaks of how postcolonial theory problematizes the idea of belonging in general. The diaspora of peoples around the world destabilizes the idea of belonging as an attachment to place or a community where all share the same values and lifestyle. While Adler's idealistic belonging strikes me as a worthy goal in many ways, one that I am loathe to abandon, I cannot fail to mention that the historical, political, and contextual dynamics that produce the yearning of be/longing often problematically disappear in his analysis. Under postmodern, globalized conditions, deep religious conflicts based on fundamentalisms that provide 'belonging' have further fractured communities and produced an increase in conflict. In painting a totalized, metaphysical view of community, Adler failed to foresee the pitfalls of masking difference, and reinforced the clinical gaze that diagnoses non-belonging as something to be cured. In this sense, I favour a reworking of Adlerian therapeutic practice similar to Gergen and Kaye's (1992) narrative therapy, deploying a hermeneutic approach that questions the positions of both therapist and client. This approach privileges dialogue and the negotiation of meaning to produce glimmers of truth, to work towards understanding and a 'healing' that does not entail suppression or denial of difference.

Holism is one of the principle epistemological tenets supporting Adler's notion of community feeling. The next and final chapter will take a more careful look at the positive and negative implications of holism. Before entering that debate, it is relevant to note some limited and perhaps previously unthought parallels between Adler's ideas and those of Julia Kristeva, a feminist post-Lacanian psychoanalyst usually perceived as having little in common with those associated with ego psychology.

Adler and Poststructuralism: Disputations of the Self and the Ego

Fuss (1989) credits Lacan for providing constructionism with some of its leading insights. In going beyond Lacan, others have introduced new ideas about subjectivity. As I have argued in this chapter, Adler was the first to provide a constructivist account in depth psychology, the first to move into the subject without recourse to a determinist-instinctual paradigm, and the first to take a constructivist approach (though hybridized through 'holism') to mind/body dualism. Unquestionably there are significant differences between Adler's psychology and poststructuralist discourses, since Adler died at the height of modernity, but to my mind some of his ideas moved in the same direction. Poststructural feminist theorists such as Fuss (ibid.), in her deconstructive discourse on essentialism, might even concur with limited aspects of Adler's later turn to metaphysics, since she concedes that 'we can never get beyond metaphysics' (p. 13). Fuss argues that the concept of constructivism itself develops out of a polarity with essentialism yet is actually reliant upon metaphysics in order to sustain its claims.

In focusing on Adler's early constructivist period, a number of parallels emerge between his insights and later poststructuralist arguments. Here I will draw attention to Adler's (1956) concept of *movement*, as parallel to Kristeva's introduction of the *subject in process / on trial (le sujet en procès)*. I will also offer an Adlerian interpretation of Kristeva's concept of *abjection*, a significant element for further understanding trans subjectivity and repudiation. It is notable that Adler and Kristeva resist a Cartesian dualism that posits a knowing subject separate from an unknowing body. Kristeva rejects the Western idea of an innate self, arguing that the birth of the human subject constitutes a 'violent separation' from the mother (Oliver, 1993). Human subjects begin by means of splitting, and the first split is from the maternal body. Later splits occur (such as the 'thetic split,' Kristeva's elaboration of Lacan's mirror phase), when subjects enter the process of identification. The overall emphasis for Kristeva, as for Lacan, is on the subject as a perpetually split subject. Although a trained psychoanalyst, Kristeva's intellectual roots are in linguistics and semiotic theory. Adler, in contrast, came to depth psychology through medicine, which he saw as both a healing art and science.

In disrupting the Cartesian dualism of mind and body, Kristeva turns to the maternal relationship as a means to explain and illustrate the subject in process. In French, this expression carries a double meaning: in process (movement, unfinished) and 'under legal duress' or on trial (McAfee, 2004, p. 30). The legislative aspect orders a relational dynamic between subject and other, and subjects are observed, coerced under 'the Law': Lacan's symbolic order, represented by the *'nom/non'* (name/no) of the Father. The mother, in contrast, is associated with the Imaginary order and what Kristeva calls the 'semiotic,' an on-going mode of less rational communication that coexists with the symbolic order of language and law. Oliver (1993) contends that the maternal body cannot, however, demarcate a clear distinction between subject and object. The process as trial points to the contextual and juridical elements that inscribe the rational, liberal self and its supposed unification, but for Kristeva (1997) this is never complete. Otherness not only surrounds us but is within us; we are strangers/aliens to and within our selves ('étrangers à nous-mêmes'). Not belonging is an essential characteristic of the postmodern condition and the globalized world, and something that could be embraced rather than 'cured.'

Perhaps an earlier recognition of stranger(s) within, Others in me, and the fundamental early splitting of the subject, may very well have been the motivation for the rise of the Adlerian fictive final goal and other unconscious fictions. Mythologies, such as belief in the rational, autonomous self, undoubtedly press for the adoption of a homogeneous self and identity. Kristeva challenges the possibility and desirability of anything approximating such a thing and uses feminist analyses (e.g., *herethics*) to undermine this ethical and juridical mythology, pointing out its negative effects on all who are othered by it. The Adlerian style of life, which is holistic in a field sense, could be prompted by early splits, such as from the maternal body, motivating in part a style of cohering which is not the same as being ontologically whole. In fact, in cases of psychopathology, the style of cohering, paradoxically, frequently incoheres.

Transpeople are subjects 'on trial' and subjects 'in process.' In TG subjectivities, with their emphasis on fluidity, crossing, and the impermanence of identity, the act of transiting (/m/f/) entails unstable identities and a refusal to belong in one category. Passing, in the case of TS ontology, is a test which some TS people (will) fail. This verdict is one that repudiates TS claims of belonging in one category. TG people, who may appear differently each time the jury convenes, also risk a derisive verdict of 'guilty by reason of insanity.' Both TS and TG people are deemed to be disturbed because they are too disturbing in a context that denies strangers/otherness in the self a place. Transpeople are potentially threatening to cherished fictions of sex/gender coherency and, whether they like it or not, challenge the fiction of the binary. Many people evidently are intolerant of the threats that transpeople pose to such deeply revered fictions and act (pass sentence / penalize) accordingly. All subjects follow fictions, which are meaningful to them, and subject to inter/intrapersonal defence.

Like Kristeva, Adler (1956) also contends that the subject is not a static, standard character: 'paltry typologies tell us nothing about the individual' (p. 196). In his conception, un/conscious dynamics are at play, governed by 'a law of movement ... without his understanding it or giving himself an account of it' (p. 195). *Movement* holds a pre-eminent position in Adler's psychology: 'the strongest step which Individual Psychology has taken ... we have always maintained that all is movement' (ibid., p. 195). This movement is not the rational unfolding of an intrinsic self since 'the individual is hardly ever able to state clearly where his way leads ... and he often states the contrary' (ibid., p. 195). On the level of interiority, Adler posits paradox as a common dynamic in subjectivity. Yet unlike Kristeva, Adler's 'movement' is not necessarily aimless, but pursues the fictive goal of overcoming the inferiority and indeterminacy of actual early fracture. The subject can 'heal,' but often strives to in mistaken ways. When mistaken or neurotic movement is apparent, this state of affairs can be altered. Adler (1998/1938) clearly states that 'everything can be something else as well' (p. 18). The fictive final goal may be experienced as a peculiar sense of fate; it may be transformed, or indeed overthrown, as in Kristeva's notion of psychotherapy as (potentially) revolutionary for the subject.

In chapter 2, I outlined the importance of Kristeva's concept of abjection to understanding trans repudiation, especially of a transphobic nature. Like the infant who vomits the mother's breast milk, expelling it as foreign to the tenuous self, repudiation of trans subjectivity likewise is a negation of the other, a refusal to accept, a projection of the abject incarnate. Abjection takes on the image of the retching of a body that wishes to expel what is harmful, what is dirty, sour, bacterial, a threat to the self, Other. As Kristeva (1982) writes, 'It is thus not lack of cleanliness or health that causes abjection but what disturbs identity, system, order. What does not respect borders, positions, rules' (p. 4). If one considers this alongside Adler's fictive final goal of overcoming defects and producing a utopian homogeneous/harmonious community, one might consider that trans repudiation is an (un)conscious attempt to protect this goal, to expel those who threaten the imago of a perfect community.

The abject hounds the subject and can never be fully expunged. Radical practices such as surgical sex reassignment aid transsexual subjects to live their lives in a body that is habitable. However, many transsexuals as 'subjects on trial' fail to pass and are rejected, thrown out, by others who consider them abject: they *are* hounded. In my interviews with transpeople, many transsexuals revealed traumatic events in their struggle to 'heal' the mis-sexed body. Otherness in the self and abjection by others complicate the striving for fictional goals (such as completion, harmony, rebirth). I maintain, however, that striving for fictions of a 'whole self' and for 'healing' is essential for those transsexuals traumatized by/as the abject. Both the *self*, based on a discourse that posits integration (which Adler favours), and the (permanently) fragmented *subject* (which Kristeva favours), pose a host of dissonant problems and hence require further analysis, the focus of the concluding chapter.

7 Conclusion: The Gendered and Trans/gendered Self

Trans Integrity / Trans Selfhood

In reflecting on the interviews conducted for this book as a whole, one particular impression stands out in counterbalance to the pain of repudiation. The notion of trans selfhood as a quest for *integrity* has struck my ear in ways that ring hopeful. In contradistinction to the psychiatric diagnosis of 'gender identity disorder,' with its implication that identification of gender requires an *order* to be imposed to produce mentally healthy individuals, I am impressed by transsexual people's narratives of their sense of, or desire for, *embodied* integrity. For TS people their identities are generally not out of order; rather, their bodies require interventions to heal the incongruity of having been mis-sexed. And for TG people, their seeming lack of an orderly identity constitutes, for them, an integrity and honesty to their own selves.

The tenuous and elusive nature of the self has long been a focus of debate: who gets to be a self, and what is the self subject to? Anti-foundationalist, poststructuralist theory, some of which draws on Foucault's thought, decries the idea of a holistic self for some very good reasons. Foucault (1984a) held a discursive interest in the topic of the self, a subject he viewed as more interesting than sex: 'I must confess that I am much more interested in problems about techniques of the self and things like that than sex ... sex is boring' (p. 340). Within the concept of the self, he found an effect of power, the self as *subject* (Latin: *subjectum*, that which is thrown under, derived from *sub* and *iaceo*).

For Foucault (1984a), the 'essence' of self is a matter of the historical and political subjugation of subjects. For transpeople, this issue is pertinent, since their selves are frequently subjugated, as I declared in the opening statement of this book. The matter of subjugation (exteriority) is important; however, so too is the subjective sense of selfhood (interiority). Transsexuals commonly cite the desire for a coherent and stable self as a basis for the necessity of healing the mis-sexed body. In contrast, transgenderists may privilege an indeterminate crossing, fluidity, and flux in ways that defy a fixed 'teleological' self. Yet I have uncovered no evidence that such multiplicity negates the importance of the self(selves) for TG people either. The gendered subject may never reach a final sense of being a man/woman, yet narratives of the self often include the avowed pursuit of such ideals.

In their sensitive and informative text that explains transsexualism to friends, families and co-workers of TS people, Brown and Rounsley (2003) inadvertently draw attention to the 'self' as a central philosophical problem in trans studies. The authors of this work do not critique the self; rather, they foreground it as crucial to TS subjects, as evidenced in the title of their book: *True Selves*. The idea of capital *T* 'true selves' poses numerous theoretical problems, in light of the discussion above. Nevertheless, in covering debates surrounding the self and the subject, I do not wish to trifle with the integrity of TS people's embodied claims. I acknowledge that many transsexuals believe SRS allows their 'true gendered self' to emerge, while shedding a false gendered self that was imposed upon them. Indeed, one of the central issues to emerge from my interviews with transsexuals entails a concept of self that differs from both the unproblematic liberal humanist 'knowing subject' and the permanently fractured poststructuralist subject. The phantom of the ideal self makes a tenuous appearance, as a 'whole' to be realized or conjured, to be brought into physical presence.

As discussed earlier, for many TS people it is a case of recognizing what is perceived as true, core identity (m/f) and making the body conform to it; whereas for some TGs, it is a struggle to escape from the rigid m/f binary and be recognized as something else. Perhaps for TGs it is a question of having multiple selves (or for Two-Spirit people, two spirits), or subject fragments within one body – yet not as in the clinical pattern of dissociative identity disorder, since the 'I' remains intact. For example, in working with a psychotherapy client who is TG, I have asked them to come to session on occasion in 'hir' alter identity (not as 'Giles' but cross-dressed as 'Gillian') in order to assist in integrating conflicts between the two sides. Speaking sepa-

rately to each subject revealed differing tastes and sexual orientations, and conflicts within the same person which produced disso-
nance and emotional distress, their primary motivation for coming to
therapy.

Prosser (1998) draws on the idea that 'narrative composes self' (p.
120) to critique what he perceives to be the poststructuralist view of
the self as only *a priori* or transcendental.[1] He demonstrates a plurality of meanings of 'self' and uses the idea of body-self integrity to
question some aspects of postmodern queer theory, asserting that
'the transsexual does not approach the body as an immaterial provi-
sional surround but, on the contrary, as the very "seat" of the self' (p.
67). For Prosser, the material body, an essential aspect of the transsexual self, is often held in a (pre-SRS) sexed abeyance, in a state of
'bodily alienation' (p. 68). For him, the refusal of the ego to claim
ownership over its corporeal terrain, perceived as the 'wrong body'
(p. 85), is more than sufficient reason to justify transsexual claims
for SRS, which ideally leads to 'attaining that feeling of a coherent
and integral body of one's own' (p. 80). Surgery is an instrument to
heal the body, 'integrating its lost parts' (p. 83). Morphological integration brings about a 'completion' of bodily image that 'reveals
sex as quite real, quite embodied' (p. 92). SRS permanently abjects
what both hounds and is foreign to the sexed and gendered self.
Prosser wants to make the body feel like 'a home' (Prosser, 1998, p.
59), a place/space in which transsexuals may be/long. The narrati-
zation of bodily alienation predicates the necessity of SRS. That
transsexuals must become expert narrators of their autobiographical
history of corporeal distress and mis-sexed trauma leads Prosser to
conclude that 'narrative has an explicitly cohering function. Like
surgery, autobiography heals the splits in plot into a transsexual
identity' (p. 121).

Not all transpeople agree with Prosser's idea of the desirability of a
fixed and gendered home. Noble (2004b), for example, argues for his
transgendered state of paradox: 'I'm a guy who is half lesbian' (p. 26).
He articulates the self as a subject who is 'engendered, racialized,
sexed, nationed, classed, etc.' (p. 23). Reading the complexities of intersectionality usually leads to recognition of a multiplicity of identities
that may never cohere. However, as a stage in Western philosophy,
postmodernism and poststructuralism must be careful not to impose a
universal theory of fragmentation (Dews, 1987). Herdt (1997) reminds
us of non-Western conceptions of ontology that celebrate wholeness

and integrity: 'Western sexuality in the modern period has come to exclude areas of ontology so critical and pervasive elsewhere across time and space: concepts of the whole person that incorporate spirit, mind, and social relations' (p. 276). Poststructuralism's rejection of the singular self produced by humanism and the Enlightenment tends to ignore a multiplicity of meanings that can be given to the embodied self. By an exclusive focus on language, the material body as *felt* tends to be under-recognized and under-theorized.

Postmodern and poststructuralist theorists tend to dispute the Western concept of the autonomous and coherent self as an historical creation, a 'technology of the self' in the Foucauldian sense that exists to answer to the power of ruling institutions (Dreyfus and Rabinow, 1982). Foucault argues that such a self arose in the thirteenth century as an effect issued by order of the Catholic Church. The requirement of *confession* served as a tool of institutional surveillance, calling individuals to account for their inner sinfulness, to be their own reflective judge, and disclose their sins to the authorities. In contemporary society, the confession continues to operate through the Law, psychiatry, psychology, and psychotherapy. As Danziger (1997) remarks, however, 'once the self is conceptualised as an entity that observes, evaluates, and controls itself, it is, in principle, a divided entity, unlike the soul, whose indivisibility was of the essence' (p. 147). Soul, mind, and body, observer and observed – the self-conscious subject was actually already divided.

Feminist theorists such as Lather (1991) remind us that the Western self is marked by Cartesian dualism, an ontological split between subject and object, mind and body. This split solidified the observing, thinking self as masculinist, to the degree that women were denied selfhood, relegated to the status of body/Other (de Beauvoir, 1952/1989). The only selfhood available to women was based on being socialized into a subordinate and self-denying role constructed under patriarchal control. For these and other reasons, some feminists such as Finke (1997) prefer the Lacanian understanding of the 'subject,' arguing that it 'more fully captures the sense of subjection, of the self's fashioning by its insertion into an already articulated symbolic economy' (p. 125). Such a self is not 'pre-existent' but results from the discursive and semiotic practices of patriarchy within and against which the gendered self fashions its "identity"' (ibid., p. 124). Others, such as liberal feminists, seek equality for women within the prevailing status quo, demanding for women equal access to a self within the institutions that were (until recently) the exclusive province of men: the forum, the academy, and the marketplace. Liberalism permits women to celebrate a self that is conflated as both instrumental (exploited) and free or exercising agency in the existential sense (Brown, 2003).

Postmodern and poststructural discourses tend to see the self as something other than an identity that one can possess, reify, and subsequently measure. Even as the speaking subject of language, the self is spoken by language, and is therefore its effect. In contrast, liberal humanism, in the guise of liberal feminism, seeks an equal female self to the 'pre-existent' male self, a self that can be weighed against his, and its valuation and representation in terms of asymmetry reformed towards an ideal of institutionalized equality. Materialist, liberal, and humanist discourses acknowledge that the self *exists* as both a discrete and tangible thing, yet is often oppressed, politically subject to the ruling relations derived from political categories of subjugation (patriarchy, imperialism, colonialism, capitalism).

McAdams (1997) proposes that the self is not necessarily unified as was thought in the past. Rather, the self has the task of creating a temporal coherence out of a multitude of experiences. McAdams refers to this process as *selfing*, entailing the task of integration and synthesis. Hence the 'I' will make sense of varying 'me's' over time. McAdams's ideas are comparable to Kristeva's concept of the subject in process. Selfing is an ongoing motion, a 'movement' in the Adlerian sense. As applied to transsexuals, 'selfing' attempts to resolve the embodied discord of having been mis-sexed into a more coherent self. To pursue SRS takes tremendous ego strength, and courage is required to both face and correct an otherwise chronically dissonant existence. Repression of the knowledge of having been mis-sexed might bring more harm to the subject than pursuing SRS. To reduce such a complex situation to issues of identity encourages pathologization of a choice that is based both on physical conviction and reasonable assessment of the gains and risks.

In favouring the concept of the self, especially for transsexuals, I do not wish to detract from the transgender activism of the 1990s that sought to deconstruct ideas of a shared and unified transgender experience, 'of decentring and disrupting identity' (Broad, 2002, p. 244). Rather, it is to address a stunning observation by Califia (2003):

> Not a single recognized authority on this issue has said that transgendered people have intrinsic value and worth, or something important to

contribute to the rest of us and our understanding of what it means to be human. Benjamin, Green, and Money would have absolutely no ethical problem with genetically engineering transsexuals out of existence. (P. 81)

It is within the context of psychology and psychiatry's reductive focus on 'identity as disorder,' as evident in the clinical diagnosis of GID, that Califia's criticism is so important. Without considering the possibility of the integrating function of the self (which may never reach its fictional goals such as 'total integration'), psychiatry and psychology lose a fundamental appreciation for the richness of transpeople's interiority and strivings. By reducing the self to an aberrant gender identity, the integrity of the person is lost. In evolutionary psychology there is no self, only an identity that expresses a genetic flaw. In GID more broadly there is no self, only a reductive focus on an identity that is 'abnormal.' What transsexuals, and perhaps some transgendered people, seem to express is the desire for the right to be whole. Since the self is posited as having an integrating function, *holism* as a concept merits closer analysis.

The Holistic Self: Problems in Holism

Lacan's idea of the *fragmented body* (*le corps morcelé*, the 'body in pieces') (Macey, 2000, p. 136) captures the sense of incompleteness or incoherence of the mis-sexed body. An (un)conscious sense of fragmentation may motivate the self to strive towards an integrity, synthesis, or 'holism' that cannot be attained and yet, for many, constitutes a very meaningful journey, the quest to be whole. The premise of a holistically striving self is crucial to schools of depth psychology such as Jung's and Adler's. Jan C. Smuts (1926), prime minister of South Africa in the pre-apartheid years, coined the term 'holism' and made the self a fundamental constituent of the phenomenon. In so doing, he declared that 'our very foundation and constitution, self of our very selves, it is yet the great mystery, the most elusive phantom in the whole range of knowledge' (p. 263). A constructivist synthesis of holism, such as Adler's, transforms Smuts's holistic self from an essentialist concept to something else, perhaps still in keeping with Smuts's curious and contradictory positing of the self as phantom, the self as selves that cannot be pinned down.

With the chronic fracturing of an untended incongruity, woundedness often prevails. Many people cannot subjectively tolerate fracture and seek to heal psychologically from deep divisions. Postmodernism and poststructuralism are pessimistic towards the idea of wholes, integration, and unity. As Dews (1987) puts it, in his critical assessment of these discourses, they prefer 'the logic of disintegration,' which leads to fragmentation (p. 269). Yet even those who practise deconstruction, such as Rose (1986), understand that this comes with limits: 'reifying the idea of a pure fragmentation would be as futile as it would be psychically unmanageable for the subject' (p. 15). She continues with the contention that 'feminism needs access to an integrated subjectivity more than its demise' (p. 15). In this sense, Rose does not relinquish, however, her strenuous objections to an idealization of wholeness. Elliot and Roen (1998) also criticize an ideal of wholeness though recognize that this ideal is what motivates many transpeople. They cite the statements of trans activist Leslie Feinberg who,

> ... writes about the connections between sexual identities and gender identities, arguing that they are aspects of a person's identity that are 'tightly braided' together ... she articulates her transgender politics as being about fighting for her '*right to be whole*.' (P. 241; italics added)

This brings us back to the idea of selfhood. Rose draws attention to the need for an integrated subject, and Feinberg to her right to be whole. In psychodynamic psychology, identity ultimately becomes a defensive manoeuvre based on projection and identification as defence mechanisms. Hird (2003) discusses Freud's papers 'Mourning and Melancholia' (1917) and 'Analysis Terminable and Interminable' (1937), summarizing his conclusions that identification is never complete and is often both traumatic and mired in resistance. Anna Freud (1966/1936) extends her father's discussion by noting the similarity and closeness between the mechanisms of introjection and identification, in her chapter entitled 'Identification with the Aggressor.' She sees such identification as a part of superego formation (the moral seat of the mind), as identification defends against paranoiac fear of the castrating or otherwise punishing parental object. My contention is that the issue of identity, while very important, is insufficient to achieve the ideal wholeness that Feinberg speaks of. There must be something more that integrates an identity that is not pre-existent but complexly acquired. Perhaps this 'something more' is what Jung (1957) referred to when discussing the archetype of the Self with its overriding transcendence of fragmentation and its spiritual concern with integration. Holism, on the contrary, is related to healing. Post-modern and poststructural discourses dismantle the whole to reveal fractures, incongruencies, splits, and absences. To heal means to make whole; it is a force with directionality, and the goal of healing is to repair painful fracture(s).

Smuts's (1926) philosophical ideas on holism filtered into Anglo-American psychology after having been endorsed by Alfred Adler, the Gestalt therapy school (Fritz and Laura Perls), and the influential psychiatrist Adolf Meyer (1951) in the early to mid twentieth century (Shelley, 2004, 2008). The holism of that period was disdainful towards the predominant reductionism espoused in science. However, holism as expressed in medicine and psychiatry produces some difficult problems. In his historical analysis of German physicians from 1890 to 1930, Hau (2000) notes that a 'synthetic gaze' based upon an intuitive holism was considered 'the hallmark of a superior physician' (p. 495). This gaze of the cultivated, educated, and hence bourgeois male physician carried forward a Romantic aesthetic. Hau argues that it became the basis of the unthought imposition of this class of men, 'the *Bildungsbürger* [who] could truly judge whether a person was normal, healthy, and beautiful' (p. 495). This aesthetic holism is associated with a specifically male gaze. The authorial male eye projects its Romanticism by equating the corporeal/body to a work of art. An ocular-centric sensibility to proper and eternal pro-portions captures forms in terms of an 'absolute norm of beauty' (p. 504). The holistic physician, a declared expert in natural science, dis-dains the reductive (and Kraepelian)[2] approach. Rather, *he* needs to adopt an artistic and holistic gaze so as to 'reveal eternal truths' (ibid., p. 512) and increase his sense of mastery. This masculinist gaze reflected a holism that decentred others: 'women and the unculti-vated were neither capable of creating great and timeless works of art nor capable of practising the art of medicine' (ibid., p. 524). In early twentieth-century Germany, holism in psychology was taken up most forcefully by the *Ganzheitspsychologie*. This school was subsequently appropriated by the Nazis, who rhetorically deployed fictions of a naturalistic unification and racist metaphors of 'blood and soil.' Holism came to justify racial exclusion (by those who 'naturally belong') and subsequent genocidal practices (to expel/extinguish aliens/others), to elevate the 'natural superiority' of certain races in a grotesque attempt at 'purification.' Hence, the grave danger of essentialist holism is that it leads to an idea of the total, to totalitarianism (Shelley, 2008).

Smuts's philosophy of the essence of wholes was opposed to the Nazi appropriation. Adolf Meyer tried to open an institute of holism in Germany, which Smuts cautioned against. As Smuts's biographer, Hancock (1968), recounts,

> Smuts told [Meyer] the idea was premature. Yet he soon found out that Germans could do worse things to his ideas than bury them in an Institute. 'Ganzheit-Theorie,' as some Nazi writers were expounding it, shocked him. He thought it a monstrous parody of everything he believed in – 'a queer compound of Holism, romanticism, racialism, ethics and religion ... a ruthless scrapping of ideas and methods which we consider part of the moral and political heritage of the human race.' (Pp. 300–1)

In his analysis, Smuts (1926) did not properly consider the dangers of holism and could only comprehend the Nazis' 'appropriation' of holism as 'queer.' Meyer, inspired by Smuts, became a monumental figure in the institutionalization of academic and clinical psychiatry: 'the Dean of American psychiatry' (Neill, 1980, p. 460). While Meyer's holism does not dominate psychiatry, it remains an important thread that he theorized in his psychiatric school of *psychobiology* (which should not be confused with the reductive school of biopsychology). His holistic epistemology may be relevant to Namaste's (2000) ethnographic account of a male psychiatrist at a gender identity clinic, in which she describes this particular psychiatrist's method of differentiating 'real' from 'pseudo' MtF transsexuals. A 'real' trans woman appeals to his aesthetic and erotic sensibilities, eliciting a 'natural' and feminine stimulation of the heterosexual male body, by sexually inciting the male psychiatrist's gaze. She does not offend his eye but elicits desire in an ocular feast – she stirs his loins. The psychiatrist Paul McHugh (2004) is offended by those MtFs with 'large hands, prominent Adam's apples, and thick facial features,' whom he sees as constituting an 'incongruous' form that is not 'persuasive' to a psychiatrist's 'superior judgement' (p. 2). Such trans women cannot possibly, in his judgment/verdict, be 'real women.' This type of holistic gaze is not limited to a masculinist repudiation. As we have already seen, it is also used by some radical cultural feminists who deploy a similar essentialist and repudiating gaze to pass the judgment/verdict (Law of the Father) that trans women are not 'whole' women (Greer, 1999). In spite of such damaging effects in its application in psychiatry and other spheres, holism, when reconfigured as a useful fiction (Slavik, 2006), seems to me a fundamentally salvageable construct. It is certainly imperative to the health sciences and healing practices such as psychotherapy – and for those psychiatrists who do more than simply diagnose and prescribe pharmaceuticals, crucial to them too.

The issue of the 'real,' in the sense of material embodiment, and the sense of having a self that is split (identity/body) can lead to repression and denial. In my interviews with John and Trevor, the self as a sense of real embodiment surfaced. John described his former life as a fundamentalist Christian and how that doctrine factored into his initial repression of his trans self:

> ... fundamentalist religion does not help you to develop your own sense of who you are. It's all about Jesus and forgetting yourself – you're regularly taught certain verses in the Bible along the lines of 'Don't trust yourself; you are too sick and sinful to trust your own thoughts.'

At the time of our interview, I recall feeling struck by John's summary and its consistency with the historically challenging and contradictory meanings of the self. The earliest reference to the term in the English language (circa 1300) declares, 'Oure awn self we sal deny, And folow oure lord god al-mighty' (as cited in Danziger, 1997, p. 143), to which the period of Lent in the Christian calendar pertains (emphasizing self-sacrifice through fasting, etc.). Throughout the ensuing seven hundred years, the contradictions between the self as sinful and the self as an object to be both known and esteemed (Socrates instructed us to 'know thyself') have been carried forward through the forces of historical tradition (Gadamer, 1960). Currently, we are instructed to indulge the self, to be a consumer, yet we are also, in a maddening contest, at times required to deny the self. The paradox is that periods of having been 'denied' motivate the (ir)rationale to consume, whether or not such depravation was real or fictional (e.g., predicated on genuine material poverty; or compensation for a fictive final goal such as 'I am undeserving ... therefore I deserve ... ' or 'I have been deprived of ... therefore I must have ... ').

For John, the genuine pain and trauma of incongruity compelled him to solidify his self. He could only achieve this by shedding those repressive dogmas that prevented this, so that he could 'bloom inside,' to heal the self (see interview with John, chapter 5). His turn away from self-denial allowed him to become, to be. And for him, to be denied the opportunity to be the man who he is in a whole sense would constitute true depravation.

Zimmerman (1981) suggests that 'to be a self in the most suitable way is to be wholly open to those possibilities which are uniquely one's own' (p. 31). For John, it is not the shedding of his skin, as if he were revealing the finished and final self within, that allows for his self to bloom. He does not declare a frozen internal male to be released, an *a priori* existing figure, the David within the marble. Rather, he sees his journey as one of growth, of becoming, an ongoing process. He altered his body to achieve a sense of 'wholeness,' to seek congruency between the material, social, and spiritual selves (James, 1890/1955). Narratives such as John's persuade me that there is something 'real' laced into the social and historical production of sexed and gendered bodies.

Foucault's (1984a) *care of the self* does not engender a quest for locating the true core of one's self. But this should not be seen as an argument against those who happen to do just that: locating their own otherness as something real, and taking care of it through acceptance, affirmation, integration, and transformation. A phenomenological sense of embodiment, inclusive of its perceived limitations, is powerfully 'real' to human subjects. The material or embodied self is more than socially constructed performativity. The flesh-and-blood body, as a body that is lived in, in a daily/nightly sense, retains prime importance for those transpeople who aspire towards sex/gender congruity. In my interview with Trevor, the issue of the body surfaced in the context of discussing performativity (which we tentatively aligned with 'gender') versus 'real' (or sexed) embodiment. Trevor made his position clear:

> Chris: So basically you do see (pre-SRS) anatomy as some kind of a limitation. Is that a self-imposed limitation or reflecting something 'real'?
> Trevor: Real. You know it's interesting how much I tell myself and what's actually out there like using urinals, using locker rooms, it's how far and how close to the edge can I go and still be safe. Can I really hang out on the beach and be safe, do I feel totally safe on the beach wearing next to nothing?
> Chris: So it's like a fear of being found out?

Trevor: Yes, but at the same time I forget, I'm living my life and I forget until I get into a set of circumstances and then I think oh – I'd better be a little more careful here ... I'm a man out in the world, and I don't think twice about it, I am and I'm just being there. I mean all those years I lived trying to be a woman, I never took off, I was always aware of having to project femaleness, and now I don't have to project maleness, I just am. I'm just myself.

Chris: You don't have to construct anything?

Trevor: I don't have to construct a thing. I mean nobody ever rushes up to me and says, 'You're not an adequate man,' and I'm not thinking that anyway. Only once in a while does it surface, like I'll think, what if this person really knew? And then I think: really knew what? Anyway, I'm here and I am myself.

Trevor's and John's narratives hinge on the idea of selfhood, the 'I' constructing the 'am' in attempts to cohere the identity(ies) of 'me.' In their conceptualizations, they have become what they believe they are – they have allowed their true selves to emerge. In an Adlerian sense, they have followed their fictions and 'real-ized' them. In having done so, material alterations of the flesh-and-blood body have solidified in the form of a liveable body. The ideals of the self have dramatically actualized in their quests to 'become,' as subjects in process. In pursuing their goals, they have overcome previous inner restrictions that imposed limitations on their lives.

'Changing sex' is a controversial act; hence, the widespread phenomenon of trans repudiation. Coming out to oneself and then to others as 'trans' is often a difficult process posing its own unique set of barriers. The stigma attached to gender transgression, which has its source in the political and social context and is not intrinsic to the self, is something that many transpeople need to untangle and overcome, even before they embark on transition: they face their own shame, guilt, and self-imposed prohibitions – their own internalized oppression.

Self-Oppression: Internalizing the Gaze of Repudiation

A disturbing aspect to emerge from my interviews with transpeople is evidence of trans self-repudiation. As a feminist psychotherapist, I kept an ear open for any distress revealed as a result of living life under the auspices of ruling relations / Law of the Father. Domination also has internalized consequences, and transpeople frequently, but not universally, evidence these through their reflexive accounts. Past instances of self-harm or other patterns of emotional, mental, or interpersonal difficulty were mentioned in many of the interviews. These difficulties were attributed to coping with life under the weight of a social order that largely repudiates trans subjectivity.

In the following interview extracts, the colloquial term 'transphobia' is utilized to refer to the problem of having internalized the gaze of repudiation. Alex acknowledged his internalized struggles:

> Something that is not an external barrier but for me is an internal barrier is internalized transphobia. Trying to work on stuff so I feel okay about being trans ... like I have some role models now but that certainly has not been the case all my life, so dealing with internalized transphobia and keeping on trying to feel okay about things is a huge issue and probably for me the more pressing issue than external incidences. Because the internal stuff is much more of a daily issue – a constant issue.

Hank offered his experience of the kind of self-oppression he continues to face, because of his fear of being 'found-out':

> I think there's always the fear of discovery, if you're not out and you can pass. That's often when people get murdered – is on the discovery of your trans-ness. When people find out, they tend to get really, really angry, so I think that fear of discovery limits your ability to fully interact with the world because you have to keep something ... There's a trust issue where you have to keep your back up at all times, to be watchful.

The self-oppression, the fear of discovery, that Hank spoke of was echoed by Keenan. As a queer trans man, Keenan fears how other gay men will react towards him:

> I fear being rejected, that I'm not good enough. There is a lot of internalized stuff too. I am afraid of being in gay male spaces. Once when I was at a gay bar, in the bathroom a man put his hand on my chest and it really freaked me out. I don't know the rules in gay male culture, like is anyone allowed to touch you in a gay bar? Can you touch anyone you want? I just don't know what to do in gay male spaces. Even going into the men's washroom, I don't know how to stand at a urinal. So, if I am at a gay bar and someone seems interested in me, I get scared. I bring a lot of baggage

with me in there ... I don't think that gay men are even aware that trans men go into gay bars.

Internalizing the gaze of repudiation creates a self-policing carefulness, a vigilance to avoid discovery. The (un)known rules that are produced under binary conditions create, in Keenan's case, an anxiety of breaching these rules. The (un)conscious comforts that most natal male-bodied people take for granted, such as using a urinal, are initially missing in perhaps most trans men. The need to repress such anxiety, to mimic conventions as closely as possible, adds a layer of psychic stress to trans men that is missing in other marginalized groups, such as gay men.

Prior to her transition, Roz revealed a history of self-oppression through strategies of denial. She explained the types of compensatory behaviour that she employed: 'I became -aholic – I was a work-aholic, I was a student-aholic, I was a study-aholic, I was a jog-aholic, I was a fitness-aholic.' Such intense overcompensations allowed Roz to cope for a time, but as strategies, in the end, they were untenable.

Aiyanna also disclosed her coping strategy in the years that she tried to live as a man, a period she had earlier referred to as 'living the lie':

Aiyanna: The years of abuse of alcohol, drugs, other things had taken their toll – by the age of 38/9 if I didn't make a major change, I was going to die ... that was my self-suicide.
Chris: And that was the way you were self-medicating for living 'the lie' and hiding?
Aiyanna: For all of those things.
Chris: And you had to make a choice then?
Aiyanna: It was life, simple as that.

Aiyanna made a choice to live, to be who she is, a woman, and to cease living life as a man, the latter an inauthentic, dangerous existence. Her previous strategy of denial, of self-medicating the pain of living in a mis-sexed body, could not continue. Like the push of Thanatos, living 'the lie' leads to death. Emerging to heal, Aiyanna identified the sources of her oppression:

Society's obstacles and restrictions and shit eventually take a toll psychologically and emotionally and debilitates you to where you do become physically and mentally ill ... it's an external force, it's a social force that's applied, that's the disabling factor.

Hence, the problem of the interior/exterior dynamic. For transpeople, trying to hide – to repress or force the interior realm of identity to conform to the external world – simply fails, in the long term, as a strategy. Indeed, there are complex feelings of guilt and shame that accompany attempts to repress trans-ness. As Kimberly elaborated:

It's much, much different growing up as a boy being treated as a boy compared to growing up as a girl being treated as a boy. Keeping the secret can just tear you apart inside, and having to perform to other people's expectations and be the person that they expected you to be, was very difficult. Very uncomfortable and very painful. For me, I had one blessing that I somehow knew that this was the way it was meant to be and I just accepted it in myself. Otherwise I would have gone down another road, either not been here anymore or other ramifications ... That didn't happen with me because I just accepted it within myself, but I felt, initially, a lot of guilt and shame.

Kimberly's disclosure of risking 'not being here anymore' points to SRS as a life-saving procedure for transsexuals. Her experience of trying to conceal her 'secret' reveals the trauma of repression and the negative effects of an internalized gaze that judges harshly and produces shame. The tyranny of normativity, and the sad examples of what happens to those who openly defy it, further reveal the threats, coerciveness, and consequences that incite self-oppression and self-repudiation. Aiyanna recalled what had happened to her sister in the 1950s upon her family's discovery that she was a lesbian, which frightened Aiyanna into self-repression of her trans-ness:

Aiyanna: I knew my older sister was a dyke, she was a butch. When my parents locked her up the first time, she was sixteen – I would have been fourteen/fifteen – and it scared me into silence. It was only a couple of years after I knew about Christine Jorgensen and it absolutely scared me into silence. They will lock you up for being too weird. That's the message that I got, though it certainly wasn't talked about ... that's what they did in the 50s, 60s, 70s to young women who professed love for other women. That's what they did to my sister, and they said it was

because of her 'promiscuity' but it wasn't – it was because of her choice
of partners.
Chris: Did this force you to keep yourself a secret, and conform on the
surface to what they expected you to be?
Aiyanna: Absolutely.

The gravity of self-oppression in the lived experiences of transpeople cannot be underestimated. Asked what were the worst barriers,
Trevor expanded:

> It's the internal ones. And certainly that whole struggle with my feminist
> perspective. It was a huge struggle. I mean at some point I had read
> Janice Raymond [anti-trans feminist], I had gone through a phase where
> I was reading everything.

In this instance, Trevor speaks of the conflicts between his feminist
consciousness and how radical cultural feminist rejection of trans-
embodied claims creates internal conflict for some pre-transition transpeople. Resolving these internal conflicts is imperative for those transsexuals who need to address the mis-sexed body and retain allegiance
to feminist aims of the emancipation of marginalized groups. For
Trevor, transitioning did not require a rejection of feminism more
broadly, but a recognition that this particular feminist position is, on
the issue of transpeople, quite mistaken.

Yossi reminded us that these issues are not just an internalized
barrier, the internal struggles of transpeople, but can also be the basis
for transpeople oppressing other transpeople: 'Often transpeople have
huge amounts of internalized transphobia ... Transpeople can be very,
very mean to each other.'

The issue of self-oppression in transpeople is a serious one. One is
reminded of the recognition of the problem in previous struggles for
liberation, as in gay liberation. The manifesto of the London Gay Liberation Front states: 'The ultimate success of all forms of oppression is
our self-oppression' (as cited in Hodges and Hutter, 1979, p. 1). Self-
oppression in transpeople underscores the need to continue to push
for their right, not just to a non-pathological subjectivity, but also to
selfhood. If self incorporates the idea of striving for a fictional whole,
for 'healing,' then it incorporates the right to be free from self-oppression. The repudiation of trans subjectivity and selfhood divides trans-

people internally, divides trans communities, and divides transpeople as a social group from other marginalized groups. The ubiquity of ruling binaries spares few, if anyone.

Drawing attention to 'self-oppression' can provoke legitimate criticisms. In her critique of 'gay affirmative psychotherapy,' Celia Kitzinger (1999; Peel and Kitzinger, 2005) contends that the concept of 'self-oppression' shifts the responsibility from the oppressor to the oppressed, delegating to the oppressed the sole responsibility for overcoming their internalized barriers and traumas. For Kitzinger, psychotherapy and self-help groups mitigate the necessity for fighting political sources that create this oppression in the first place. She suggests that 'therapy' siphons off the necessary rage needed for organized, radical transformation of society. Therapy draws 'self-oppressed' lesbians and gays into liberal/humanist-based 'solutions' that individualize the problem of oppression.

Kitzinger's criticism has merit but sets up an either/or conundrum that places gays and lesbians, and also transpeople, in a double bind. Many pre-transition transpeople are deeply traumatized, conflicted in such a way that their very survival is threatened, often by potential suicide. Many transpeople may very well need to prioritize their mental health over activism, as they may not be able to manage both at once. This is why allies are so important for the political struggles that marginalized people face. Without allies, the full burden of inciting social change would rest solely with transpeople. I believe that Kitzinger's stance, as applied to transpeople, imposes an unreasonable burden on them. Moreover, not all transpeople want to be activists.

The aim for those pre-transition transpeople who have difficulty accepting their trans-ness is to overcome their self-oppression, to heal psychologically so as to live a life that is resilient and authentic. In focusing on psychotherapeutic strategies for therapists working with these clients, St Claire (1999) contends that they must accept their split-off identity, one that is often mired in shame, and reclaim it from the Jungian archetype of the Shadow.[3] In doing this, 'the false gendered ego-identity dies,' to be replaced by an authentically integrated 'gendered persona' (p. 5). The process is not, in her experience, an easy or comfortable one. She argues that for transsexuals 'the journey from self-hatred and paralytic fear, through death, transformation, and rebirth is daunting' (p. 8). As a Jungian, St Claire favours an ideal of 'the whole,' of integration and completeness. This psychic integration mitigates and inoculates against dangerous potentialities in pre-transition transsexuals, such as suicide. She believes that for these individuals to heal, they must accept and affirmatively endorse their selves by developing an integrated identity, enabling them to 'establish a functioning transgendered persona by which the person can meaningfully live with others in an authentic life' (p. 3).

Conclusion: The Enigma of Self-Estrangement

In summary, the 'self' is a contestable concept. Poststructuralists, in their favouring of the 'subject,' correctly draw attention to the uncertainty that the concept of the self poses. However, a rethinking of the self as both multiple and more than identity, containing an 'I' and 'me's,' allows the self to re-emerge as a useful fiction that speaks to the integrating function as expressed in 'holism.' Transsexuals especially, seeking to correct their mis-sexed bodies, often adopt a discourse of the 'right to be whole.' Concepts such as 'selfing,' 'movement,' and 'subject in process' all allow for a multiplicity that accounts for the complexity of trans lives. This complexity is evidenced not only by external social barriers, where the trans self is always in process and on trial, but also by internal ones that impede self-acceptance.

The intricate intersections of interiority and exteriority that challenge transpeople's everyday/night lives surface in this book through hermeneutic dialogue. The eradication of trans repudiation requires an end to unwarranted institutionalized oppression, which is also the ultimate source of internalized oppression. The shift away from a pathological 'gender identity disorder' moves the location of gender 'symptoms' from the individual as the aberrant source to the social world as the correct origin of unnecessary harm. Until the eradication of trans repudiation occurs, transpeople may very well need fictions of healing, to recover from trauma that is not intrinsic to them, so that they may – like most of the rest of us – be accepted and valued as (them)selves. So long as trans repudiation prevails, transpeople remain foreigners, and 'the foreigner has no self' but is 'constantly other' (Kristeva, 1997, p. 270). As Others, the strange(rs) become the screens upon which unwanted reactions/projections are hurled; they are targeted as the 'phobogenic object.'

Freud refers to an aspect of this interpersonal dynamic using the German term *unheimlich*, which Kristeva (1997) translates as 'uncanny strangeness,' representing the strange as encountered through projection, what is not recognized as 'my ("own and proper") unconscious' (p. 283). As Tim Dean (2001) points out, 'it is not the recognizable other but the unrecognizable Other ... that most urgently calls for an ethical attitude' (p. 131). In confronting the phobogenic object, perpetrators of trans repudiation have their fear/desire stirred up. In fearful reactions, the archaic aspects of the narcissistic self are provoked to abject, to throw out of the self what is deemed dangerous, alien 'uncanny and demonical' (ibid., p. 283). It is the return of the repressed that provokes this self-estrangement. Whether it is pre-transition transpeople who may try to vanquish their 'secret' through repression but cannot abject it, or their attackers whose gender certainty is challenged, an anguish is provoked by the 'weird ... by death ... an untouchable universe ... the strange within us' (ibid., p. 289). Transpeople often unknowingly provoke a response to the *unheimlich*, rattling perpetrators' deepest gender fictions, in an encounter that may affectively flood their 'ego' with feelings that transpeople are '"too good" or "too bad"' (ibid., p. 287), in a manner akin to the Adlerian inferiority/superiority dynamic, a consequence of the lack of equality: they are fascinating/desirable, they trans-fix the gaze, and they become an object of fear/dread. This is the essence of the phobogenic object, whether expressed in xenophobia, homophobia, transphobia, fear of the dis/abled, or misogyny.

The self intersects the interior and the social-exterior, where selves are read through role identification, institutional inscription, and attempts at social coherence. Transpeople may (un)consciously utilize the idea of selfhood as a means to guide healing of the mis-sexed or mis-gendered body. Whether transpeople need a 'self' or not, the right to selfhood includes, I contend, the right to retain or reject it. An appreciation of difference, regardless of debates surrounding the 'self,' requires acceptance with acknowledgment that other people, too, no matter how different they may seem, ought to be constituted as subjects in their own right.

Trans repudiation, whether through utterance, erasure, gaze, spectacle, alienation, phobia, sexual objectification, or violence, requires the solidarity of others to eradicate it. The lessons of depth psychology, moreover, speak to the necessity of reconciling the 'stranger within' so that we may better know our own shadow, account for our own fears, and contain the potential spilling-out of noxious fragments that do not belong on the skin of others. Gadamer's hermeneutics speaks of dialogue, of conversation, interpretation, and understanding as a means to better comprehend one's own and others' 'truths.' If transpeople disrupt our fixed sense of the order of things, this may actually be perceived and received as a positive event, rather than as something that arouses fear and loathing. Transpeople have something profound to teach us, yet unless we take down our defences we may not hear them and hence miss something that would benefit our own self-understanding. Feminism speaks of gender justice and often strategizes through solidarity to challenge barriers and advance the rights of women. As a broad spectrum of discourses, feminism has much to offer to transpeople in terms of experience and expertise in facing seemingly insurmountable barriers.

In a book that focuses on the negative aspects of repudiation as it pertains to the interiority (intrapersonal) and exteriority (interpersonal/institutional) of trans subjects, I am wary that an impression of victimization may linger, paradoxically curtailing the agency of these subjects. Transpeople's activism on the local and international levels (the latter especially facilitated through the Internet) clearly demonstrates the exertion of their social agency. They are not necessarily or only the passive recipients of repudiation, transphobia, and social exclusion. Rather, from the inception of the availability of SRS to the formation of groups that provide social space to advocate for crossdressing and the rights of TG people, transpeople have a long and active history of coming together to advance their rights. On the local level in Vancouver and the Lower Mainland of BC, groups such as the Cornbury Society, the Zenith Foundation, the Trans Women Dialogue Committee, the BC FtM Network, the annual Trans Day of Remembrance, and others have worked tirelessly to provide assistance, support, and advocacy for transpeople in ways that clearly exert their agency. Moreover, the demise of the gender clinic at the Vancouver Hospital (a program cancelled due to neo-liberal austerity cuts) has given rise to a unique trans-run health referral and support program (Transgender Health Program) funded by Vancouver Coastal Health. This program, located at the Three Bridges Health Centre, recognizes and advocates for the essential medical needs of this group.

Transgendered people, in a tentative umbrella sense, challenge many of the deepest convictions that a pervasive and naturalistic common-sense discourse holds dear. That many feminists, queer, dis/ability, anti-racist, and anti-psychiatry activists, critical psychologists, and social theorists are now paying attention to the rumblings below suggests that the ground may be about to shift, especially if we pay attention to trans challenges and their convictions. The narratives shared in this book point to the necessity of a deep shift. These narratives are, for me, a beginning and not an end, as the quest for understanding, undoing estrangement, and concrete social change continues, in struggle and in solidarity.

Notes

1. Introduction: Transpeople and the Problem of Re/Action

1 Pfäfflin's review of follow-up literature spanning thirty years found that 1–1.5 per cent of MtFs regret surgically transitioning, while the incidence/incidents of FtM regret is less than 1 per cent.

2 Critics of sex assignment surgery for intersex babies acknowledge the medical necessity to proceed with surgery when serious health risks are evident for the infant/child. These instances are, however, rare (Preves, 2002).

3 The majority of intersex babies are surgically assigned/sexed to conform to the female genital form (Preves, 2002).

4 Preves (2002) notes that Western medical standards codify acceptable clitoral size as between 0–0.9 centimetres. Any 'phalloclit' larger than 0.9 centimetres 'is considered ... unacceptable by Western clitoral standards,' requiring surgery to 'recede' or 'trim [it] back' (p. 530). Normative codification for an acceptable penis requires a minimum measurement of 2.5 centimetres.

5 Psychoanalytic thinkers such as Jean Laplanche (1996) dispute the compatibility of psychoanalysis and hermeneutics. Indeed, Laplanche's essay on the topic is titled 'Psychoanalysis as Anti-hermeneutics.'

6 Namaste (2005) overlooks the significant influence that French poststructuralist theory has had on Anglo uses of 'transgender' within queer theory. Without the underlying influence of several French theorists, philosophers, and psychoanalysts, it is doubtful that an anglophone writer such as Judith Butler (1990, 1993, 2004) could have produced her well-known analyses.

7 LGBTTQQI = lesbian–gay–bisexual–trans–Two-Spirit–queer–questioning–intersex.

8 In Namaste's otherwise impeccably drawn arguments, the term 'erasure' seems somewhat problematic. Erasure assumes that TS people had a diachronic presence that was taken away (erased). In the West, this has never been the case, though it certainly was for the Two-Spirit subjects and their violent and colonial domination by British and French imperialists.

9 Notable examples of trans autobiography include works by Christine Jorgensen (1967), Mario Martino (1977), Rene Richards (1983), Jan Morris (1986), Leslie Feinberg (1993), and Erica Rutherford (1993).

2. Repudiation and Transphobia: Concepts, Theory, and Experience

1 As recently as 1998 the term 'transgender' was not yet a part of the Oxford dictionary.

2 In reproducing the Oxford dictionary definition of 'trans,' I have omitted sub-definitions numbers 6a and 6b since they relate specifically to 'trans' as used in chemistry and physics.

3 Although the phrase 'Law of the Father' has terminological specificity in Lacanian discourse, my usage pertains to the general internalized conception of the superego as one that has *patriarchal* roots/implications in a *feminist* sense. My utilization of the phrase should not be confused with its more commonly known meaning in Lacanian scholarship.

4 Namaste (2005) defines imperialism thus: '(1) economic practices outside the United States that are destined to benefit the interests of American business ... (2) to designate the imposition of a particular world view and conceptual framework across nations, languages, and cultures' (p. 103). In the Canadian context, Namaste cites the early twentieth-century feminists Nellie McClung and Emily Murphy, arguing that they were racists who entwined women's rights with the project of British imperialism and empire building.

5 In the United States, Steinberg (2005) notes that the trans panic defence has been successfully used by perpetrators and their counsel to mitigate punishment of their crimes. This was not the case in the Gwen Araujo murder; two of the defendants were found guilty of second degree murder on 13 September 2005 (a successful 'trans panic' mitigation would have produced a judgment of manslaughter) (Marshall, 2005). However, the prosecution had unsuccessfully sought conviction for first degree murder and confirmation of the hate crime status with which the perpetrators were initially charged.

6 SIN = social insurance number.
7 What was known as 'hysteria' has been reconfigured in diagnostic rubric as 'conversion disorder' (APA, 2000).

3. Social Repudiation

1 The Harry Benjamin International Gender Dysphoria Association (HBIGDA) first drafted standards of care and protocol for the administration of hormones and SRS in 1979. These standards are widely applied at gender clinics and recommend the controversial *real life test*, requiring applicants for SRS to live in their desired sex full-time for one to two years (depending on jurisdiction) (see Israel and Tarver, 1997, for a comprehensive discussion).
2 Some questions that demand answers surface for those who are categorically shut out of the public health system in Canada: How many transpeople have been coerced into the sex or pornography trades to finance the treatments they require to heal the mis-sexed body? How many transpeople have subsequently contracted HIV/AIDS as a result of systematic repudiations? Namaste (2000) reports that levels of HIV seroprevalence, especially among trans women, are 'astronomical' (p. 237).
3 In neighbouring, conservative Alberta, phalloplasty is publicly insurable as a medical procedure for qualifying provincially resident FtMs. British Columbians who travel to Alberta for these procedures must, however, pay the full cost of the procedure themselves (between $40–50,000).
4 This example, of an Alzheimer's patient able to know and not-know at the same time, seems to be consistent with Adler's (1956) contention that the unconscious is 'present' in the conscious. In this sense, the unconscious dimensions can aid, for a time, even those with serious degenerative diseases of the brain.
5 The problems that younger transpeople face in primary school are poignantly dramatized in the French film *Ma Vie en Rose* (Berliner and Scotia, 1997).

4. The Political Repudiations of Trans Subjectivity

1 Conservatives sometimes rely on evolutionary principles when it suits their aims (e.g., conceptions of breeding, pedigree, etc.), especially in light of their broad rejection of evolution in favour of 'intelligent design.'
2 Second-wave feminism is not limited to radical cultural or radical libertarian variants. It also includes Marxist, socialist, and anarchist feminist threads.

3 Radical cultural feminist organizations such as Vancouver Rape Relief
  have, however, taken such criticism seriously. For example, they have
  a strong non-white representation in their membership cadre, which is
  certainly due to outreach efforts in communities such as the South-
  Asian-Canadian. These are laudable efforts, and they ought to be com-
  mended.
4 The acronym R.E.A.L. signifies Real Women's political standpoint: 'Real-
  istic, Equal, Active, for Life.'
5 I maintain that most queer people are in a less vulnerable position than
  are transpeople. At the same time, the matter is complicated by the fact
  that many non-queer transpeople are nevertheless misread as queer.

5. Talking Back: Historicizing the Repudiation of Transsexualism

1 Recently, this problem appears to have improved with more support and
  information sites appearing at the top of the Internet search results, while
  pornography sites begin to appear two to three search pages down. That
  the word *sex* appears within the search word 'trans*sex*ual' no doubt contributes to the pornography sites yielded.
2 Ringo (2002) suggests that the media provoke three general effects on
  pre-transition trans men (trans status as initially unconscious/repressed):
  '(1) Formative awareness: A respondent became aware of a gendered
  aspect or aspects of himself that eventually became a basis for his gender
  identity or identities; (2) Sudden awakening: A respondent experienced a
  comprehensive change in his understanding of his gender within a short
  period of time; (3) Gradual awakening: a respondent experienced a
  change in his understanding of his gender over an extended period of
  time' (p. 17).
3 Chiland (2005) argues that Freud's use of bisexuality is confusing and
  that 'it would be better were we to use a neologism such as "bisexua-
  tion," [or] "bi-sexed" disposition' (p. 49).
4 Important alternate discussions of Kimberly Nixon's legal case against
  Vancouver Rape Relief have appeared in Elliot (2004b), Namaste (2005),
  and Scott-Dixon (2006). Vancouver Rape Relief's website also provides
  their own perspective on the dispute: www.rapereliefshelter.bc.ca/
5 The specific *DSM*-IV-TR diagnostic code numbers pertaining to gender
  identity disorder (GID) are the following: 302.6 = GID in children; 302.85
  = GID in adulthood; and 302.6 = GID-NOS ('not otherwise specified'),
  where some IS and TG people are categorized.
6 Nietzsche is popularly considered to be a philosopher, yet his self-
  declared position was that of a psychologist: 'Ich bin ein Psychologe' (as

cited in Golomb, 1999, p. 1). In his later period, Nietzsche repeatedly emphasized his identity as a psychologist, remarkably defining himself as one 'without peer or precedent ... unlike those clumsy [empirical] "English psychologists"' (Conway, 1999, p. 51). His position was at times provocative, as when he claimed that 'there was no psychology at all before me' (ibid., p. 51). Unsurprisingly, Anglo-American psychology rejects Nietzsche's claim, as evidenced in texts tracing the historical development of the discipline that generally elide all references to Nietzsche. Indeed, Nietzsche was certainly not a psychologist as conventionally understood, not an experimentalist, a clinician, a pedagogic scientist, a lover of measurement, or a statistical analyst. However, his influence on psychodynamic depth psychology, in contrast to empirical psychology, was profound. It was Nietzsche who first posited a 'depth psychology,' a precursor to the development of the later psychodynamic psychologies of Freud, Adler, and Jung, who were all familiar with his writings.

7 St Claire's (1999) Jungian position, which affirms transpeople and their need for healing, is encapsulated in the following summary: pre-transition transpeople may hold adverse internalized feelings, placing them at risk of 'paralytic fear' leading to self-destructive behaviours, including suicide. She contends that (1) the trans self/soul is independent of culture; (2) the trans self manifests regardless of the Western sex/gender binary system; (3) transpeople inevitably come into conflict with the binary; (4) trans children are at risk of learning that gender transgression is 'bad,' which may facilitate repression through forms of splitting and relegation of split-off material into the 'shadow'; (5) a false gender identity takes the place of the split-off identity, functioning to hide one's trans-ness from others *and* oneself; (6) a 'transphobia complex' forms that can produce self-deprecation; and (7) the transgendered self must integrate its split-off parts in order to heal, to reclaim it from the shadow. In doing this, 'the false gendered ego-identity dies,' to be replaced through an authentically integrated 'gendered persona' (p. 5). The process is not, in St Claire's experience, an easy or comfortable one. She argues that 'the journey from self-hatred and paralytic fear, through death, transformation, and re-birth is daunting' (p. 8).

6. Adlerian Theory

1 The German title of Adler's first monograph is translated as *Health Book for the Tailor Trade*.

2 Adler was characterized as 'the socialist' in Wilhelm Stekel's sketch of the original Wednesday Society members.

3 In Heinz and Rowena Ansbachers's otherwise excellent systematization of Adler's writings, their conflation of self/soul is problematic.

4 Orthodox Adlerians reject Freudian metapsychology, including the notion of ego, in favour of the self and the style of life, which, in a field sense, includes the un/conscious.

5 *Mise en abîme*: A term from heraldry (the design of shields) introduced by French writer André Gide to evoke a story within a story, or the reflection of the creative process within a work of art. In French the phrase means: 'placing into the abyss' or 'placing into infinity.' It literally implies an anti-foundationalist nihilism *ad infinitum* as when used as a device in photography (e.g., the 'Droste Effect' after a famous Dutch advert for Cocoa, an effect easily invoked by the use of two mirrors reflecting into each other). Alternatively, my use of the term is consistent with the meaning of the concept in the humanities, the narrative aspect of stories-within-stories that are not necessarily nihilistic.

6 It was common practice for Adler to take a generally accepted psychoanalytic concept and rename it. The unconscious is a case in point. At various points in time, Adler referred to the unconscious as the 'not understood,' 'unawareness,' and the 'non-conscious.' His habit of renaming psychoanalytic concepts is clearly related to the animosity he developed towards Freud but also reflected his desire to reframe these concepts within his own theoretical understanding of the psyche.

7 One could, however, counter that such individuals would be better able to facilitate social change with their symptoms under control: an agoraphobic individual, for instance, would probably be of little use to revolutionaries.

8 Adler's view of phenomenology differs from Edmond Hüsserl's discourse, since the latter focuses on 'pure' descriptions of consciousness through mind/body dualism (Bowie, 2003). In contrast, Adler's 'phenomenological' discourse maintains that the body is still present, including its gendered/sexed aspects; it speaks.

9 In a letter to Jung (2 February 1910) Freud writes: 'Adler promises a paper on psychosexual hermaphroditism which will probably be rich in substance' (as cited in Fiebert, 1997, p. 246). A definite shift in attitude emerges in a letter Freud wrote to Ferenczi (25 February 1910) expressing disappointment in Adler's presentation, describing the thesis of psychic hermaphroditism in mocking tones as 'packed with will-of-the-wisps' (as cited in Fiebert, 1997, p. 246).

10 The 'character disorders,' non-adaptive patterns of personality which Adler conflated in his profile of 'the neurotic,' are contemporarily

referred to within various clusters of 'personality disorders' (see APA, 2000).

11 One need only peruse the diagnostic criteria for personality disorders (e.g., the 'antisocial' or 'narcissistic' personality disorders in men or the 'histrionic' and 'dependent' personality disorders in women) to see that the criteria are heavily gendered. Psychiatric epidemiology cites sex ratio prevalence rates that consistently predominate in one group or the other (APA, 2000). Luce Irigaray (2002) exploits this division in her account of the discourse of psychiatric patients, *Parler n'est jamais neutre* (to speak is never neutral/neutered).

12 Adler was ambiguous about homosexuality and homosexuals, often writing about them in pathological terms, yet at other times instructing professionals, such as those who consulted him for supervision in the 1930s, to basically leave them alone (Manaster et al., 1977). We are reminded that virtually all mental health and medical professionals in the early twentieth century held the view that homosexuality constituted a mental disorder/illness.

13 My critical comments on the concept of belonging, posed as an Adlerian, are not intended to detract from the significance of *a feeling of belonging*, which in many cases relates to states of mental health. The former tells us that people 'have a proper place,' with which I disagree; whereas the latter speaks to fellowship and social connection, the opposite of alienation and estrangement.

14 Freud's letter to Einstein, 'Why War?' (*Warum Krieg?*), was published posthumously in 1957.

7. The Gendered and Trans/gendered Self

1 By emphasizing language, poststructuralists usually agree that the 'self' is a narrative. This is a point that Prosser (1998) overlooks in his critique.

2 Emil Kraepelin (1856–1926), influential German psychiatrist.

3 In touching on Jungian *analytical psychology*, I shall steer clear of the debates surrounding contrasexuality (the popular Anima/Animus archetypes) and mention instead two particularly useful concepts for understanding trans repudiation: the *shadow* and the *persona*. The shadow, which is an 'archetypal tendency' said to be present in the human subject from birth, makes its appearance solely through projection. Jung claims that of all the archetypes, the shadow is actually the most accessible, representing moral problems that challenge the whole ego-personality. In dealing with shadow manifestations, an emotional reaction is elicited that

evinces 'dark characteristics' (CW9ii, 1951, para. 14). Transpeople become
the screens on which others project their own unconscious gender doubts
or failings. Others, including effeminate queer men, butch dykes, and
other gender outlaws will also, according to the Jungian scheme, be in
danger of having to carry unwanted projections. Yet, it is not and never
has been the gender outlaws who are 'the problem.' People may feel so
threatened by their own projections that they act in irrational ways
towards the (phobogenic) object of their contempt/fear. Repudiation of
those perceived to have failed is a projective outcome of the defensive
need to disengage from what we, as a political culture, (unknowingly)
create. Transpeople are *forced* to carry psychic burdens as a result of
unwarranted projections of inadequacy and primordial fears of loss of
sexual organs, or that the body will fall to pieces.

References

Adler, A. (1956). *The individual psychology of Alfred Adler*. H.L. Ansbacher and R.R. Ansbacher (eds.). New York: Harper Torchbooks.

– (1978). *Co-operation between the sexes: Writings on women and men, love and marriage, and sexuality*. H. Ansbacher and R. Ansbacher (eds.). New York: Anchor Books.

– (1993). *Das Problem der Homosexualität und sexueller Perversionen: Erotisches Training und erotischer Rückzug*. Frankfurt am Main: Fischer, Taschenbuch, Verlag. (Originally published 1930.)

– (1998). *Social interest: Adler's key to the meaning of life*. C. Brett (trans.). Oxford: Oneworld. (Originally published 1938.)

– (2002). *The neurotic character: Fundamentals of individual psychology and psychotherapy*. H.T. Stein (ed.). C. Koen (trans.). Classical Adlerian Translation Project. San Francisco: Alfred Adler Institute. (Originally published 1927.)

Ahmed, S. (2004). *The cultural politics of emotion*. London: Routledge.

American Psychiatric Association. (2000). *Diagnostic and statistical manual of mental disorders*. 4th ed. Text revision. Washington, DC: American Psychiatric Association.

Ansbacher, H.L. (1965). Sensus privatus versus sensus communis. *Journal of Individual Psychology* 21(1): 506–9.

– (1999). Alfred Adler's concepts of community feeling and social interest and the relevance of community feeling for old age. In P. Prina, C. Shelley, and C. Thompson (eds.). *Adlerian yearbook 1999*, pp. 5–19. London: ASIIP.

Bailey, J.M. (2003). *The man who would be Queen: The science of gender-bending and transsexualism*. Washington, DC: Joseph Henry Press.

Barrows, K. (2002). *Envy: Ideas in psychoanalysis*. Cambridge: Icon Books.

Batty, D. (2004). Mistaken identity. *Manchester Guardian*, 31 July. Retrieved 31 July 2004 from: http://society.guardian.co.uk/health/story/0.7890.1273045.00html

Berger, J. (1997). Trauma and literary theory. *Contemporary Literature* 3: 569–82.

Berliner, A. (director), and C. Scotia (producer). (1997). *Ma vie en rose.* [Motion picture.] France.

Billings, D.B., and T. Urban. (1982). The socio-medical construction of transsexualism: An interpretation and critique. *Social Problems* 29(3): 266–82.

Blackwood, E. (1997). Native American genders and sexualities: Beyond anthropological models and misrepresentations. In S.E. Jacobs, W. Thomas, and S. Lang (eds.). *Two-Spirit people: Native American gender identity, sexuality, and spirituality,* pp. 284–94. Chicago: University of Illinois Press.

Bly, R. (1990). *Iron John: A book about men.* New York: Addison-Wesley.

Bottome, P. (1957). *Alfred Adler: A portrait from life.* New York: Vanguard Press.

Bowie, A. (2003). *Introduction to German philosophy: From Kant to Habermas.* Cambridge: Polity.

Boyd, N. (2004). *Big sister: How extreme feminism has betrayed the fight for sexual equality.* Vancouver: Greystone Books.

Broad, K.L. (2002). GLB+T?: Gender/sexuality movements and transgender collective identity (de)constructions. *International Journal of Sexuality and Gender Studies* 7(4): 241–64.

Brown, L.B. (1997). Women and men, not-men and not-women, lesbians and gays: American Indian gender style alternatives. In L.B. Brown (ed.). *Two Spirit people: American Indian lesbian and gay men,* pp. 5–20. Binghamton, NY: Hayworth Press.

Brown, L.S. (2003). *The politics of individualism: Liberalism, liberal feminism, and anarchism.* 2nd ed. Montreal: Black Rose Books.

Brown, M.L., and C.A. Rounsley. (2003). *True selves: Understanding transsexualism – for families, friends, coworkers, and helping professionals.* New York: Jossy-Bass.

Bullough, V. (1994). *Science in the bedroom: A history of sex research.* New York: Basic Books.

Burnham, C.W.G. (1999). *Analysis and commentary: Transsexual/transgendered needs assessment survey (1998) report.* Vancouver: GC Services.

Busfield, J. (1996). *Men, women and madness: Understanding gender and mental disorder.* London: Macmillan Press.

Butler, J. (1990). *Gender trouble: Feminism and the subversion of identity.* London: Routledge.

– (1993). *Bodies that matter: On the discursive limits of 'sex.'* London: Routledge.

– (2004). *Undoing gender.* London: Routledge.

Cadello, J. P. (1999). *Psychology as the 'great hunt.'* In J. Golomb, W. Santaniello, and R. Lehrer (eds.). *Nietzsche and depth psychology*, pp. 23–36. Albany, NY: State University of New York Press.

Califia, P. (2003). *Sex changes: Transgender politics*. 2nd ed. San Francisco: Cleis Press.

Campbell, A., and S. Muncer. (1995). Men and the meaning of violence. In J. Archer (ed.). *Male violence*, pp. 332–51. London: Routledge.

Carrigan, T., B. Connell, and J. Lee. (1987). Hard and heavy: Toward a new sociology of masculinity. In M. Kaufman (ed.). *Beyond patriarchy: Essays by men on pleasure, power and change*, pp. 139–92. Toronto: Oxford University Press.

Cartwright, D. (2002). *Psychoanalysis, violence and rage-type murder*. New York: Brunner-Routledge.

Chase, C. (2000). Intersex activism, feminism and psychology: Opening a dialogue on theory, research and practice. *Feminism and Psychology* 10(1): 117–32.

– (2002). Affronting reason. In J. Nestle, C. Howell, and R. Wilchins (eds.). *Gender queer: Voices from beyond the sexual binary*, pp. 204–19. Los Angeles: Alyson Books.

Chiland, C. (2005). *Exploring transsexualism*. D. Alcorn (trans.). London: Karnac Books. (Originally published in French [2003]: *Le transsexualisme*.)

Collier, R.M. (1964). A figure-ground model replacing the conscious-unconscious dichotomy. *Journal of Individual Psychology* 20(1): 3–16.

Connell, R.W. (1995). *Masculinities*. Cambridge: Polity Press.

Conway, D.W. (1999). The birth of the soul: Toward a psychology of decadence. In J. Golomb, W. Santaniello, and R. Lehrer (eds.). *Nietzsche and depth psychology*, pp. 51–72. Albany, NY: State University of New York Press.

Cromwell, J. (1997). Traditions of gender diversity and sexualities: A female-to-male transgendered perspective. In S.E. Jacobs, W. Thomas, and S. Lang (eds.). *Two-Spirit people: Native American gender identity, sexuality, and spirituality*, pp. 119–42. Chicago: University of Illinois Press.

Currie, D.H. (1999). *Girl talk: Adolescent magazines and their readers*. Toronto: University of Toronto Press.

Danziger, K. (1997). Historical formation of selves. In R.D. Ashmore and L. Jussim (eds.). *Self and identity: Fundamental issues*, pp. 137–59. Oxford: Oxford University Press.

Darke, J., and A. Cope. (2002). *Trans inclusion policy manual: For women's organizations*. Vancouver: Trans Alliance Society.

Datler, W. (1999). Adler's ambiguity about the concept of the dynamic unconscious and the identity of individual psychology. In P. Prina, C. Shelley, and C. Thompson (eds.). *Adlerian yearbook 1999*, pp. 20–44. London: ASIIP.

Dean, T. (2001). Homosexuality and the problem of otherness. In T. Dean and C. Lane (eds.). *Homosexuality and psychoanalysis*, pp. 120–43. Chicago: University of Chicago Press.

de Beauvoir, S. (1989). *The second sex*. New York: Vintage. (Originally published 1952.)

Demara, B. (2004). Transsexual ex-cop claims shoddy treatment. *Toronto Star*, 16 July. Retrieved 18 July 2004 from: http://www.thestar.com

Denny, D. (1998). Introduction. In D. Denny (ed.). *Current concepts in transgender identity*, pp. ix–xx. New York: Garland Publishing Co.

Devor, H.[A]. (1997). *FTM: Female-to-male transsexuals in society*. Bloomington, IN: Indiana University Press.

Dews, P. (1987). *Logics of disintegration: Post-structuralist thought and the claims of critical theory*. London: Verso.

Dreikurs, R. (1973). The private logic. In H. Mosak (ed.). *Alfred Adler's influence on psychology today*, pp. 19–31. Park Ridge, NJ: Noyes Press.

Dreyfus, H.L., and P. Rabinow. (1982). *Michel Foucault: Beyond structuralism and hermeneutics*. London: Harvester Wheatsheaf.

Edwards, E. (2003). In the supreme court of British Columbia: Vancouver Rape Relief v. Nixon et al. [The Honourable Chief Justice Mr E.R.A. Edwards]

Ehrenwald, J. (ed.) (1991). *The history of psychotherapy*. London: Jason Aronson Inc.

Ellenberger, H.F. (1970). *The discovery of the unconscious: The history and evolution of dynamic psychiatry*. London: Penguin Press.

Elliot, P. (2004a). What's that smell? Bailey, backlash, and the 'science' of transsexuality. Paper presented at Resolutions, and ruptures: Sexual and gender diversity and the spaces in-between, UBC, Vancouver, BC, 7 March 2004.

– (2004b). Who gets to be a woman? Feminist politics and the question of trans-inclusion. *Atlantis: A Women's Studies Journal* 29(1): 13–20.

Elliot, P., and K. Roen. (1998). Transgenderism and the question of embodiment: Promising queer politics? *GLQ: A Journal of Lesbian and Gay Studies* 4(2): 231–61.

Elshtain, J.B. (1981). *Public man, private woman*. Princeton, NJ: Princeton University Press.

Engels, F. (1972). *The origins of the family, private property, and the state*. New York: International Publishers. (Originally published 1845.)

Fanon, F. (1967). *Black skin, white masks*. C.L. Markmann (trans.). New York: Grove Press.

Fathi, N. (2004). As repression lifts, more Iranians change their sex. *New York Times* (on-line newspaper). Retrieved 2 August 2004 from: http://www.nytimes.com/2004/08/02/international/middleeast/02iran.html?ex=1092 41483

Fausto-Sterling, A. (2003). The five sexes: Why male and female are not enough. In S. LaFont (ed.). *Constructing sexualities: Readings in sexuality, gender, and culture*, pp. 166–71. Upper Saddle River, NJ: Prentice Hall.

Feinberg, L. (1993). *Stone butch blues: A novel*. New York: Firebrand.

Ferguson, A. (1984). Sex war: The debate between radical and libertarian feminists. *Signs: Journal of Women in Culture and Society* 10(1): 106–12.

Fiebert, M.S. (1997). In and out of Freud's shadow: A chronology of Adler's relationship with Freud. *Individual Psychology* 53(3): 241–69.

findlay, b. [*sic*] (2003). Real women: Kimberly Nixon v Vancouver Rape Relief. *UBC Law Review* 36(1): 1–31.

Finke, L. (1997). Knowledge as bait: Feminism, voice, and the pedagogical unconscious. In S. Todd (ed.). *Learning desire: Perspectives on pedagogy, culture and the unsaid*, pp. 117–40. London: Routledge.

Firestone, S. (1972). *The dialectic of sex*. London: Paladin.

Foucault, M. (1978). *The history of sexuality: An introduction*. Vol.1. New York: Vintage Books.

– (1984a). *The care of the self: The history of sexuality III*. R. Hurley (trans.). Harmondsworth, UK: Penguin.

– (1984b). *The Foucault reader*. P. Rabinow (ed.). New York: Pantheon Books.

French, M. (1985). *Beyond power: On women, men and morals*. New York: Summit Books.

Freud, A. (1966). *The writings of Anna Freud: The ego and the mechanisms of defense*. Vol. 2. Rev. ed. Madison, CT: International Universities Press. (Originally published 1936.)

Freud, S. (1905). *Three essays on the theory of sexuality*. Standard ed. London: Hogarth.

– (1915). Instincts and their vicissitudes. In *Standard edition of the complete psychological works of Sigmund Freud*, vol. 14, pp. 117–37. London: Hogarth.

– (1925). *Some psychical consequences of the anatomical distinction between the sexes*. Standard ed. London: Hogarth.

– (1933). *New introductory lectures on psychoanalysis*. London: Hogarth.

– (1957). Why war? In J. Riviere (trans.). *Collected papers*, vol. 5, pp. 197–215. London: Hogarth.

– (1985). *Civilisation and its discontents*. London: Hogarth Press and Institute of Psychoanalysis. (Originally published 1930.)

Frosh, S. (1994). *Sexual difference: Masculinity and psychoanalysis.* London: Routledge.

Fuss, D. (1989). *Essentially speaking: Feminism, nature and difference.* London: Routledge.

Gadamer, H.G. (1960). *Truth and method.* J. Weinsheimer and D. Marshall (trans.). New York: Continuum.

Gallagher, S. (1992). *Hermeneutics and education.* Albany, NY: State University of New York Press.

Gergen, K.J., and J. Kaye. (1992). Beyond narrative in negotiating meaning. In S. McNamee and K.J. Gerger (eds.). *Therapy as social construction,* pp. 166–85. London: Sage.

Gilligan, C. (1982). *In a different voice.* Cambridge, MA: Harvard University Press.

Goffman, E. (1963). *Stigma.* Englewood Cliffs, NJ: Prentice-Hall.

Goldberg, J. (2002). *Trans people in the criminal justice system: A guide for criminal justice personnel.* Vancouver, BC: Trans Alliance Society.

Goldstein, R. (2002). *Homocons: The rise of the gay right.* London: Verso.

Golomb, J. (1999). *Introductory essay: Nietzsche's new psychology.* In J. Golomb, W. Santaniello, and R. Lehrer (eds.). *Nietzsche and depth psychology,* pp. 1–22. Albany, NY: State University of New York Press.

Goodwin, B. (1998). *Using political ideas.* 4th ed. New York: John Wiley and Sons.

Gooren, L.J.G. (1993). Concepts and methods of biomedical research into homosexuality and transsexualism. *Journal of Psychology and Human Sexuality* 6(1): 5–21.

Gorten, D. (1987). Gestalt therapy: The historical influences on F.S. Perls. *Gestalt Theory* 9(1): 28–39.

Greer, G. (1999). *The whole woman.* London: Transworld publishers.

Griffith, J. (2006). Adler's organ jargon. In S. Slavik and J. Carlson (eds.). *Readings in the theory of individual psychology,* pp. 83–92. New York: Routledge.

Guettel, C. (1974). *Marxism and feminism.* Toronto: Women's Press.

Hainsworth, J. (2005). Rape relief wins again. *Xtra West* 322: 7–9.

Halberstam, J. (1994). F2M: The making of female masculinity. In L. Doan (ed.). *The lesbian postmodern,* pp. 210–28. New York: Columbia University Press.

Hale, J. (2004). Suggested rules for non-transsexuals writing about transsexuals, transsexuality, transsexualism, or trans__. Retrieved 4 February 2004 from: http://www.transfeminism.org/nontrans-rules.html

Hall, C.M. (1997). You anthropologists make sure you get your words right.

In S.E. Jacobs, W. Thomas, and S. Lang (eds.). *Two-Spirit people: Native American gender identity, sexuality, and spirituality*, pp. 272–5. Chicago: University of Illinois Press.

Hancock, W.K. (1968). *Smuts: The fields of force.* Vol. 2. Cambridge University Press.

Handlbauer, B. (1998). *The Freud-Adler controversy.* Oxford: Oneworld.

Haraway, D. (2004). Situated knowledges: The science question in feminism and the privilege of partial perspective. In S. Harding (ed.). *The feminist standpoint theory reader: Intellectual and political controversies*, pp. 81–101. London: Routledge.

Hari, J. (2004). Outcast heroes: The story of gay Muslims. Retrieved 21 May 2004 from: http://www.johannhari.com/archive/article.php?id=395

Harper, D. (2001). Repel: Online etymology dictionary. Retrieved 12 April 2005 from: http://etymonline.com/index.php?term-repel

Hau, M. (2000). The holistic gaze in German medicine, 1890–1930. *Bulletin of the History of Medicine* 74(3): 495–524.

Helgeson, V.S. (2005). *Psychology of gender.* 2nd ed. Upper Saddle River, NJ: Pearson-Prentice Hall.

Herdt, G. (1997). The dilemmas of desire: From 'berdache' to Two-Spirit. In S.E. Jacobs, W. Thomas, and S. Lang (eds.). *Two-Spirit people: Native American gender identity, sexuality, and spirituality*, pp. 276–83. Chicago: University of Illinois Press.

Highcrest, A. (1997). *At home on the stroll: My twenty years as a prostitute in Canada.* Toronto: Knopf.

Hillman, J. (1983). *Healing fiction.* Putnam, CT: Spring Publications, Inc.

Hillman, J., and M. Ventura. (1992). *We've had a hundred years of psychotherapy and the world's getting worse.* San Francisco: Harper.

Hird, M.J. (2000). Gender's nature: Intersexuality, transsexualism and the 'sex/gender' binary. *Feminist Theory* 1(3): 347–64.

– (2003). A typical gender identity conference? Some disturbing reports from the therapeutic front lines. *Feminism and Psychology* 13(2): 181–99.

Hodges, A., and D. Hutter. (1979). *With downcast gays: Aspects of homosexual self-oppression.* London: Pomegranate Press.

Hoffman, E. (1994). *The drive for self: Alfred Adler and the founding of individual psychology.* New York: Addison-Wesley.

Hook, D. (2005). Postcolonial psychoanalysis. Paper presented at the 11th Biennial conference of the International Society for Theoretical Psychology, 20–4 June 2005, University of Cape Town, Cape Town, South Africa.

– (2006). 'Pre-discursive' racism. *Journal of Community and Applied Social Psychology* 16: 207–32.

Horney, K. (1937). *The neurotic personality of our time.* New York: W.W. Norton.

Horrocks, R. (1994). *Masculinity in crisis.* London: Macmillan.

– (1998). Paradigms of homosexuality. In C. Shelley (ed.) *Contemporary perspectives on psychotherapy and homosexualities,* pp. 14–43. London: Free Association Books.

Human Rights Watch. (2001). Hatred in the hallways: Violence and discrimination against lesbian, gay, bisexual and transgender students in US schools. Retrieved 5 August 2004 from: http://www.hrw.org/reports/2001/uslgbt/toc.htm

Irigaray, L. (1985). *This sex which is not one.* C. Porter (trans.). Ithaca, NY: Cornell University Press.

– (2002). *To speak is never neutral.* G. Schwab (trans.). London: Continuum.

Israel, G.E., and D.E. Tarver II. (1997). *Transgender care: Recommended guidelines, practical information and personal accounts.* Philadelphia: Temple University Press.

Jacobs, S.E., W. Thomas, and S. Lang. (1997). Introduction. In S.E. Jacobs, W. Thomas, and S. Lang (eds.). *Two-Spirit people: Native American gender identity, sexuality, and spirituality,* pp. 1–18. Chicago: University of Illinois Press.

Jacoby, R. (1975). *Social amnesia: A critique of conformist psychology from Adler to Laing.* Boston: Beacon Press.

Jaggar, A.M. (2004). Feminist politics and epistemology: The standpoint of women. In S. Harding (ed.). *The feminist standpoint theory reader: Intellectual and political controversies,* pp. 55–66. London: Routledge. (Originally published 1983.)

Jagose, A. (1996). *Queer theory: An introduction.* New York: New York Universities Press.

James. W. (1955). *The principles of psychology.* Mineola, NY: Dover. (Originally published 1890.)

Jeffreys, S. (2003). *Unpacking queer politics.* Cambridge: Polity Press.

– (2005). *Beauty and misogyny: Harmful cultural practices in the West.* London: Routledge.

Jordan, N. (director), and S. Wooley (producer). (1992). *The crying game.* [Motion picture]. UK.

Jorgensen, C. (1967). *Christine Jorgensen: A personal autobiography.* New York: Bantam.

Josselson, R., A. Lieblich, and D. McAdams (eds.). (2002). *Up close and personal: The teaching and learning of narrative research.* Washington, DC: American Psychological Association.

Jukes, A. (1993). *Why men hate women.* London: Free Association Books.

Jung, C.G. (1931). *The structure of the psyche.* Collected Works, 8. Princeton, NJ: Princeton University Press.

– (1951). *Aion.* Collected Works, 9 (part II). Bollingen Series. New York: Pantheon Books.

– (1957). *The undiscovered self.* Collected Works, 10. Bollingen Series XX. New York: Pantheon Books.

– (1961). *Memories, dreams, reflections.* London: Routledge and Kegan Paul.

Kaufman, M. (1987). The construction of masculinity and the triad of men's violence. In M. Kaufman (ed.). *Beyond patriarchy: Essays by men on pleasure, power and change,* pp. 1–29. Toronto: Oxford University Press Canada.

Kaufmann, W. (2003). *Freud, Adler, and Jung: Discovering the mind, volume three.* London: Transaction Publishers.

Kehoe, A.B. (1997). On the incommensurability of gender categories. In S.E. Jacobs, W. Thomas, and S. Lang (eds.). *Two-Spirit people: Native American gender identity, sexuality, and spirituality,* pp. 265–71. Chicago: University of Illinois Press.

Khosravi, P. (director/producer), and B. Yousefi (director/producer). (2005). *I know that I am.* [Motion picture.] Iran/Canada.

Kimmel, M. (1994). Masculinity as homophobia. In H. Brod and M. Kaufman (eds.). *Theorizing masculinities,* pp. 119–41. London: Sage.

Kimura, D. (1999). *Sex and cognition.* Cambridge, MA: MIT Press.

King, R.A., and C.A. Shelley. (2008). Community feeling and social interest: Adlerian parallels, synergy, and differences with the field of community psychology. *Journal of Community and Applied Social Psychology* 18: 96–107.

Kitzinger, C. (1987). *The social construction of lesbianism.* London: Sage.

– (1996). Speaking of oppression: Psychology, politics, and the language of power. In E.D. Rothblum and L.A. Bond (eds.). *Preventing heterosexism and homophobia,* pp. 3–19. London: Sage.

– (1999). Lesbian and gay psychology: Is it critical? *Annual Review of Critical Psychology* 1: 50–66.

Klein, M. (1975). *Envy and gratitude and other works 1946–1963.* New York: Free Press.

Kristeva, J. (1982). *Powers of horror: An essay on abjection.* L.S. Roudiez (trans.). New York: Columbia University Press.

– (1989). *Black sun: Depression and melancholia.* L.S. Roudiez (trans.). New York: Columbia University Press.

– (1997). Strangers to ourselves. In K. Oliver (ed.). *The portable Kristeva,* pp. 264–94. New York: Columbia University Press.

Kulkani, C. (1997). *Lesbians and lesbianisms: A post-Jungian perspective.* London: Routledge.

Kurzweil, E. (1995). *Freudians and feminists.* San Francisco: Westview Press.

Lacan, J. (1977). *Écrits: A selection.* A. Sheridan (trans.). London: W.W. Norton.

Lang, S. (1997). Various kinds of Two-Spirit people: Gender variance and homosexuality in Native American communities. In S.E. Jacobs, W. Thomas, and S. Lang (eds.). *Two-Spirit People: Native American gender identity, sexuality, and spirituality*, pp. 100–18. Chicago: University of Illinois Press.

Laplanche, J. (1996). Psychoanalysis as anti-hermeneutics. *Radical Philosophy* 79: 7–12.

Laplanche, J., and J.B. Pontalis. (1972). Appendices: [Vocabulaire de la psychanalyse]. *Yale French studies* 48: 179–202.

Lather, P. (1991). *Getting smart: Feminist research and pedagogy with/in the postmodern*. London: Routledge.

Lawrence, A. (2000). Transsexual surgery: Its pros and cons. Comprehensive exam, Institute for Advanced Study of Human Sexuality. Retrieved 2 January 2004 from: http://jenellerose.com/htmlpostings/transsexual_surgery_its_pros_and_cons.htm

Lehrer, R. (1999). Adler and Nietzsche. In J. Golomb, W. Santaniello, and R. Lehrer (eds.). *Nietzsche and depth psychology*, pp. 229–46. Albany, NY: State University of New York Press.

Leung, Y. (2004). From Australia to Canada: A conversation with Sneja Gunew. *Tamkang Review* [Taiwan] 35(2): 141–60.

Levinas, E. (1990). Intersubjectivity: Notes on Merleau-Ponty and 'sensibility.' In G.A. Johnson and M.B. Smith (eds.). *Ontology and alterity in Merleau-Ponty*, pp. 55–66. Evanston, IL: Northwestern University Press.

Linden, G.W. (1997). Adler and organ music. In P. Prina, C. Shelley, and C. Thompson (eds.). *Adlerian yearbook 1997*, pp. 29–45. London: Adlerian Society (UK) and Institute for Individual Psychology.

Lorber, J. (1994). *Paradoxes of gender*. London: Yale University Press.

Lorber, J., and L.J. Moore (2007). *Gendered bodies: Feminist perspectives*. Los Angeles: Roxbury.

Macey, D. (2000). *The Penguin dictionary of critical theory*. London: Penguin.

Manaster, G.L., G. Painter, D. Deutsch, and B.J. Overholt (eds.). (1977). *Alfred Adler: As we remember him*. Chicago: North American Society of Adlerian Psychology.

Marcuse, H. (1955). *Eros and civilization*. Boston: Beacon Press.

Marshall, C. (2005). Two guilty of murder in death of a transgender teenager. *New York Times*, 13 September. Retrieved 16 September 2005 from: http://www.nytimes.com/2005/09/13national/13transgender.html

Martino, M. (1977). *Emergence: A transsexual autobiography*. New York: Crown.

McAdams, D. (1997). The case for unity in the (post)modern self. In R.D. Ashmore and L. Jussim (eds.). *Self and identity: Fundamental issues*, pp. 46–78. Oxford: Oxford University Press.

McAfee, N. (2004). *Julia Kristeva*. London: Routledge.

McDougall, J. (1995). *The many faces of eros*. London: Free Association Books.

McHugh, P. (2004). Surgical sex. *First Things: The Journal of Religion, Culture and Public Life* 147. Retrieved 26 November 2004 from: http://www.first things.com/ftissues/ft0411/articles/mchugh.htm

Meyer, A. (1951). *The collected papers of Adolf Meyer: Volume III medical teaching*. E. Winters (ed.). Baltimore: Johns Hopkins University Press.

Meyerowitz, J. (2002). *How sex changed: A history of transsexuality in the United States*. Cambridge, MA: Harvard University Press.

Millett, K. (1977). *Sexual politics*. London: Virago.

Mitchell, J. (1974). *Psychoanalysis and feminism*. New York: Vintage Books.

Mohanty, C.T. (1991). Under western eyes. In A. Russo and L. Torres (eds.). *Third World women and politics of feminism*, pp. 51–80. Bloomington, IN: Indiana University Press.

Money, J. (1986). *Venuses, penuses: Sexology, sexosophy, and exigency theory*. Buffalo, NY: Prometheus Books.

Moran, L.J., and A.N. Sharpe. (2004). Violence, identity and policing: The case of violence against transgender people. *Criminal Justice* 4(4): 395–417.

Morris, E. (2005). Sexual anatomy, reproduction, and the menstrual cycle. In Boston Women's Health Collective (eds.). *Our bodies: Ourselves*. 8th ed. Chapter 13. [On-line book.] Retrieved 31 May 2005 from: http://www.our bodiesourselves.org/book/inside/

Morris, J. (1986). *Conundrum*. 2nd ed. New York: Henry Holt and Co.

Namaste, V.K. (2000). *Invisible lives: The erasure of transsexual and transgendered people*. Chicago: University of Chicago Press.

– (2004). Beyond leisure studies: A labour history of female to male transsexuals and transvestite artists in Montréal, 1955–1985. *Atlantis* 29(1): 4–11.

– (ed.). (2005). *Sex change, social change: Reflections on identity, institutions, and imperialism*. Toronto: Women's Press.

Neill, J.R. (1980). Adolf Meyer and American psychiatry today. *American Journal of Psychiatry* 137(4): 460–4.

Newitz, A. (2004). Gender slumming. *Bad subjects* 7. Retrieved 25 April 2004 from: http://eserver.org/bs/07/newitz.html

Nicki, A. (2006). Women's spaces are not trans spaces: Maintaining boundaries of respect. In K. Scott-Dixon (ed.). *Trans/forming feminisms: Transfeminist voices speak out*, pp. 154–60. Toronto: Sumach Press.

Nietzsche, F. (1972). *Beyond good and evil*. R.J. Hollingdale (trans.). London: Penguin. (Originally published 1886.)

Noble, B.J. (2004a). *Masculinities without men*. Vancouver: University of British Columbia Press.

– (2004b). Sons of the movement: Feminism, female masculinity and female to male (FTM) transsexual men. *Atlantis* 29(1): 21–8.

Noddings, N. (2003). *Caring: A feminist approach to ethics and moral education.* 2nd ed. Berkeley: University of California Press.

Nunberg, H., and E. Federn (eds.). (1962–74). *Minutes of the Vienna psychoanalytic society.* M. Nunberg (trans.). Vols. 1–3. New York: International Universities Press.

Nuttbrock, L. (2002). Transgender identity affirmation and mental health. *International Journal of Transgenderism* 6(4): 1–13.

Oberst, U.E., and A.E. Stewart. (2003). *Adlerian psychotherapy: An advanced approach to individual psychology.* New York: Brunner-Routledge.

O'Connor, N., and J. Ryan. (1993). *Wild desires and mistaken identities: Lesbianism and psychoanalysis.* London: Virago.

Oliver, K. (1993). *Reading Kristeva: Unravelling the double-bind.* Bloomington, IN: Indiana University Press.

Paris, B. (1994). *Karen Horney: A psychoanalyst's search for self-understanding.* London: Yale University Press.

Parker, I. (1997). Discursive psychology. In D. Fox and I. Prilleltensky (eds.). *Critical psychology: An introduction,* pp. 284–98. London: Sage.

– (2004). *Qualitative psychology: Introducing radical research.* Buckingham, UK: Open University Press.

Peel, E., and C. Kitzinger. (2005). Challenging heterosexism in psychology. *Lesbian and Gay Psychology Review* 6(2): 83–8.

Perelle, R. (2007). Rape relief wins: Supreme Court refuses to hear trans woman's appeal. *Xtra West* 352 (15 Feb.): 7, 9.

Pevin, D.E. (1996). Sexual disorders from the viewpoint of individual psychology. In L. Sperry and J. Carlson (eds.). *Psychopathology and psychotherapy: From DSM IV diagnosis to treatment,* 2nd ed., pp. 391–413. Washington, DC: Accelerated Development.

Pfäfflin, F. (1992). Regrets after sex reassignment surgery. In W.O. Bockting and E. Coleman (eds.). *Gender dysphoria: Interdisciplinary approaches in clinical management,* pp. 69–86. New York: Haworth Press.

Popper, K. (1976). *Unended quest: An intellectual autobiography.* London: Fontana Press.

Pratt, M.B. (1995). *S/He.* Ithaca, NY: Firebrand Books.

Preves, S. (2002). Sexing the intersex: An analysis of sociocultural responses to intersexuality. *Signs: Journal of Women in Culture and Society* 27(2): 523–56.

Prosser, J. (1998). *Second skins: The body narratives of transsexuality.* New York: Columbia University Press.

Raymond, J. (1994). *The transsexual empire: The making of the she-male.* 2nd ed. New York: Teachers College Press.

Reich, W. (1946). *The mass psychology of fascism.* London: Penguin.

Rennie, D.L., A.M. Monteiro, and K.D. Watson. (2002). The rise of qualitative research in psychology. *Canadian Psychology* 43(3): 179–89.

Rich, A. (1980). Compulsory heterosexuality and lesbian existence. *Signs: Journal of Women in Culture and Society* 5(4): 631–90.

Richards, R. (1983). *Second serve.* New York: Stein and Day.

Ringo, C.P. (2002). Media roles in female-to-male transsexual and transgender identity formation. *International Journal of Transgenderism* 6(3): 1–22.

Robinson, P. (1993). *Freud and his critics.* Berkeley: University of California Press.

Roen, K. (2001). Transgender theory and embodiment: The risk of racial marginalisation. *Journal of Gender Studies* 10(3): 253–63.

Rose, J. (1986). *Sexuality in the field of vision.* London: Verso.

Ross, B.L. (1995). *The house that Jill built: A lesbian nation in formation.* Toronto: University of Toronto Press.

Rothblatt, M. (1996). *The apartheid of sex: A manifesto on the freedom of gender.* New York: Crown.

Rudy, K. (2001). Radical feminism, lesbian separatism, and queer theory. *Feminist Studies* 27(1): 191–209.

Rutherford, E. (1993). *Nine lives: The autobiography of Erica Rutherford.* Toronto: University of Toronto Press.

Salecl, R. (2003). Success in failure, or how hypercapitalism relies on people's feeling of inadequacy. *Parallax* 9(2): 96–108.

Salisbury, J., and D. Jackson. (1996). *Challenging macho values: Practical ways of working with adolescent boys.* London: Falmer Press.

Samuels, A. (1989). *The plural psyche: Personality, morality and the father.* London: Routledge.

– (1993). *The political psyche.* London: Routledge.

Scott-Dixon, K. (ed.). (2006). *Trans/forming feminisms: Trans-feminist voices speak out.* Toronto: Sumach Press.

Shelley, C.A. (1998). A feeling of community? Individual psychology and homosexualities. In C. Shelley (ed.). *Contemporary perspectives on psychotherapy and homosexualities*, pp. 117–55. London: Free Association Books.

– (2004). Holism, personality theory, and the self: The contribution of the holistic perspective of Jan Christiaan Smuts to Anglo-American psychology. *From Past to Future: Clark Papers on the History of Psychology* 5(1): 40–53.

– (2006). Phenomenology and the qualitative in individual psychology. In J.

Carlson and S. Slavik (eds.). *Readings in the theory of individual psychology*, pp. 595–604. New York: Brunner-Routledge.

– (2008). Jan Smuts and personality theory: The problem of holism in psychology. In R Diriwächter and J. Valsiner (eds.). *Striving for the whole: Creating theoretical syntheses*, pp. 89–109. Somerset, NJ: Transaction Publishers.

Slavik, S. (2006). Therapeutic strategy in a holistic psychology. In P. Prina, K. John, A. Millar, and C. Shelley (eds.). *Adlerian yearbook 2006*, pp. 137–53. London: Adlerian Society (UK) and Institute for Individual Psychology.

Smith, D.E. (1987). *The everyday world as problematic: A feminist sociology*. Boston: Northeastern University Press.

– (1999). *Writing the social: Critique, theory, and investigations*. Toronto: University of Toronto Press.

– (2004). Women's perspective as a radical critique of sociology. In S. Harding (ed.). *The feminist standpoint theory reader: Intellectual and political controversies*, pp. 21–33. London: Routledge. (Originally published 1974.)

Smith, G.A. (1990). Introduction: Alterity as a reversibility. In G.A. Johnson and M.B. Smith (eds.). *Ontology and alterity in Merleau-Ponty*, pp. xvii–xxxiv. Evanston, IL: Northwestern University Press.

Smuts, J.C. (1926). *Holism and evolution*. London: Macmillan.

Socarides, C.W. (1969). The desire for sexual transformation: A psychiatric evaluation of transsexualism. *American Journal of Psychiatry* 125(10): 1420–3.

Southam, H. (2001). Ban sex change ops, says church. *Independent on Sunday*. 14 January. Retrieved 25 July 2004 from: http://www.pfc.org.uk/cgi/printit.pl?/news/2001/ea-ios1.htm

Staeuble, I. (2005). Entangled in the Eurocentric order of knowledge: Why psychology is difficult to decolonize. Paper presented at the 11th Biennial conference of the International Society for Theoretical Psychology, 20–4 June 2005, University of Cape Town, Cape Town, South Africa.

St Claire, R. (1999). A Jungian analysis of transgender identity development and internalised transphobia. Paper presented at the Harry Benjamin international gender dysphoria association symposium XVI, 17–21 August 1999, Imperial College, London, England.

Steinberg, V.L. (2005). A heat of passion offense: Emotions and bias in 'trans panic' mitigation claims. *Boston College Third World Law Journal* 25(1): 1–26.

Stoller, R. (1968). *Sex and gender: The development of masculinity and femininity*. London: Karnac.

Stoltenberg, J. (1989). *Refusing to be a man: Essays on sex and justice*. New York: Penguin.

Stryker, S. (1998). The transgender issue. *GLQ: A Journal of Lesbian and Gay Studies* 4(2): 145–58.

Sullivan, A. (1996). *Virtually normal: An argument about homosexuality.* New York: Vintage books.

Tacey, D.J. (1997). *Remaking men: Jung, spirituality and social change.* London: Routledge.

Tong, R.P. (1998). *Feminist thought: A more comprehensive introduction.* 2nd ed. Boulder, CO: Westview Press.

United Nations. (1948). Universal declaration of human rights. Retrieved 29 September 2003 from: http://www.un.org/Overview/rights.html

Vaihinger, H. (1965). *The philosophy of 'as if.'* London: Routledge and Kegan Paul. (Originally published 1911.)

Webster, R. (1996). *Why Freud was wrong: Sin, science and psychoanalysis.* London: Fontana Press.

Weedon, C. (1987). *Feminist practice and poststructuralist theory.* Oxford: Basil Blackwell.

Wheeler, A. (director), and S. McGowan (producer). (1999). *Better than chocolate.* [Motion picture.] Canada.

White, C. (2002). Re/defining gender and sex: Educating for trans, transsexual, and intersex access and inclusion to sexual assault centres and transition houses. Unpublished M.A. thesis, University of British Columbia. Retrieved 30 April 2004 from: www.barbarafindlay.com

White, M., and D. Epston. (1990). *Narrative means to therapeutic ends.* New York: W.W. Norton.

Wilchins, R. (2002a). A continuous nonverbal communication. In J. Nestle, C. Howell, and R. Wilchins (eds.). *Gender queer: Voices from beyond the binary,* pp. 11–17. Los Angeles: Alyson Books.

– (2002b). Queerer bodies. In J. Nestle, C. Howell, and R. Wilchins (eds.). *Gender queer: Voices from beyond the binary,* pp. 33–46. Los Angeles: Alyson Books.

Winnicott, D. (1958). *Collected papers: Through paediatrics to psychoanalysis.* London: Tavistock.

Wittig, M. (1988). One is not born a woman. In S.L. Hoagland and J. Penelope (eds.). *For lesbians only: A separatist anthology,* pp. 439–48. London: Only Women Press.

Zhou, J.N., M.A. Hofman, L.J. Gooren, and D.F. Swaab. (1997). A sexed difference in the human brain and its relation to transsexuality. *International Journal of Transgenderism* 1(1). Retrieved 5 August 2004 from: http://www.symposion.com/ijt/ijtc0106.htm

Zimmerman, M.E. (1981). *Eclipse of the self: The development of Heidegger's concept of authenticity.* London: Ohio University Press.

Name Index

Subject Index